THE
BIG
EARTH
BOOK

THE
BIG
EARTH
BOOK

IDEAS AND SOLUTIONS FOR A PLANET IN CRISIS

James Bruges

Alastair Sawday's

Fragile Earth Series

Author: James Bruges

Editor: Emily Walmsley

Design: Derek Edwards, Patwa (patwa.co.uk)

Original cover design concept: CompanyX (thecompanyx.com)

Project Manager: Lyn Hemming

Production Manager: Julia Richardson

Picture Research: Tom Germain

First edition

Copyright © September 2007

Fragile Earth an imprint of Alastair Sawday Publishing Co. Ltd

Published in 2007 by Alastair Sawday Publishing

The Old Farmyard, Yanley Lane,

Long Ashton, Bristol BS41 9LR

Tel: +44 (0)1275 395430

Fax: +44 (0)1275 393388

Email: info@sawdays.co.uk or info@fragile-earth.com

Web: www.sawdays.co.uk or www.fragile-earth.com

Printing:

Butler & Tanner, Frome, UK

UK Distribution:

Penguin UK, 80 Strand, London

ISBN-13: 978-1-901970-87-6

The purpose of this book

I WANT TO provoke you – emotionally and intellectually. I also want to illuminate some dark corners of our world and to give you the tools with which to tackle the great and pressing issues of our time.

The Big Earth Book brings together an impressive collection of global issues, and shows the connections between them. Each chapter, each subject, is the result of some Herculean condensing of vast amounts of material. As a result, I have, of course, sometimes failed to balance strong opinions. But humankind has now reached the stage when opinion, allied to careful research, is desperately needed. Sitting on fences is no longer an option.

Global issues must not be viewed in isolation. The physical and biological environments, trade, militarism, genetics, debt and our own philosophies all act upon each other. Please don't skip the chapters on economics – hardly the most seductive of subjects. A faulty money system is at the root of most of our problems. I have, I hope, made this easy to understand.

We have never been able to predict the future, but each step we take can be towards, or away from, social justice and environmental survival. I believe that a better world is possible, and that we can be part of its creation. Politicians, currently the missing link, will take action when they see that voters are already doing so.

CONTENTS

Foreword
we can make a difference

A SINGLE, TINY mosquito can make a very large person uncomfortable all night. A single human being, each one of us, can make a whole society sit up and think. But first we must understand where we are going and, more importantly, why.

As climate change unfurls before our eyes, ignorance allows us to be optimistic rather than intelligently active. Humankind finally triumphed over evil during the Second World War. Surely scientists and technologists will deliver us from this new danger? But humankind has never had to triumph over forces as vast as market capitalism, globalisation, technology running riot, and our empty-headed addiction to 'things'. Meanwhile, we grow accustomed to bad news and our leaders avoid frightening us. We must be allowed to believe that our comfort is not threatened, that someone will invent a clever technical way to enable us to continue as we are. We must be allowed to be positive.

There are, of course, many reasons to be positive. The earth is very beautiful, and full of wonderful people. In *The Little Earth Book*, I wrote of the Scottish musician whose work with the town's wind band transformed a sleepy Spanish town. Most great campaigning organisations have been founded by one inspired person. Remember the transforming power of

Nelson Mandela. But if there is so much positive work, so many fine people, so much high-level discussion of climate change and other problems facing us, why is there still so little action?

The message I want to convey is not just that matters are in our own hands, but that time is now frighteningly short. We have had decades of being alerted to the crises. Twenty years ago we knew that intensive cotton cultivation had drained and dried much of the vast Aral Sea in the old Soviet Union, leaving fishing fleets rusting on sand. For years we have watched as our politicians have signed treaties consciously allowing the further depletion of fish stocks.

So can we trust our existing institutions, political and financial systems to provide leadership and solutions after decades of doing the opposite? I think not. Governments, industry, those at the head of great institutions and businesses find it hard to absorb a profound sense of crisis. Great tankers change course very slowly. But we must make them change, we must galvanise them, engage with them – and sometimes bypass them.

Our individual responses are doubly important. Every time we welcome a new technology, a new miracle cure, we tend to abandon our critical faculties. If something is new, sleek and shining we are not interested in evidence of its value, neither do we consider its potential long-term effects – especially if it is profitable and 'scientific'. Modern technology provides us with deadly risks, both to ourselves and to the planet.

My own engagement with these questions stems from an irrepressible resentment at the stupidity of much of what we do. Our addiction to cars, for example, is breathtakingly silly. I have watched as governments have caved in to the motor lobby and built more roads. It is known as a 'predict and provide' policy, one which countless official reports have condemned as pointless. We are now doing it with airports. I have watched as lovely towns have yielded to invasions of banality and ugliness. I have worked overseas and seen poverty made worse by ill-conceived aid. All these things clash with an ingrained sense of justice, with a longing for common sense and a convivial society. It is nothing more complicated than that.

It was common sense that provoked me to create eco-offices for my publishing company. We store rainwater to flush the loos, heat the water with solar power, use as little energy as possible and avoid fossil fuels. Why are we not all obliged and helped to do these things?

Thirty years ago I was an environmental activist with Friends of the Earth, popularly seen as barmy. We were the small boy shouting that the emperor had no clothes. We battled to stop whaling, the destruction of the countryside, the dominance of the car over public transport, the world's dependence on oil. We are still asking for these things to stop – and time is shorter.

There is no power on earth that can utterly destroy the human spirit. Whatever the calamity, however profound the oppression, some flicker of life, courage or enterprise will remain. But we must not allow humanity to get to that stage. The first step is for each one of us to look up from our comforts and to learn some inconvenient truths. Then we can get angry and shout from the rooftops. This book will help us to get angry, positive and active.

Alastair Sawday
Publisher and environmental activist

Introduction
anger can lead to change

A HUGE LAKE in the Himalayas was once contained by the Pir Panjal mountain range. Local mythology tells of a struggle involving the demon Jalod Bowa and the saint Kashyap, who shattered rocks at Baramulla sending water cascading down to the plains of India. The fertile valley created was in Kashmir: from the Sanskrit 'ka', meaning 'water', and 'shimeera', dried-up land.

The Valley of Kashmir is one of the most beautiful places on earth with lakes, poplars and willows surrounded by snow-capped mountains. Thousands of years later the Mughal emperors, for their summer retreat, laid out Shalimar Bagh and other gardens with lawns and fountains stepping down to the lakeside, fed by mountain streams and populated with golden orioles and paradise flycatchers. They introduced magnificent chenar trees (oriental plane) from Persia and executed anyone who harmed them. Draconian environmental regulations are not new.

My childhood, until the age of 12, was spent exploring bazaars, swimming in lakes and climbing mountains, with a little schoolwork thrown in. This left me belonging, emotionally, to a country that contains a quarter of the world's poor as well as to a rich country – Britain – that has over-exploited global resources. More recently, with my wife, I have visited India annually and become involved with a number of organisations that derive their inspiration from Gandhi and his spiritual successor, Vinoba Bhave.

Our friend Rajesh and his wife Divya are architects in Kerala. They fenced in a large family estate on the east side of the western ghats to keep out the deer and goats, then they planted indigenous trees and dug check trenches to prevent rainwater runoff. Already the microclimate is improving and the level of groundwater has risen – a barren hillside has been transformed into fertile ground that can now be cultivated without irrigation. Rajesh talked to me about his wish to buy a stretch of the east coast of Tamil Nadu and reintroduce mangroves to protect farmland from the sea and prevent salt seeping into the groundwater. That was a year before the Boxing Day tsunami that claimed hundreds of lives in areas where the mangroves had been cleared for tourism and shrimp farms.

Rajesh invited us to stay at the family home. His father, who had been a member of parliament was polite but distant until he asked, "Why is India poor and England rich?" I risked a provocative answer: "We found India rich in the 17th century with 25% of world trade and left it poor in the 20th century with only 4%."

"You admit it!" he cried. Having now engaged his full attention we worked on the question. India is rich in basic commodities, it produces enough food to feed itself, it has wide ranging industrial and service sectors, its IT rivals Silicon Valley with Bangalore becoming the nerve centre of original research, it virtually runs the accountancy of banks and companies in Britain and the US. And Britain? It imports over a third of its food, it does not even make washing machines and its service industry is demonstrated by the state of the railways. So why does India have such poverty while Britain retains a high standard of living?

There are probably three reasons. Britain has been close to the heart of banking (for how much longer?). Second, we are a knowledge-based society that prevents poor countries benefiting from this knowledge through a worldwide framework for patents – the notorious TRIPS agreement (though India and China may soon overtake us in this respect). Third, trade and money regulations have allowed western companies to plunder the agrarian wealth of Asia, the mineral wealth of Africa and the labour wealth of Latin America.

Cletus Babu, who runs an organisation in Tamil Nadu called Social Change and Development, once said to me, "We have struggled to achieve change for 25 years and every step forward is pushed back by global issues outside our control." India, after 60 years of development and in spite of its new high-tech wealth, now has more people in grinding poverty than its whole population numbered at independence. Africans, meanwhile, must be wondering what they have gained from opening their mineral wealth to foreign exploitation.

My criticisms in this book are directed at the policies of the dominant west, without implying that others are blameless. The criticisms are not always the received opinion of environmental groups but I hope that they will contribute to the general discussion about the exploitation of the weak by the strong. The persistence of exploitation can make one feel helpless, but I prefer the attitude of Shalmali Guttal, an Indian activist, who said to me, "Don't despair. Get angry. Anger can lead to change."

Engagement with people who are suffering from global injustice led me to think about more abstract theory. There is a graph – as an architect I like graphs – that represents our civilisation: the line runs for millennia almost horizontally, then gradually rises and finally zooms upwards as a spike. This graph looks the same whether referring to the economy, oil extraction, carbon emissions, extinctions, consumption, population and many other fields. It is obvious that the spike can't rise forever, yet further growth remains the panacea of economists and politicians. We know the future of only one of these graphs for certain, that of oil extraction. It is not a spike but a rise to a peak followed by a steep descent. It is possible that the other graphs may all follow the same bell-shaped curve.

Our money system has been driving the spike, which is why I have tried to lay emphasis on this aspect. Economists try to cloud economics in mystery. My reluctance to engage with it was removed by Richard Douthwaite who, with the Irish group Feasta, has shown how a sane money system could introduce a tendency towards equality and reduce carbon emissions, prevent over-exploitation of global resources, strengthen communities and enable individual enterprise to flourish.

For tens of thousands of years humans were enclosed in nature, and I feel privileged to know adivasi people in India who retain some indigenous wisdom. Then, as civilisations developed, homo sapiens subjected itself to various gods made in its own image, and in modern times adopted concepts of the

Enlightenment. However, the current threats from climate and environmental degradation provide a new perspective on our species as among the shortest lived and the most destructive of any that has ever evolved.

We need to change the way we relate to the environment, to other animals, to other cultures and to society's 'housekeeping' – the economy. Marginal changes will not achieve survival. In this book I have drawn attention to thinkers who define these profound changes; they are found in all walks of life and their ideas connect across a wide variety of subjects. There is no point in being optimistic or pessimistic, we must work for radical change, change that is dismissed as impractical by 'realists' but that is essential for the real world.

The end of the Cold War brought hope for a better world, briefly. This hope was dashed by the new elite's resort to force and competition rather than dialogue and cooperation. But recently there has been a sea change in public awareness. We have just one last chance to achieve a fair and peaceful civilisation that retains our foothold on earth.

"A single tiny island [Britain] is keeping the world in chains. If an entire nation of 300 million took to similar economic exploitation it would strip the world bare like locusts." Mahatma Gandhi, 1928

Women in Udaipur, Rajasthan, India

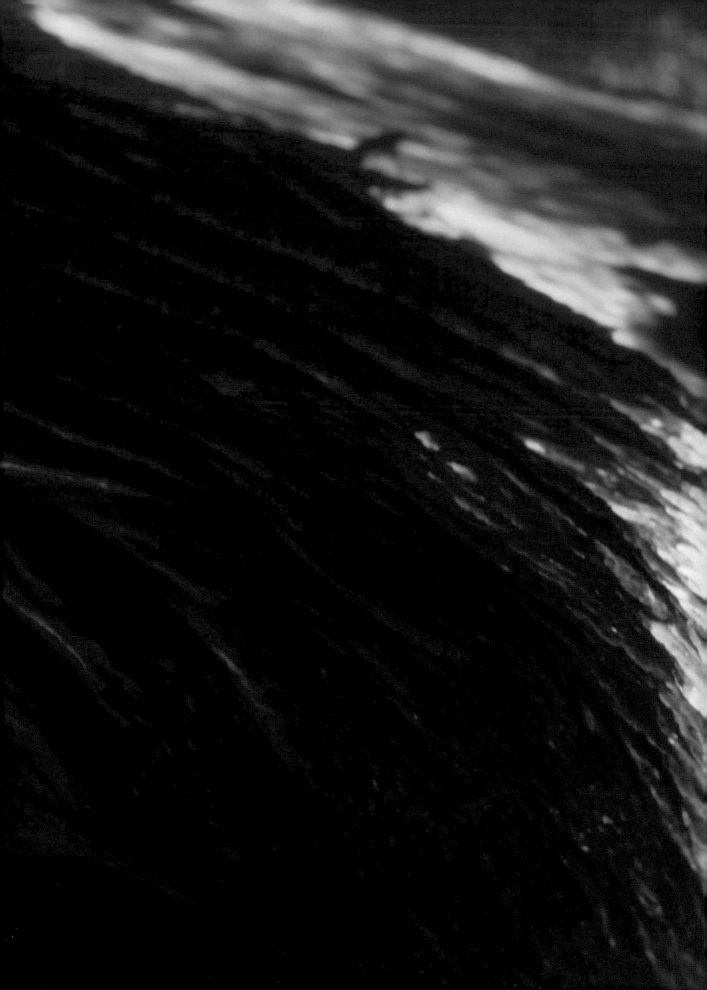

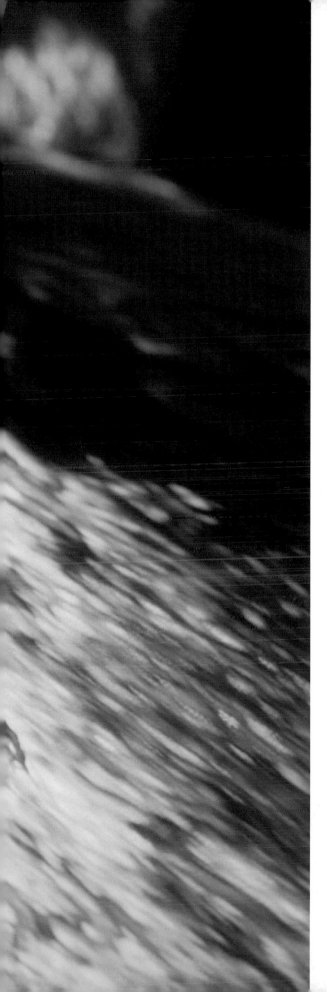

The Elements
Air, earth, fire and water

THREE BILLION YEARS ago, when the sun was not too bright, life established a foothold on earth.

Since then, radiant heat from the sun has increased by a quarter. Our planet would be a rocky waste, too hot on the sunny side and frozen on the other, if it had not become clothed in plants. There is a seemingly magical process by which the earth maintains the conditions necessary for life.

However, our species has multiplied and colonised the world to such an extent that we now affect all its natural systems, and many of them are threatened. This is a global crisis, no longer just an issue for environmentalists.

We are beginning to realise that simply correcting faults as they appear is not an adequate response. A fundamental change is needed in our way of life and in our attitude to society, to animals and to plants – to all aspects of our relationship with the planet.

Increasingly, individuals are adjusting their lives to the new reality. The overwhelming need now is for radical political and economic action on a national and international scale.

Atmosphere
the global duvet

"Beyond there is only emptiness, coldness and darkness. The blue sky, which gives us breath and protects us from endless black and death, is but an infinitesimally thin film. How dangerous it is to threaten even the smallest part of this gossamer, this conserver of life."

Vladimir Shatalov, cosmonaut, one of the few people to have passed through the atmospheric duvet, 1969

FORESTS ONCE COVERED the land. The atmosphere once contained large amounts of carbon dioxide and methane. It was warmer and the sea level was 60 metres higher than today. Gradually algae, plankton and plants captured the carbon and released oxygen. In some places the fossil remains of plants became coal, gas and oil. The concentration of greenhouse gases reduced; the earth cooled and sea levels fell.

But over the last 250 years we have reversed the process. By digging up and burning coal, oil and natural gas we are putting their captured carbon back into the atmosphere.

The atmosphere preserves life. Various gases envelope the earth in a 'duvet', distinguishing our planet from the moon which has a surface temperature 35°C colder than the earth. Half the duvet is water vapour, mostly clouds; carbon dioxide makes up over a quarter of it.

Ice ages are the normal state of the planet but the earth's orbital variations kick start interglacial periods every 100,000 years. This triggers feedback effects – such as the release of carbon dioxide – that amplify the warming

process. The current interglacial period, which started 10,000 years ago, has enabled humans to cultivate land and build civilisations.

Other phenomena also determine the climate: cosmic rays affect the clouds, the earth tilts during a period of 40,000 years, it wobbles over a period of 23,000 years and the sun's intensity varies. Since these periods are so long they are of only academic interest. Sunspot activity is more frequent but has only a marginal impact.

The science of climate change is 180 years old. In 1827 Joseph Fourier, a French mathematician, was the first to identify the influence of various gases on the atmosphere. John Tyndall, an Irish scientist, later took on the idea. Then, in 1898 Svante Arrhenius, a Swedish scientist, coined the phrase 'greenhouse effect' and predicted that if concentrations of carbon dioxide in the atmosphere doubled, the global climate would warm by 4°C to 6°C, figures remarkably close to recent predictions.

In 1985 an international group of scientists met with climate modellers and were shocked by what they heard. They attended the meeting as

A melting iceberg in the South Atlantic

individuals so their report was unconstrained by commercial or political pressure. They predicted "substantial warming" that was unambiguously "attributable to human activities". No ifs, no buts, no maybes.

This led to the Rio Earth Summit in 1992, then to Kyoto in 1997. Big Oil, fearing damage to its business, gave massive grants to any scientist or pseudo-scientist who would add a few ifs and buts. Donations helped the friends of Big Oil into political power, from the president of the United States downwards.

The problem of climate change began with the Industrial Revolution. The burning of coal released carbon back into the atmosphere. Then oil extraction, which began in earnest about 100 years ago, released even more. Now, early in the 21st century, the concentration of carbon dioxide in the atmosphere exceeds the highest levels in the period for which data exists, covering the past 650,000 years. This means that it is probably higher than at any other time during the past 20 million years.

- **CO_2 concentrations**
  Before the Industrial Revolution in the 19th century the atmosphere contained 280ppm (parts per million) of carbon dioxide. This has now risen to 384ppm.

  Between 2001 and 2005, CO_2 concentrations rose at the rate of 2.2ppm a year. In 2006 the increase was 2.6ppm, much more than scientists were expecting. In January 2007 scientists predicted that they would rise more than 3ppm during the year. This rate of increase would bring us to the danger threshold of 400ppm within six years.

- **CO_2 emissions**

  Carbon dioxide stays in the atmosphere until oceans, plants and plankton absorb it. But once saturated they may become a source, rather than a sink, of carbon emissions.

  In the 1990s emissions increased at the rate of 0.8% a year. From 2000 to 2006 the annual rate of increase rose to more than 3.2%. Ten years of negotiations to reduce emissions have only seen them rising at an increasing rate.

Cattle cross the dried-up Lake Ambroseli in Kenya

Professor Peter Cox, a climate-change expert, said in January 2007: "Over the past few years the concentration of carbon dioxide has been going up faster than we would expect based on the rate that emissions are increasing." This could be due to the increase in forest fires, heat waves and the Amazon drought.

Carbon dioxide takes time to permeate the atmosphere and cause global warming, so present temperatures are the result of 30-year-old emissions. Today's emissions will therefore raise temperatures during the coming 30 years.

Africa is already suffering from the changing climate. Kenya faces desertification of the Mandera district, home to three million pastoralists whose way of life has sustained them for thousands of years.

A quarter of the earth's surface is now susceptible to moderate drought. This will rise to half the world's surface by 2100, with extreme drought affecting a third.

Carbon dioxide concentrations will therefore rise above 400ppm whatever we do. This concentration will remain in the atmosphere for about 150 years.

Most climate events are more extreme and happen sooner than expected. In 1990 scientists predicted that temperatures might soon rise 3°C above pre-industrial levels if we carried on with business as usual, but later they doubled that figure. They then realised that tiny aerosol particles from exhausts and chimneys had blocked out sunshine and suppressed the temperature, so their measurements had to allow also for this short-term effect, called global dimming. They upped the figure to 11°C. And yet scientists are constantly reported as being "surprised" or "astonished" by incidents such as the collapse of the Larson B ice shelf in the Antarctic or methane bubbling from permafrost. The Greenland ice sheet was expected to lose 80 cubic kilometres in 2006, but NASA's Grace satellite has shown that it actually lost 287.

The oil-lubricated deniers of climate change are now seen to have had no evidence for their disgraceful campaign. It has wasted many years during which action could have been taken.

"Scientists are screaming from the rooftops," says Al Gore, former US vice president and environmental campaigner, "The debate is over."

However, we may still be caught unawares. The media usually assumes that temperatures will rise evenly through the coming century, but major climate changes have not always happened gradually. At the end of the last Ice Age, global temperatures flipped up and down several degrees within a decade. A destabilised atmosphere could do the same

"We can say with confidence that the trends in sea surface temperatures and hurricane intensity are connected to climate change."

Judy Curry, *Science Journal*, Vol.309 (2006)

now. "An abrupt climate change," stated the US National Academy of Sciences, "occurs when the climate system is forced to cross

Uncharted territory

Carbon dioxide concentrations during the past 400,000 years and current predictions
(Vostok ice core data)

Predicted concentrations under present policies, including introduction of renewables and greater energy efficiency:
700 ppm by 2100

Predicted concentrations if carbon dioxide emissions are reduced by 70% globally: 550 ppm

Present concentrations:
370 ppm

2 —
0 —
- 2 —
- 4 —
- 6 —
- 8 —

local temperature at Vostok, °C

ice-age

settled agriculture

300

200

100
parts per million (ppm) by volume

400,000 years ago
300,000 years ago
200,000 years ago
100,000 years ago
1000 CE
1500 CE
2000 CE

some threshold, triggering a new state at a rate determined by the climate system itself and faster than the cause. On the basis of the inference from the paleoclimatic record, it is possible that the projected change will occur not through gradual evolution, proportional to greenhouse gas concentrations, but through abrupt and persistent regime shifts affecting sub-continental or larger regions."

In other words, the danger is not from gradual change over the coming century but from a sudden tipping point.

Hurricanes

Thomas Knutson, a climate modeller at the US National Oceanic and Atmospheric Administration (NOAA), suggested in 2004 that increases in atmospheric carbon dioxide would lead to more intense hurricanes. A year later, when further research supported this link, Knutson was invited to comment on it on television. Before he could appear however, his slot was cancelled, apparently because "the White House said no" to his appearance. All further media enquiries were sent to a researcher who was known to doubt the link between hurricane intensity and global warming.

The number of serious hurricanes (category 4 and 5) has doubled since the 1970s. In 2005 a hurricane developed south of the equator off Brazil for the first time, and scientists say that this can only be due to global warming. In the same year, New Orleans was destroyed as a result of rising temperatures by Hurricane Katrina. Previously, Hurricane Mitch killed 18,000 people in the Caribbean and Central America. Hurricane Rita led to the evacuation of Houston. With present trends, insured losses will outstrip global GDP in 50 to 60 years' time. But we cannot spend all our wealth on repairing disasters, so the crunch will come much earlier.

Devastation in New Orleans caused by Hurricane Katrina

Runaway warming
positive feedbacks

"If we don't take action very soon we could unleash runaway global warming that will be beyond our control, and will lead to social, economic and environmental devastation worldwide."

Tony Juniper, Director, Friends of the Earth, 2006

SNOW AND ICE are white and reflect sunshine. When they melt, the dark ground, trees and water become exposed and start to absorb heat that would otherwise be reflected back to the sky. This causes more warming, so more melting, more dark surfaces, more warming, and more melting. This is a 'positive feedback' effect.

Once it has gone beyond a tipping point there is nothing we can do to stop it. Scientists do not know how close we are to this point. Referring to the melting of Arctic ice, Dr Nghiem of NASA said that, "Over the long term we find a reduction of about 7% a decade. What we have here is 14% in one year."

Before

After

The Muir Glacier, Alaska, in 1941 and in 2004

The Toboggan Glacier, Alaska, in 1909 and in 2000

Methane, in the form gas hydrates, is trapped in even larger quantities than fossil fuel reserves under continental shelves, in ocean depths and underneath the permanently frozen subsoil of the tundra. It was formed over millions of years from the decay of organic matter. Methane (CH_4) is a carbon greenhouse gas 20 times more damaging than carbon dioxide (CO_2) and scientists used to think it was the real problem. They may have been right.

As the snow that covers the tundra recedes, the warmth of the sun on dark ground is causing permafrost to melt. Frozen soil used to provide a stable foundation but now roads crack, houses and trees settle at alarming angles, pipelines break, lakes form and other lakes, once held by the frozen ground, disappear.

In August 2005 methane was found bubbling up in western Siberia over an area larger than France and Germany combined. These bogs contain a quarter of the methane stored on the land surface worldwide. Of all positive feedback effects this could be the one that causes the global climate to collapse. When this news broke scientists described it as an "ecological landslide that is probably irreversible" and "a major source of feedbacks." Governments around the world, however, made no comment.

Scientists differ on the rate at which sea levels will rise. Polar temperatures are increasing faster than elsewhere in the world. The melting of the three-kilometre thick ice on Greenland could raise sea levels by six metres. This would take thousands of years if it melted from the top down, but meltwater is now dropping down crevasses. This lubricates the base and causes massive chunks of ice to slide into the ocean. The West Antarctic land-based ice sheet used

Climate and ocean currents

The pumps are powered by high salt concentrations near the water's surface. Melting ice dilutes the salt and weakens the pump.

As the pumps weaken, the current slows down and may suddenly switch off.

The system depends on so-called "natural pumps" around Greenland that draw warm water up towards northwest Europe and send cold water back southwards.

The Gulf Stream brings warm water from the tropics as part of a worldwide network of ocean currents.

to be buttressed by the Larson B floating ice shelf, but this suddenly collapsed in 2002. The sheet now rests on land below sea level, which means that warmer seawater could penetrate it, increasing the rate of melt and making the bottom of the ice slippery. "We could be seeing the start of a runaway collapse of the [land-based] ice sheet," said Chris Rapley of the British Antarctic Survey. "This is a real cause for concern. We need to marshal world resources to find out what is going on." The melting of the West Antarctic sheet alone could raise sea levels by five metres.

The Greenland ice cap has a positive feedback of a different kind: as the height drops, the surface is exposed to warmer air at the lower altitude and it starts to melt faster. Melting of this ice cap is now irreversible. The only question is: how quickly will it go? Jim Hansen, former director

of NASA's Goddard Institute and adviser to the US president, said that the collapse could be "explosively rapid" with sea levels rising "a couple of metres this century and several more in the 21st century." Not surprisingly, he did not remain long in NASA employment.

Doing what is necessary to prevent runaway global warming will be expensive. Reducing the use of coal, natural gas and oil will give

a huge shock to the global economy. So is it more practical to allow the climate to adapt? "The world can't afford it," says John Harte of the University of California. "Even the most outrageously high estimates of what it would cost to do something about this are way, way less than what it would cost if it happened."

The 2007 *Stern Review* confirmed that the cost of taking action to avoid runaway global

warming is manageable, whereas the cost of allowing it to occur is not. Imagine the flooding of coastal cities, islands and even whole countries. Imagine the loss of all low-lying agricultural land, with the consequent breakdown of law and order as populations become desperate to grab food or migrate. Imagine the extinction of plants and animals unable to adapt to a climate changing at great speed. Assessing such catastrophes in terms of money is meaningless, but by pointing out their effect on the economy the *Stern Review* has at least grabbed the attention of policy makers and businessmen.

Runaway warming, once it has passed a tipping point, cannot be stopped. We do not know how close we are to that point, but there is scientific consensus that we have well under ten years to start reducing carbon emissions substantially.

Glofs

As Himalayan glaciers melt they form lakes held in by packed ice. These lakes, some of them over two and a half square kilometres in area and 100 metres deep, are getting bigger. At some stage the ice dams will burst and a wall of water will destroy everything in its path – settlements, bridges and dams.

These 'glofs' (glacial lake outburst floods) will affect Nepal, Bhutan, India and Pakistan. Will the industrial world, grown rich on its profligate use of fossil fuels, undertake massive and urgent remedial action to reduce the level of the lakes? Its response is simply, "Tough! We need to burn more fossil fuels; how else can we maintain our standard of living?"

Imja Tsho glacier, Khumbu Himal, Nepal

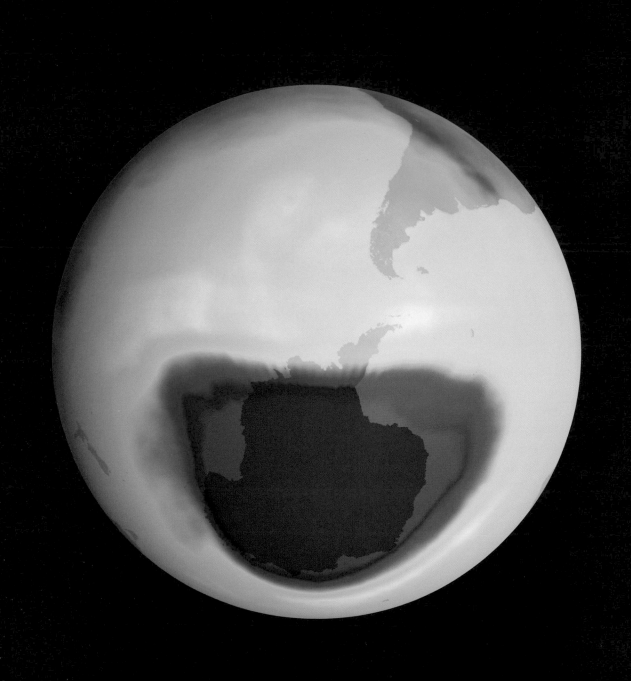

These humans have at last acted sensibly. Let's hope they can do so again.

Ozone layer
a ray of hope

BY TAKING ACTION to reduce the release of ozone-depleting gases, global society proved that it was capable of acting to avert a major environmental threat.

If there were no ozone in the stratosphere, there would be little life on earth. Ozone is a gas dispersed across a 32-kilometre layer of the upper atmosphere, where it shields us from ultraviolet radiation from the sun. The gas is so dilute that if it were all brought down to sea level it would be no thicker than a china plate.

Ultraviolet radiation has had a lot of publicity because it causes skin cancers. But it also reduces resistance to AIDS, tuberculosis and herpes, it causes cataracts and blindness and it reduces the growth and yield of most food crops. It kills plankton in the sea, which affects the fish population and reduces plankton's pivotal role in extracting carbon dioxide from the air. With increased exposure to ultraviolet radiation the genes in some plants relocate in the genome, causing mutations and disrupting the plant's development and fertility. Changes to the DNA of plants and animals could permeate the food chain. Ozone holes are seriously bad news.

The major culprits are chlorofluorocarbons (CFCs), which are artificial chemicals that have been widely used in propellants, refrigerants, insulation, cleaning agents and packaging. They are non-toxic, have no smell and are non-flammable, so for 40 years they were considered benign and there seemed to be no reason to restrict their use. But they are stable gases that are not found in nature and the processes of evolution have not developed ways to neutralise them. Somehow, sometime, they were bound to cause problems.

When fears about the ozone hole became widely accepted companies stopped building new CFC facilities. Then, in 1987, the Montreal protocol required industrial countries to halt CFC production altogether and banned trading in products containing CFCs. The protocol was based on a precautionary principle even before all scientists agreed that there was a problem. CFCs are depleting year on year and it is anticipated that the ozone layer will be back to normal by 2065 – a hugely encouraging thought. This shows that when politicians impose appropriate legislation the planet can be saved from the forces of commerce.

The Antarctic ozone hole in 2002

Public policy
positive inaction

"The risks of outcomes much worse than expected are very real and they could be catastrophic ... if and when the damages appear it will be too late to reverse the process."

Stern Review: The Economics of Climate Change (2007)

WHAT SCIENTISTS ARE saying is downright scary. The summary of the latest report by the Intergovernmental Panel on Climate Change (IPCC) was published in February 2007. It was based on the work of 2,500 climate scientists and 800 contributing authors from 130 countries, and it was prepared over a period of five years. The report is therefore conservative by definition as it included only statements that received consensus agreement. Nevertheless, it calls for drastic action.

Scientists, of course, deal in probability not certainty and this allows the message to be softened. But what was probable 20 years ago is virtually certain now. Those 20 years of warning, during which action could have been taken, have been lost. We are now at crisis point.

A temperature rise of 2°C is considered the critical threshold. In 1996 the European Union said that the average global temperature must not be allowed to increase more than 2°C above pre-industrial levels and it has repeated this statement frequently. A symposium called by Sir David King, the UK government's chief scientific adviser, was charged with informing the 2005 G8 summit in Gleneagles, Scotland. The symposium met the February before in Exeter and concluded: "If we go beyond 2°C we will raise hell."

Its report warned that, with temperatures above this, the worst-case scenario could see the Gulf Stream stop, a ten-metre rise in sea levels, the collapse of the Amazon rainforest, conversion of soil from a carbon sink to a carbon source and widespread desertification. Above all, runaway global warming might kick in and we would be unable to stop it. These comments were made with varying degrees of probability, but the risks of ignoring them are obviously frightening.

Economists like to do cost/benefit analyses in order to advise governments whether to invest a lot of money now, or to invest a little now and then spend more on repairing the damage when it happens later. However, doing a cost/benefit analysis of the effects of a 2°C compared with a 3°C rise is rather like a financial adviser saying: "You can choose between a pension or a lethal injection on retirement; your premiums will, of course, be lower if you choose the latter."

A report by the Tyndall Centre in September 2006 said that at a concentration of 400ppm (parts per million) there is a very high chance of keeping below the 2°C temperature rise. At 550ppm the probability drops to between 10% and 20%. It added: "According to current scientific understanding, to have a very high probability of not exceeding 2°C would require a complete cessation of carbon emissions from today." Since policy makers would deem it impossible to stop emissions immediately, the report set a target of 450ppm, even though this

"is likely to provide a medium-to-high (35% to 65%) probability of exceeding 2°C." If this were a game of craps it would mean that between two and four of the six dice markings were weighted against you.

This was not an isolated report; it was mainstream science. But these things can be expressed in different ways. The Institute for Public Policy Research, described as the UK's leading progressive think tank, said in November 2006 that if we want a very low risk of exceeding 2°C, then concentrations of carbon dioxide in the atmosphere must "peak at between 410ppm and 421ppm by around 2050 before falling to between 355ppm and 366ppm

What climate change?

'Climate denial' is strong in the US. "Every time one of these assessments [by the Intergovernmental Panel on Climate Change, IPCC] is released, about every five years, some of the American scientists who have played a part in producing it become the targets of concerted attacks apparently designed to bring down their reputations and careers," says Fred Pearce, a science commentator. "If the acrimony were to become so intense that American scientists were forced to stop helping in the preparation of IPCC reports, it could seriously dent the organisation and rob the world of some significant voices in the climate change debate."

Carbon dioxide concentrations in the atmosphere

- 210 ppm: minimum ice-age level
- 281 ppm: pre-industrial level
- 300 ppm: maximum for 650,000 years
- 368 ppm: concentrations in 2000
- 384 ppm: concentrations in 2007

by 2100 … For the rich countries (Europe, for example) that could essentially mean preparing to build a zero-carbon economy by 2050."

Other gases such as methane and nitrous oxide currently add about 15% to the warming effect. The terminology 'CO_2e' refers to 'carbon dioxide equivalent' and includes the effect of these gases. Scientists' publications are often unclear about which definition applies, but the uncertain figures and implications reflect a scientific understanding based on probability not certainty. One thing that is certain, however, is that humanity today is up against the biggest threat it has ever faced.

Politicians like long-term targets. They will have moved on by the time their distant targets fail to be met. Britain accepted the goal of a 12% reduction from 1990 figures by 2012 and then revised it to a more ambitious 20% reduction. Ten years have passed and it is becoming clear that even the original target will not be reached. This shows that the only target that has any real validity is an annual commitment, or a two-year rolling commitment to allow adjustment for a cold winter.

Government figures are also deliberately designed to mislead the public. "The government's carbon reduction policies continue to be informed by a partial inventory which omits the two important and rapidly growing sectors of air transport and shipping," stated the Tyndall Centre. "There is a clear void between the scale of the problem and the actual policy mechanisms proposed … The real challenge is making a radical shift within four years and driving down carbon intensity at an unprecedented 9% a year." Keep this in mind when the government next claims that it is on target.

Keep in mind also that some economists live in a make-believe world. Economic models produced in the US, based on normal discounted cash-flow accounting, claim that future generations will be vastly more wealthy than today's, and therefore able to cope with problems presented by a changing climate. On this basis there is little need to make sharp reductions in emissions in the near future, though they may be necessary later. If these flat-earth economists had the remotest contact with the real world they might question their basic assumption that prosperity will grow ad infinitum on a finite planet subject to catastrophic climate change. Unfortunately, they have had the preseident's ear.

A *New Scientist* editorial in December 2005 highlighted the scale of the threat facing us, and the failure of leaders to prioritise it:

"The latest international climate conference [in Montreal] closed in a mood of euphoria … even normally hard-boiled environmental campaigners were misty-eyed. 'Historic,' said Greenpeace, 'a big step forward … the US has been shamed.'

"With Green groups playing politics, scientists seem to stand alone. In recent months, they have reported compelling evidence that climate change is a real and present danger, and that the global climate system may be on the brink of dangerous positive feedbacks.

"At this magazine we regularly meet climate and earth-system scientists who harbour real fears for themselves and their families about what the 21st century will bring. Jim Hanson, George Bush's top climate modeller, said last week that we have 'at most 10 years' to make drastic cuts in emissions that might head off climate convulsions."

Threats of this magnitude should override all other considerations for world leaders. However, they were ignored by the G8 at Gleneagles, indicating that this gang of eight rich-country leaders cannot be trusted with world affairs. Under George W. Bush, carbon emissions in the US have risen steadily. Britain switched from coal to gas for economic reasons and its emissions reduced for a time, but under the Blair/Brown government emissions between 1997 and 2007 have risen 5.5% – back to 1990 levels – and are now increasing by 3% annually, driven by government policies for new roads, airport extensions and increased international trade.

However, in March 2007 the UK government became the first country to propose a legally binding limit on carbon dioxide emissions, requiring cuts of 60% by 2050 relative to 1990 levels. This is a step in the right direction. It does not, however, commit the present government to any action, and it is questionable whether emissions could be measured accurately enough for prosecution if the target is not met. Should the government of the day fail to achieve the projected cuts, it is allowed to buy additional allocations from other countries.

The Bush administration knows that climate change would be an ecological and humanitarian catastrophe that vastly exceeds the threat of terrorism, but it has published only one official document that acknowledges the fact. The report, commissioned by Donald Rumsfeld and made public in February 2004, was called 'Climate Change as a National Security Concern' and dealt with global warming as a purely military issue.

The report said that "the focus on climate research is slowly shifting from gradual to rapid change," and it "urged policy makers to consider the implications of possible abrupt climate change within two decades." The report questioned how to protect borders from environmental refugees, how to overpower nations collapsing under environmental pressures, how to maintain access to food, water and energy when other parts of the world go hungry and thirsty, and how to maintain

What about taxes?

Taxes cannot reduce greenhouse gas emissions to a safe level because taxes in a recession would be totally inadequate in a boom period. The Stern Review suggested that energy costs should rise by a factor of six to have an adequate effect on people's habits. This, however, would cause a recession and the tax would immediately have to be revised downwards.

nuclear pre-eminence while nuclear capability
falls into the hands of insurgents. The Bush
administration has therefore prevented action
being taken on climate change for ten years
in the full knowledge of its dangers. Its only
concern has been how best to use the ensuing
mayhem to assert US dominance.

Runaway warming has happened once before.
At the end of the Permian period, 250 million
years ago, volcanic eruptions in Siberia emitted
carbon dioxide that raised global temperatures.
Permafrost and polar ice melted, and tundra
released methane that caused the runaway
warming. Temperatures rose to 8°C warmer
than today. Ocean currents stalled, depriving
deep water of oxygen; topsoil, unrestrained
by plant roots, washed away into the oceans;
deep-sea stagnation produced clouds of
hydrogen sulphide that led to mass extinctions
on land. Over 90% of marine life and 70%
of terrestrial life was wiped out. Evolution
stalled for ten million years while planet earth
took time to recover.

And yet we squabble. A Martian would be
bewildered by our inaction and would surely
wonder: "Are the elders of this planet mad,
bad or just totally incompetent?"

Rio and Kyoto
initial good intentions

Well, at least the negotiatiors enjoyed themselves!

"We have everything we need to save the earth with the possible exception of political will, but in the United States of America political will is a renewable resource." Al Gore, *An Inconvenient Truth* (2006)

AT KYOTO IN 1997, countries representing 95% of the world's population agreed that, by 2012, industrialised countries should reduce greenhouse gas emissions by an average of 5.2% below 1990 levels. The reduction was not enough but it showed that the majority of the world wanted to take action on global warming. At the same time, the United States was denying the science of climate change, confusing the negotiations, watering down requirements – and ultimately refusing to sign.

In spite of its good intentions, the Kyoto Protocol is among the weirdest of international agreements. It allocates property of incredible value arbitrarily, on no basis of ownership whatsoever, to various rich countries. The property is the sky; or, to be more specific, the ability of the atmosphere to handle carbon emissions until these gases are absorbed by oceans, plants and plankton.

Having received this bonanza, countries are allowed to trade it. Not only that, but rich countries are allowed to increase the value of their property by using land in poor countries to absorb some of their emissions. This amounts to a new form of colonialism as poor countries will not be able to use this land in future at their own discretion and for their own benefit.

The date of 2012 for achieving the reductions avoided controversy because it was beyond the tenure of the politicians involved. As a result, they could make promises that would be broken only after they had gone. It is clear that politicians in rich countries have no intention

The Rio Earth Summit in 1992 was the most remarkable meeting of heads of state that has ever taken place. Leaders acknowledged a threat to the planet, and they set an agenda:

• "To achieve stabilisation of greenhouse gas concentrations in the atmosphere at a level that could prevent dangerous anthropogenic interference with the climate system." (Article 2)

• To "protect the climate system for the benefit of humankind on the basis of equity." (Article 3.1)

Fifteen years of negotiations have failed on both counts. Greenhouse gas concentrations have not been stabilised and the requirement for equity has been ignored.

of achieving the promised reductions if this in any way compromises their nations' competitiveness. "The blunt truth about the politics of climate change," said Tony Blair, "is that no country will want to sacrifice its economy in order to meet this challenge." Their purpose was to enable business to carry on as usual, and their chosen mechanism was emissions trading.

'Emissions' is a weasel word beloved of negotiators. It is notoriously difficult to measure or monitor emissions because they come as a mixture of several different gases from a multitude of different outlets, both massive and tiny. Your car, for instance: can you measure the fumes that come out of its exhaust? Research by Christian Aid in early 2007 estimated that 40% of the emissions of the top 100 firms in the UK are missing from their official figures.

The Kyoto Protocol lumps all types of emission together – from fossil fuels, agriculture and landfill, each of which has different causes and requires totally different mechanisms to control – making a dense fog of bureaucratic complexity that can keep negotiators groping in the dark for decades. This absolves politicians from making difficult decisions, secures work for bureaucrats and creates endless business opportunities for expert advisers; all are happy to extend their lucrative careers and make it virtually impossible for more simple and sensible ideas to be introduced from outside the establishment.

Since 2000, emissions in general have been rising at the rate of 3.2% a year, four times the pre-Kyoto level. The negotiators have failed. Emissions are spiralling out of control and humanity faces extinction.

The Kyoto Protocol is due for revision in 2012. It must not be allowed to sink further into the bureaucratic morass, nor must it be influenced by vested interests. And no country should be allowed to opt out.

There are signs of hope, even in the US. For years the most powerful voice on the environment in the senate was James Inhofe who famously stated that, "global warming is a hoax," and compared warnings about climate change to Nazi propaganda. In January 2007 he was replaced by Barbara Boxer, who considers global warming "a potential crisis of a magnitude we have never seen." Thirty-one US state governments, meanwhile, are following the example of California, which passed a law in September 2006 to cut greenhouse gases by 25% by 2020, and 370 US cities signed a climate protection agreement by the end of 2006 in defiance of the White House.

Contraction and convergence
for climate justice

"We hold these truths to be self-evident, that all men are created equal."

United States Declaration of Independence (1776)

THE GLOBAL COMMONS Institute developed the principle of contraction and convergence (C&C) as a negotiating tool for the 1997 conference in Kyoto.

Under C&C, countries could achieve a safe level of greenhouse gas emissions on the basis of equity, as required by the Rio summit. It would work like this:

- A figure for total global emissions would be set. It would start at current levels and contract year on year until emissions no longer pose a threat to the climate.

- Within this contracting figure, emission rights or permits would be distributed to countries on the basis of their population – converging to an equal distribution per person.

C&C provides a framework – contraction to sustainability, convergence to equality – within which the details can be negotiated. It is a simple concept, but it has huge implications.

If the permits were traded, countries that emit more than their allocation would have to buy emission rights from countries that do not use their full allocation. Rich, over-emitting countries would have the incentive to reduce emissions so that they needed to buy fewer permits. Poor countries would also wish to reduce their emissions so that they would have more permits available for sale. Money would flow from rich nations to poor nations as a right, not as aid or as cancellation of debt.

Poor countries could argue that they deserve a higher allocation of emission rights because the rich have already used their share and are responsible for the global crisis that is now harming poor countries more than the rich. Although this is true, it would be better to move to future equality through C&C and seek redress for the past in law.

Imagine living in a village where everyone dumps garbage into a giant hole. For years this causes no discernible harm, but then it starts to produce noxious smells and seep into an adjacent well. From this point on anyone continuing to dump harmful waste can be fined. Such a scenario has been used in legal matters since John Locke's Second Treatise on Civil Government – in 1690. Like those continuing to dump waste in the hole, rich countries have failed to curb their emissions, though they have known since 1992 that these emissions are causing harm. Those suffering the effects of global warming should seek redress from rich nations that are guilty of such negligence.

It is not the responsibility of the Bangladeshi government, for example, to compensate its farmers for the loss of their land when sea levels rise. It is the duty of the west, and in particular of the individuals, companies and governments that have blocked international agreements that could have reduced the damage.

"The UK should be prepared to accept the contraction and convergence principle as the basis for international agreement on reducing greenhouse gas emissions."

Royal Commission on Environmental Pollution (2000)

Children recycling rubbish at a landfill site in South America

Cap and Share
ownership of a right

IF YOUR BATHROOM is flooding what is the first thing you do? You turn off the taps. Our atmosphere is flooding – with gases from fossil fuels – so the obvious first step would be to stop any more gases being released.

But our present policy is more like struggling to keep the water in the bath while leaving the taps on – allowing, even encouraging, companies to extract as much fossil fuel as possible – rather than turning the supply off. This is the starting point for Cap and Share.

The Cap
Excessive emissions of carbon dioxide are resulting in greenhouse gases concentrating in the atmosphere, where they destabilise the climate system.

Emissions must be capped. This should be repeated again and again because so many conferences, speeches and learned papers are devoted to avoiding hard decisions and obfuscating this essential, urgent, stark and inconvenient truth.

There is a solution. Most carbon emissions come from coal, oil and natural gas. Once these fuels leave the ground their carbon will be released somehow, somewhere, sometime. Only a few large companies mine coal, or have gas fields and oil wells. A way must be found to reduce the amount of fossil fuels that they extract. By going upstream and controlling carbon fuels at source there is no need to measure and regulate the many points at which emissions are made downstream by industry, agriculture, airlines, railways, cars, tractors, power-tools, heating, cooking and our many other energy-consuming activities. The idea of regulating at the point of emission is absurd.

> It's easier to limit the supply of fossil fuels than to control demand for them.

The Share
Who owns the sky? The atmosphere, with its ability to handle carbon emissions, is a gift of nature to all living beings. We all have an equal stake in it and its benefits should be evenly distributed between everyone.

The sky's ability to handle carbon is limited, so emissions should be valued in terms of this limit. This idea gave rise to the concept, introduced at Kyoto, of buying and selling the right to emit carbon dioxide. Europe's 2005 Emissions Trading Scheme (EU-ETS) allows emission rights to be traded but it gives these rights, free of charge, only to large polluting companies.

British power companies are receiving an annual windfall profit of £800 million from the scheme. It is worth looking at this system in order to understand the problems associated with carbon trading. The EU-ETS has three basic faults – philosophical, economic and political.

It is philosophical nonsense: what right have corporations to trade a property of the sky that belongs to everyone – you and me? **It is economic nonsense**: restrictions on the use of fossil fuel (as well as the depletion of these fuels) will cause the cost of living to rise dramatically. A means must be found to use the escalating monetary value of the fuels to compensate individuals against these costs, not to benefit big business. **It is political nonsense**: imagine the backlash when corporations reap huge benefits while more and more people struggle to get by.

The faults of the EU-ETS demonstrate why the Cap and Share concept insists, first, that everyone has a right to the properties of the sky; second, that an equal distribution of income from the sale of these rights makes economic sense; and third, that this method would be politically sustainable.

Cap and Share – how it works

An independent Regulator – the equivalent of the World Bank or the IMF – would define the level of emissions that will not harm the atmosphere and allocate emission coupons on the basis of equity.

An agency in each country, independent of government, would either:

- auction the coupons to extractor companies and distribute the proceeds equally to every adult in the country; or
- issue equal emissions entitlement coupons to each adult to sell through the banking system.

Companies that extract coal, oil or natural gas would bid for sufficient coupons from the agencies to cover the emissions that their fuels release. Without adequate coupons they would not be allowed to sell fuel. They would then surrender the coupons to the Regulator's inspectors for cancellation.

If a country failed to distribute coupons equally to all its citizens, its next allocation would be withheld until it did so. Supply and demand would determine the price of the coupons. Their value would rise as the supply of fossil fuels was progressively restricted.

Under Cap and Share only a limited amount of fossil fuel would be available. The distribution of equal-per-capita shares would ensure that

Cap and Share applied to transport in Europe

Each adult in Europe would be given eight tonnes (reducing annually) of emission entitlement coupons. They could sell their surplus to banks or post offices at the going rate.

Companies that introduce fossil-based transport fuels in the EU would bid for the coupons to cover the environmental damage their products would cause (aviation fuel would need more coupons than petrol).

The coupons would be returned, checked and cancelled. This would limit the amount of all forms of travel in Europe to sustainable levels. The cost of travel would rise and those that travel least would benefit most.

poor countries would not lose out. It would be up to governments to regulate these fuels within a country; for example, they might allocate half the available petrol to ambulances and public transport, and half to the market. There would be a level playing field for all businesses. A convergence fund should be held back from the process to cover the costs of adaptation.

Cap and Share has variations that would allow it to be adopted as a revision to the EU-ETS, or to be pioneered unilaterally by Britain. Friends of the Earth said in 2006, "Committing the UK to operate the economy within a defined carbon budget would make us a world leader in tackling climate change."

Other emissions

Other sources of carbon emissions need to be dealt with separately. Deforestation is a major reason for the rise in atmospheric carbon concentrations, since tropical rainforests are the lungs of the earth, an essential control mechanism. But logging cannot be lumped together with the extraction of fossil fuels in a single regulation. The logical solution is to ban, totally, the logging and trade in old-growth timber from rainforests – a global ban similar to that on ivory. The loss of income should be compensated using the convergence fund.

Aircraft exhausts contain nitrogen oxides, steam and particulates, which, when emitted in the stratosphere, cause three times more damage than the emission of CO_2. The cost of fuel for use in aircrafts should therefore be multiplied (that is, taxed) by a factor of three. Separate schemes should be devised for agriculture and landfill, which both have the different problem of emitting methane.

The concentration of wealth

Vast wealth is accumulating in the hands of oil-producing companies and countries, particularly in the Middle East. The Cap would prevent such accumulation because there would be limited emission coupons available for the companies to buy in order to sell their fuel. The amount of oil that companies could sell would decrease each year and their profits would be reduced by the cost of the emission permits.

But surely the US would never join a scheme that limits its use of oil? Don't be so sure. The US, apart from the Bush administration, is taking more action on climate change than other countries. And there are reasons why all countries, including the US, might wish to prevent an ever-increasing concentration of wealth in oil-producing regions. Most oil comes from state-controlled companies in the Middle East, the Caspian, Russia, the Gulf of Guinea and Venezuela, none of which are particularly friendly with Washington. The US would welcome a scheme that prevents them accumulating yet more wealth.

At last – they have an idea that could do the trick.

The Chinese government is worried about social unrest due to widespread poverty. But under Cap and Share its large rural population would receive income from selling their allotted emissions coupons. The same would happen in India and other countries with poor communities whose standard of living would significantly improve with this extra income.

Europe would also suffer drastically with oil depletion and restrictions on the availability of fossil fuels. The cost of most goods, including food, would escalate, causing runaway prices and increasing hardship for many people, which would then lead to public outrage if there was no compensation. The Share is an essential economic mechanism to pre-empt this hardship.

But the producing countries would never agree! They might. As the global demand for crude oil exceeds supply, the price will rise and there is likely to be a deep recession whether or not restrictions are placed on the extraction of fossil fuels. The price of oil would then crash and remain low for several years. Producing countries might prefer a lower but more regular return that lasts for longer. An organisation of petroleum importing countries might control the trade, and any country attempting unilateral deals with oil producers would forego the benefits of Cap and Share.

Perhaps the greatest benefit of the scheme, however, would be the peace dividend. When the income from oil production is astronomical, as it is at present, industrialised countries often secure supplies by taking military action.

More than
75% of the
electricity
made
by power
stations
is wasted
through
inefficient
generation,
transmission,
and end use.

Energy
how we waste it

"The energy crisis has not yet overwhelmed us but it will if we do not act quickly."

US President Jimmy Carter, 1977

ENERGY IS LIFE. It is the ability to work, to move, to heat and to cool. Atoms are full of energy and without it everything would collapse into dust. But only a certain amount of energy arrives on the planet each day from the sun and almost all our activities are based on the withdrawal not of current but of historical energy – energy that came from the sun and was laid down in the earth millennia ago.

Wood, water, wind and muscle used to be our energy sources. But coal provided us with greater power, enough to drive the industrial revolution. Coal was then replaced by more accessible fuels, like oil. Easy to extract, oil has created and encouraged our habit of using excessive energy. Then came natural gas, gushing out of the seabed and providing a bonanza of cheap electricity. In Britain we used it with such haste that after 30 years our gas fields are nearly exhausted. What will we use next?

Scientists say that if we rule out fossil fuels we cannot meet our energy 'needs' without hi-tech solutions, which include nuclear power. If we rule out nuclear power we will have to reduce our demand for energy massively. Future solutions are not only technological, therefore, but also social, economic and organisational.

The root of our problem is waste. It has become our mindset. Goods are now deliberately made to fail, so we continually have to buy replacements. Advertising is a huge generator of waste, persuading us to buy new things to keep up with fashion. Governments rarely regulate energy use. Our houses leak energy like sieves. More than three quarters – yes, three quarters – of the electricity made by power stations is wasted through inefficient generation, grid transmission and end use.

Even our food system is hugely wasteful. Folke Günther, a Swedish scientist, studied the energy used by a typical family of four on food, heating and car travel. The family expends 40 (comparative energy) units on food management, 17 on house heating and 15 on car use. It would therefore save more carbon emissions by sourcing locally grown organic food than by adding insulation to its home or getting rid of its car. Industrial agriculture, however, is only concerned about profit.

Globalised free trade is another obvious candidate for energy reform. Most utensils in the US are flown or shipped from China. Identical foodstuffs, like biscuits and tinned soups, move in opposite directions across the Atlantic: their recipes could simply have been sent by email.

Less obvious, but perhaps the biggest cause of wasted energy, is the money system. Many economies in the past functioned by remaining stable, but our present economy would collapse without growth. Growth has become the measure of success and governments encourage their populations to consume more and more and more. Projects to generate economic growth are responsible for half the energy we use.

Now, suddenly, there is a panic. Oil may no longer flow from the Middle East. Russia might turn off the gas tap. And global warming requires us to stop using fossil fuels. How shall we find the energy we 'need'? And more energy for future growth? Many studies have shown that, with sensible legislation, we could reduce our energy use by up to a half.

There is no energy crisis, just a crisis of intelligence and competence. The miserable amount spent on reducing the use of fossil fuels contrast with sums spent elsewhere. In the UK the chancellor has earmarked just £1 billion "for spending policies that tackle climate change," despite admitting that it is "the most pressing problem in the world." But he is happy to spend £3.5 billion on widening the M1 motorway.

The UK has invested £7 billion – or £70 billion depending on how you count it – on nuclear research. The nuclear programme will need a further £125 billion for cleanup and decommissioning; renewing Trident nuclear submarines will cost £75 billion. Would Britain not be more secure if its military budget was devoted to promoting permanent, non-polluting sources of energy rather than fighting for oil in the Middle East? Countries that have invested in alternative energy sources have a healthy economic future. Denmark, where the government has encouraged wind projects, has huge contracts in China. Sweden aims do without oil imports by 2020.

Where governments fail to act, individuals can take the initiative – in how they travel, how they heat their homes, how they eat. Their choice of lifestyle will contribute to climate survival. It will also influence politicians who, having failed to lead, will be forced to follow.

Why not build segregated cycle tracks instead of roads?

An energy policy
a question of survival

"We must even face the prospect of changing our basic ways of living."

Jimmy Carter, announcing his candidacy for US president, 1974

A NEW SOCIETY, should we survive to see it, will be founded on energy that is constantly renewed and does not harm the planet. Historic energy, captured from the sun and laid down millions of years ago as coal, natural gas and oil, belongs to a dark age, whose time is passing.

It is not possible for individuals, whether in the city, suburb or remote countryside, to reduce all their responsibility for carbon emissions independently. Our housing, transport, maintenance of streets and roads, refuse system and other public services all produce emissions: everyone shares responsibility for them. We can only go some way to being carbon neutral by spending money on insulation and solar panels, by travelling only on foot or bicycle and by growing our own food. For those without the means it is very difficult.

If committed individuals cannot prevent catastrophic global warming on their own, it is essential that governments take radical action. This goes beyond party politics. In 1939 Churchill recognised that Hitler's threat was more dangerous than any other. Everyone, from King to pauper, accepted an equal food ration.

Hitler's threat was only to national survival; this one is to human survival. If the government realised the severity of our situation our economy would be put on a wartime footing.

A radical energy policy is the key weapon required in this war. We need a statesperson at the head of a political party or a coalition, and we should only vote for politicians who define how they will achieve the necessary reduction in carbon emissions. But, tragically, we and our politicians have instead been determined to walk backwards into the future, fighting wars to prop up yesterday's technology. (The Iraq war for oil looks like it may cost $2,000 billion, according to the former World Bank economist, Joseph Stiglitz.)

New technologies already exist – wind, wave, sea currents, solar-thermal-units, solar-photovoltaic-cells, co-generation, hydrogen-fuel-cells, soil-heat-exchange, geo-thermal energy – and research is progressing fast, even in the absence of government support. However, we should not pin our hopes on some magical new technology that might allow us to carry on as usual. The crisis is immediate and our policy must be based on existing technologies, not on a wing and a prayer and a 'technofix'.

Scientists have told us unequivocally what to do: carbon emissions must be reduced globally by 60% within 23 years to allow any hope of avoiding runaway global warming. Since Britain uses a disproportionate amount of fossil fuel our share of carbon emission reductions needs to be as much as 90% by 2030.

The *Stern Review* made it clear that to continue as usual will have devastating economic consequences. We are so locked into carbon technologies, it said, that cost-mechanisms alone will not achieve the required change. Government-funded research and regulation for a raft of measures is essential, including the rationing of emission allowances. Many campaign groups have been saying the same.

Friends of the Earth suggested a cap on the use of fossil fuel that reduces 3% each year – a good start but not enough. The Energy Savings Trust and the Oxford Environmental Change Unit calculated how to achieve, in the UK, a 60% reduction in CO_2 emissions by 2030 simply by grants and regulation for insulation, micro-generation and efficiency. Again, part of the solution but not enough. The most specific suggestions have come from George Monbiot, the environmental campaigner and journalist. Monbiot accepted the scientists' stipulation – 90% by 2030 – and asked himself whether we can achieve it without totally disrupting our present way of living. His book *Heat* is well researched, fully referenced and not afraid to challenge exaggerated claims for alternative sources of energy.

Monbiot concludes that the goal can indeed be achieved, but only with decisive government action. First a target has to be set for an immediate steep drop in emissions, which is then distributed equally among all citizens. New buildings must be so energy efficient that heating systems are unnecessary. All inefficient energy equipment should be banned. Regressive military expenditure should be redirected to permanent energy generation. The transport system should be totally transformed. All out-of-town supermarkets should be closed.

He argues that far from crippling our lifestyle, these measures would improve our quality of life. There is, however, one exception: we cannot continue our love affair with flying. Airport expansion should be frozen immediately, most planes should be grounded and runways drastically reduced.

To achieve the necessary reduction in emissions the government has to make human survival its primary objective. In the absence of other coordinated blue-sky thinking, Monbiot's book could act as a guide for action.

We are close to a psychological tipping point as people despair of their leaders' refusal to take action against the biggest threat humanity has ever faced. If politicians continue to prevaricate, widespread non-violent disobedience might be the only way to persuade them.

The choice

"Either we go on as usual, enjoying life and pretending we didn't know that we are actually destroying the lives of our grandchildren.

"Or we tell the people we elected as stewards of our planet to get their heads out of the sand of self-deception and set up the necessary legislation."

Oliver Postgate, 2006, creator of children's films

Trees
and carbon offset schemes

WE FEEL INCREASINGLY guilty about using aeroplanes. But some flights, for business or staying in touch with family, may be essential in today's world.

Many people try to compensate for emissions resulting from their travel by contributing to schemes that absorb carbon dioxide or prevent it being emitted. These carbon offset programmes can be a good answer if they really remove carbon immediately, safely and permanently, and if they are the only way any action will be taken. These are big 'ifs'.

Companies make a lot of money from these schemes and regulation is lax, so it is important to be sceptical. Remember, too, that emissions from aircraft flying at 10,000 metres are considerably more damaging than emissions at ground level. The CER (Certified Emission Reduction) tag is given to schemes that satisfy the strict UN guidelines.

Better than paying for carbon offset would be to spend the same money on improving the insulation of your house or installing solar panels. You would thus reduce the emissions you are responsible for in the first place.

Meanwhile, the popular belief that planting trees is a useful offset is mistaken. Although a tree absorbs carbon dioxide from the atmosphere through its leaves, it also releases

the carbon stored in the ground from its roots when it absorbs nutrients. This is especially true of younger trees. Ernst-Detlef Schulze, one of the world's leading experts in the study of carbon cycles, believes that a typical tree growing outdoors in a moderate climate "would have to be at least 60 years old before it became a net consumer of carbon dioxide from the atmosphere." The urgent need is for emissions to be reduced in the coming decade or two.

The ancient forests are an essential part of the carbon cycle. Their wholesale destruction is having a devastating effect on the atmosphere because it removes a critical carbon sink. The damage is as great as that done by emissions made by the entire global transport sector.

Reforestation does not compensate for deforestation. Planting trees in other people's countries has its advantages. But it can also be a form of colonialism as land is taken out of local control for the benefit of rich carbon offsetters. It is essential that tree-planting initiatives arise from the local communities themselves.

Planting a tree sounds simple. You dig a hole, put in a sapling and that's that. But, of course, it's not. In poor countries there are many social and economic pressures that also have to be taken into account.

One success story is the organisation SCAD (Social Change and Development) in south India. It started out by gathering bucketfuls of seeds from indigenous trees and scattering them in the surrounding barren hills. After 20 years the hills have become green with vegetation, the micro-climate has improved, the reduced run-off has resulted in less flooding and the water table has risen.

SCAD now works in 400 villages with an ongoing tree-planting scheme. Farmers who want to participate are given a week's training in the planting and caring of trees. Ponds or bore wells are dug on their land, soil samples are analysed and suitable trees selected.

"Telling people to plant trees, makes about as much sense as suggesting they drink more water to offset rising sea levels."

Oliver Rackham, Cambridge University, 2006

At the onset of the monsoon the farmers receive saplings, dig holes, prepare the soil and erect protection against goats. SCAD provides all the materials and during the first year supervisors make regular visits to provide advice, organic pesticides, manure and replacement saplings. It can take a minimum of three years before the trees provide any income, so farmers are given a cow that provides them with milk they can sell in the meantime. Failure to maintain the trees results in the cow being withdrawn.

Fruit trees like tamarind, sapota and aonala begin to yield after three years. Forest trees can eventually be used as timber; other species, like the famous neem, have medicinal properties. And there are further benefits too: fallen leaves and the cow manure improve the soil, roots protect from erosion, the micro-climate slowly improves, the water table rises. The cost of the scheme works out at about £5 a tree.

Natural gas
held to ransom

"Having ignored all the warnings and squandered two decades of planning time, the United States is left with gas from across the oceans as the only possible business-as-usual option. But it is too late."

Julian Darley, *High Noon for Natural Gas* (2004)

NATURAL GAS APPEARS to have a bright future. So what do we do? We burn it, using up the last great non-renewable hydrocarbon.

Coal-fired plants used to produce all of our electricity in Britain. Then we switched to natural gas when we found our own, cheaper, supplies beneath the North Sea. This switch had nothing to do with concern for global warming. Rather, it enabled Britain to reduce emissions for a time without having to do anything about limiting the increasing emissions from its other activities.

Emissions from gas- and coal-fired power stations could be captured and buried if appropriate regulations, research and funding were provided (don't hold your breath). But when gas is piped to houses its carbon cannot be captured. Natural gas is largely methane, a greenhouse gas that does at least 20 times more damage than carbon dioxide.

As with oil, the United States led the way with exploiting natural gas, first using it for street lighting, then home heating and then for generating electricity. Starting in the 1940s, the US gradually became an addict, knowing that it had its own vast gas fields.

But it is more difficult to know what lies underground with gas than with oil, and even more difficult to know how much is left while a field is being worked. With oil there is plenty of warning because the rate of extraction rises and gradually declines. Gas fields, once tapped, give a regular output but when the decline comes it is often sudden and with very little warning.

Optimists believe we have almost inexhaustible reserves. Pessimists expect unforeseen shocks. Gas and oil companies are optimists, or pretend to be – they regard data as confidential and hide it even from the authorities. In the US

Oil showed us the perils of fossil fuels. We should handle gas more wisely.

their message was so persuasive that no one contemplated a shortage until, in early 2003, the companies suddenly reported that output was reducing. That summer three massive blackouts showed that not enough power had been stored to tide the country over peak demand. Since then the US has become dependent on imports. The North American Free Trade Agreement (NAFTA) prevented Canada from regulating its reserves or preventing the export of natural gas to the US. So it too is now in crisis. A serious shortage of natural gas may hit the US earlier and harder than its shortage of oil.

Britain found its North Sea fields in 1969 and by the mid-1970s natural gas was providing most of our energy supply. We built gas-fired power stations and by the late 1990s were even exporting gas to Europe. As a result of Margaret Thatcher's deregulation this huge natural resource was exploited at record speed while prices were at an all-time low due to the glut in production. This gave us a bonanza of cheap energy for a short time and prevented serious investment in permanent energy sources. The party was over by 2003 just as prices were moving up. It has left us addicted to natural gas and dependent on a supply from Russia that crosses a number of other countries before reaching us.

Norway, by contrast, has extended the life of its oil and natural gas by regulating its use. We are now receiving a temporary supply from there with a new pipeline across the North Sea.

The industry insists that plentiful global gas reserves will last until at least 2050, and this period might be extended **if** new large gas fields are discovered, **if** safe ways are found to tap methane hydrates and **if** a global economic slowdown reduces demand. But, of course, that's not the whole story.

The huge fields of natural gas, which they say will last for several decades, were discovered in one decade – between 1965 to 1975. Later discoveries have been much smaller. Since 2001 the amount extracted has exceeded the amount being found each year.

A major disadvantage of gas is that most reserves are found in hostile environments far away from the end users. Of industrialised countries only Russia, Norway and Australia still have sizeable reserves of their own; other countries depend on imports.

Natural gas is easy to transport in pipes, but 60% of reserves are located in places that cannot be served by pipelines. It is too bulky to store in containers in its gaseous state so it has to be converted into a liquid – liquefied natural gas (LNG) – which is 600 times denser. The gas is then refrigerated to minus 160°C, before being

transported in insulated double-hulled tankers. It is then converted back to gas at its final port. A single 'train' – the word they use to describe the three processes – costs between $4 billion and $13 billion, uses about 15% of the energy of the gas and takes several years to plan and install. It is doubtful, therefore, whether the global economy could support the astronomical costs of LNG if it were to become a major source of energy.

In 2004 an accidental explosion destroyed three out of six LNG plants at Skikda, Algeria. They had recently been given a clean bill of health by an expert US company that services the energy industry. If a tanker carrying LNG were to explode in port, whether by accident or through an act of terrorism, the resulting firestorm could bring the whole LNG project to a halt, as the Hindenburg fire in 1937 did for the Zeppelin airship project.

Countries that have large gas fields will use them to gain political and economic power just as the US used oil in the 20th century. Iran shares with Qatar one of the largest fields in the world. Russia has a third of the world's natural gas and excludes western companies from exploiting its reserves. It also prefers the low-tech option of using pipelines to Europe, China and India rather than hi-tech LNG terminals for transporting it to the US. Many poorer countries that have natural gas cannot afford LNG terminals and will depend on the receiving countries to make the investment. The fragility of LNG as a major energy source may result in the US using even more desperate measures than it currently uses to secure oil supplies.

Natural gas provides more energy for fewer emissions than coal or oil. If regulated properly, it would be the best fossil fuel for making the transition to a zero carbon economy.

Hydrogen
the future of energy?

"Yes, my friends, I believe that water will one day be employed as fuel, that hydrogen and oxygen which constitute it, used singly or together, will furnish an inexhaustible source of heat and light, of an intensity of which coal is not capable." Jules Verne, *The Mysterious Island* (1874)

HYDROGEN PROVIDES THREE quarters of the sun's fuel and makes up more than 90% of atoms in the universe. On earth it is best known in combination with oxygen, as water (H_2O). It does not contain carbon so it might eventually replace natural gas in the fight against global warming. But in the last couple of years, doubts about its potential have been raised. If widely used, scientists say, it could act as a greenhouse gas in the troposphere, the lowest layer of the atmosphere, and damage the ozone layer as well. Still, some countries are now investing heavily in developing the use of hydrogen.

Hydrogen fuel cells – motors with no moving parts that convert chemical energy into electricity and vice versa – were developed for space technology but have, so far, had a bumpy landing on earth. Japan and the US are leading the field but China could soon overtake them.

Hydrogen can be extracted from water using electricity (by electrolysis). The hydrogen can then be combined with oxygen from the air and thereby generate electricity (and only water will come out of the exhaust pipe). But hydrogen, as a gas, is bulky. It has to be stored either under very high pressure or as a liquid at −253°C. In both forms it could easily explode, so storage must be kept to a minimum. Both processes of storage use a lot of energy: a full hydrogen economy might need three times more electricity than our present one.

Reversible hydrogen fuel cells have been suggested for electric cars. When parked at a kerbside rank or in the garage, they can be connected to a water tap and power point to refill the fuel cell. This would do away with the need for bulk storage at filling stations. The same principle can be applied to the workplace or at home. Electricity during off-peak periods can be used to fill a hydrogen tank; the hydrogen can then be used to heat buildings and for generating stand-by power. Similarly, if fuel cells are provided beside wind turbines, excess electricity generated when the wind is blowing in off-peak periods could produce a store of hydrogen, which could later be used to generate electricity when there is no wind.

Although Jules Verne outlined the potential of hydrogen 133 years ago the technology is still in its infancy and we do not yet know if it will be the energy of the future. The age of cheap oil intervened. It seems that we will always go for the cheap and easy option, however damaging and short-term it may be.

Biofuels
a dangerous distraction

"We are facing an epic competition between 800 million motorists who want to protect their mobility and the 2,000 million poorest people in the world who simply want to survive." Lester Brown, *Fortune* magazine, August 2006

A POLICEMAN IN Llandovery, Wales, once smelled chip fat when there was no fish-and-chip shop in sight. The culprits, who were mixing the waste cooking oil with diesel, were identified and prosecuted. They should have been given a medal. The re-use of waste materials is a key principle of the new economy.

This incident spread word that we don't need oil from the Middle East after all: we can grow our own. Suddenly knees jerk under desks. The supermarket chain Tesco smells a profit stream. Scientists set up new faculties. The EU wants 10% biofuel content at every pump. A new age of carbon-free mobility is promised. Clean, green, renewable!

The reality is very different. Corn (maize) for bioethanol is the favourite in the US, but it is grown with vast amounts of fertiliser and pesticides (both made using fossil fuels). As a result, the net reduction of emissions from using bioethanol instead of petrol is at most 10%. The extra demand is already raising global grain prices and reducing emergency stocks for famine relief. The poor need grain to eat.

The production of sugar cane is more efficient than that of corn but its use as a biofuel would cause world sugar prices to rocket. It is a thirsty crop too; in one state in south India it already

absorbs two thirds of the water and has lowered water tables by 50 metres. Sugar companies say that farmers will benefit from growing cane because it fetches higher prices than food crops. This only highlights the companies' ignorance: most Indian farmers grow crops primarily to feed themselves, selling only the surplus. Pushing these farmers into the market economy would make them highly vulnerable to fluctuating national and international prices. Most would have to sell their land and migrate to city slums.

In Indonesia and Brazil rainforests are being felled to plant palms for their oil, and peat bogs are being used for sugar cane – a process that releases huge amounts of trapped carbon. The US energy department is subsidising the conversion of fish oil into biodiesel. Fish stocks around the world are already crashing and this will only hasten their demise.

Biodiesel and bioethanol could be more destructive of the climate than fossil fuels. The biofuel industry cannot be left to market forces because the cars of the rich will always out-compete the poor. According to the Earth Policy Institute, the corn required to fill a large car's tank just once could feed a person for a year.

Appropriate regulations within each country are the best way forward. Bioethanol makes some sense for Brazil, where only 3% of its current farmland is providing a tenth of its fuel. By contrast, three quarters of Europe's farmland would be needed to produce just 10% of its fuel.

International trade in biofuels is already responsible for the dispossession of small farmers and the destruction of rainforests. The trade must be banned. The Global Forest Coalition in a joint petition with other NGOs (non-governmental organisations), has called the trade "a disaster in the making ... There is nothing green or sustainable about imported or exported biofuel."

But it's not all bad. A new experiment is feeding emissions from coal-burning power stations into translucent containers of water, in which algae convert the carbon dioxide into fuel. The technology is in its infancy and the potential for permanently neutralising the greenhouse gas is yet to be studied. Some scientists suggest, however, that the future for biofuels is not with crops but rather with microbes such as algae.

Pollution

Pollution from petrol engines causes 10,000 deaths in the US each year. Ethanol fuel is an even greater threat because of the acetaldehyde it emits.

New Scientist, April 2007

←——— energy captured as fossil fuels over millions of years (line extends for eight kilometres) ———→

The future of oil
half empty or half full?

IMAGINE A LINE eight kilometres long that represents the millions of years in which solar energy has been captured and laid down as coal, gas and oil. Then imagine a small blip near the end of the line. That blip represents the time we are taking to steal this resource from future generations. We are half way through the blip.

Oil was formed in two periods, 90 million and 150 million years ago, when warm conditions caused excessive flowering of algae. This produced carbon-based organic matter that was converted into oil as it became buried inside rifts. Geologists have now located all the large oil fields in the world. New, isolated discoveries are getting smaller and smaller.

These days we have a material standard of living that previous generations could never have imagined. We put this down to enlightened market-based economics, but it is nothing of the sort. It is entirely due to fossil fuels, particularly oil. They drive our cars, lorries and aeroplanes. They heat our homes. They give us plastics, medicines, cosmetics, computers, CDs, fertilisers. They also cause wars that create massive upheaval across the planet. Even George W. Bush eventually admitted in 2006 that, "We

are addicted to oil." He added, "the best way to break this addiction is through technology." What technology? We have developed few technologies that are not dependent on oil. That was an addict's hallucination.

Coal gave Britain an Empire. The US gained global power by having a tenth of the world's oil and by being the first to exploit it. Our grandchildren will have to manage without oil altogether, or only oil for specialised uses.

In 1956 M. King Hubbert, then director of the Shell research laboratory, said that oil discoveries in the US had peaked in 1930 and extraction would peak in 15 years. The oil companies said he was mad. In 1971 US oil extraction duly peaked and started its long decline in spite of a desperate hunt for new fields and the most sophisticated extraction equipment. Outside the US, the discovery of oilfields reached a peak in the 1960s and new discoveries have been declining ever since. Extraction is now at its peak.

While the amount of oil that can be produced is falling, demand is rising. China is increasing its use of oil by 15% a year. India's consumption

energy extracted over the past 200 years ⟶

is booming. The developed world crows that energy-efficiency will reduce demand, forgetting Jevons' paradox that increased efficiency has always led to an increase, not a reduction, in the use of a resource.

The first half of the age of oil – the upward slope of our blip – is at an end. Oil production during this period has been driven by a growing global economy. There have only been brief periods, as in the 1970s, when the economy was held back by an oil shortage. The second half of the oil age will be profoundly different. The global economy will be determined by the limited amount of energy available, and

the economy of each country will depend on how much energy it can command. Trade, manufacturing, services, exchange, everything will be limited not by money but by its energy use. Energy will replace money as the dominant currency for human affairs.

Jimmy Carter (US president 1976–1980) said that the US should never have to fight wars to seize other people's oil. A couple of decades of transition to renewable energy sources, he believed, would ensure the stability and future of America without destabilising the rest of the world. He put in place incentives to achieve solar-heated homes and windmill-powered

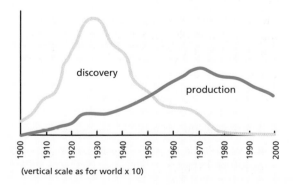

United States discovery and production of oil

discovery

production

1900 1910 1920 1930 1940 1950 1960 1970 1980 1990 2000

(vertical scale as for world x 10)

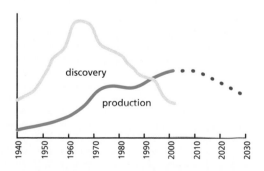

World discovery and production of oil

discovery

production

1940 1950 1960 1970 1980 1990 2000 2010 2020 2030

communities. Ronald Reagan, on achieving office in 1981, immediately removed Carter's solar panels from the roof of the White House, repealed his tax incentives and set the US on an unparalleled programme of waste and consumption. The US, still addicted to oil, has military bases around the globe to help it grab the dwindling supplies.

Production Sharing Agreements (PSAs) are part of this aggressive energy colonialism. They were forced on Russia following the demise of the Soviet Union, when prices for oil were low and the country was too weak to defend its interests. PSAs hand over development of oil and gas fields to energy corporations for 20 to 50 years, only allowing profits to the host country after production costs have been recovered. Most oil nations have repudiated this process and Russia, not surprisingly, has taken back control of the large fields on its Pacific seaboard. The US is now forcing PSAs on its puppet regime in Iraq.

Oil carries a curse. The more valuable a resource, the more conflict surrounds it. The richest oilfields are in the Middle East and the Caspian zone where oil-lubricated despots are bribed for their friendship and society is exploding with hatred of the west. Iraq has descended into civil war. Afghanistan, which spans the proposed route of a pipeline pumping oil from the Caspian, is hardly more stable.

Venezuela has the largest oil fields outside this region. Under the leadership of Hugo Chávez it now uses some of its oil income for the benefit of its poor. The state provides free preventative medicine, free eye operations, cheap food for slum dwellers, 100% literacy programmes and cheap oil exports for poorer neighbouring countries. It is re-igniting the social aspirations of Simón Bolívar and the great Latin American reformers of the 1960s and 1970s who were consistently undermined by the US.

Angola has vast reserves too, but its people do not benefit because of the widespread corruption caused by oil company practices. Luanda, the capital, is the second most expensive city in the world and hosts foreigners who fly between opulent gated enclaves and offshore rigs. Yet two-thirds of Angolans have no access to clean drinking water, and the country languishes near the bottom of the UN Human Development Index.

It is a similar story elsewhere in Africa. "Oil has brought death," said Malony Kolang, a chief of the southern Nuer people. "When the pumping began, the war began. Antonov aircraft and helicopter gun-ships began attacking the villages. Everything around the oilfields has been destroyed." Congo's conflict is blamed on linguistic and ethnic differences but, again, the underlying reason is resources; not oil this time but diamonds and cobalt. By contrast, the more stable African countries, such as Senegal, Tanzania, Mozambique or Ghana, are those of little interest to prospectors.

A still more alarming threat may be waiting. In the early 1800s, before fossil fuels, the world could support only one billion people. Oil-based development has enabled the population to rise to over six billion. After the damage oil-based agrochemicals have inflicted on fertility, the world may be able to support even fewer than it could two centuries ago.

It will take time to accept that 2000 years of modernity are at an end. Community life, destroyed by oil-based mobility, will have to be re-invented. The massive mis-investment in vertical cities, urban sprawl and industrial farming will somehow have to be transformed into balanced agri-urban settlements. We will all need to adopt a deep and comprehensive belief that society, bereft of quick-fix gadgets, is worth carrying on.

The price of oil fluctuates, depending on conflict, natural events and recession but, in due course, it will rise remorselessly.

The central dogma of the neoliberal religion is that demand will raise the price of any commodity and this in turn will result in alternatives, or in more being found or produced. The financial gurus at *The Economist* have repeatedly had to alter their predictions: when crude oil prices reached $38/barrel they said it would stabilise at $20. When it reached $70 they said it would stabilise at $60. Yet, as the price rises, there is no sign of an increase in production.

As the price of oil has risen, the oil-producing countries have become fabulously wealthy, enabling them to build ski resorts in the desert and the highest buildings in the world. But we have seen nothing yet. When oil prices double or triple, these countries will absorb much of the world's wealth. No one knows what this will do to the global economy or its power base.

The good news is that roughly half the world's oil is still in the ground.

Intelligent Homo sapiens would extract as little as possible, using this to establish wind, water and solar installations for permanent non-polluting energy. It would empower local communities to be self-supporting, self-feeding and self-governing. Homo fatuus, on the other hand, would centralise power and let the oil go to the strongest. It would invest in technology to extract it as quickly as possible and would let profit determine its exploitation. World affairs are in the hands of Homo fatuus.

Oil in Venezuela

Venezuela, with the largest reserves outside the Middle East, is liquidating its US Treasury stocks and converting its $30 billion reserves to euros and other currencies. It is offering oil on favourable terms to the Caribbean region and cementing oil alliances with Brazil, Argentina, Colombia, Ecuador, Cuba, Peru and Bolivia. It has also signed contracts with China, who is helping Venezuela with its housing programme.

Oil platform in Lake Maracaibo, Venezuela

The US orchestrated an attempted coup d'état in 2002 against the Venezuelan president Hugo Chávez, and continues to provide funding for political groups that oppose him. The right-wing Christian fundamentalist, Pat Robertson, even called for his assassination, but he has not been charged with incitement to violence.

Nuclear power
a safe option?

THE UK IS RUNNING short of long-term supplies of electricity. We knew we would. But during those heady days of North Sea oil we gorged ourselves on cheap energy and did nothing for the future. We could have been investing in sustainable energy systems, such as renewables. We wisely rejected nuclear power – even the City accepted that it was intolerably expensive. But having wasted our early opportunity we are now in danger of falling back on a technology that we once rejected. The arguments against it have not changed; our situation has. We need new solutions for a new situation, not a panicky and expensive retreat to an old, abandoned position.

Nuclear power comes from splitting fissile atoms, a process that releases energy. The two most suitable substances to use are U235 (uranium of atomic weight 235) and Pu239 (a form of plutonium). Less than 1% of uranium ore is U235 and this needs to be enriched to 5% in centrifuges before it is used in nuclear reactors. The vast majority of uranium ore is U238, which is radioactive but not fissile, so the enrichment process results in large amounts of leftover depleted uranium (DU) that either has to be expensively stored or given to the military.

Fast-breeder reactors (FBRs) will become increasingly attractive as the price of uranium rises. They have a blanket of uranium around the core that changes to plutonium Pu239 when irradiated, producing more fissile material than was originally present. Until recently FBRs were

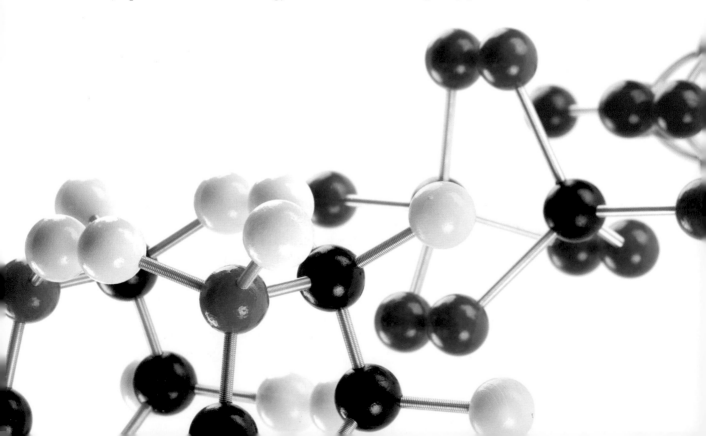

thought to have too many problems and be inherently unsafe, but India and China are now aiming to build them.

Pluto was the mythical God of Hell: plutonium is named after him. It is the deadliest substance ever made by humans; it has virtually no peaceful uses. Two kilograms of highly purified plutonium – about the size of a golf ball – is enough for a bomb of the size dropped on Nagasaki in 1945. Frank Boulton, of the Oxford Research Group and chair of the global health charity Medact, points out that FBRs are likely to come on stream just as the pressures of global warming, oil depletion and mass migration create extreme tensions between countries.

After 50 years of nuclear activity, the UK now has 10,000 cubic metres of high-level nuclear waste and 250,000 tonnes of intermediate waste on sites around the country. All will remain toxic for thousands of years and none is stored in long-term safety. The government has said it will be buried but no sites have yet been chosen, partly because there are still questions over the stability of geological strata and the possibility that the groundwater we drink may become radioactive. Parents usually tell their children to clear up one mess before starting another.

Storing waste and dismantling reactors will use vast amounts of fossil fuel, which will halve their net energy output. Old reactors will need to be dismantled and probably covered in earth, thus resembling the mounds that Odysseus raised for the honoured dead. What will future civilisations make of these tumuli with their ghostly and ghastly magical properties?

At the Sellafield nuclear power station, 80 cubic metres of radioactive liquid leaked for nine months in spite of hundreds of warnings. If the UK, with all its wealth and sophisticated institutions falls short, how on earth can poorer countries deal with the nuclear industry safely?

President Carter banned the reprocessing of spent nuclear fuel in 1977 on the grounds that it created pure plutonium. The ban was lifted. Reprocessing plants in just a few countries, including the Thorp plant in the UK, separate plutonium from used reactor fuel. The plutonium is then sent back to the country of origin by ship, air, rail and road, providing a tempting opportunity for terrorists. A cupful of plutonium in a van containing conventional explosives could contaminate an entire city. Remember the alarm raised when minute traces of polonium-210 were found in London during the Litvinenko affair in 2007?

Nuclear storage dumps and reactors, of course, provide a sitting target. If a plane crashed into Sellafield, which has the world's largest stockpile of radioactive material, all of northern England could be contaminated. It would only take a single such incident for civil freedoms in the UK to be severely curtailed; already, the Civil Nuclear Constabulary have powers to arrest anyone on suspicion and to enter any house at will. Habeas corpus, the bedrock of the UK legal system, is not compatible with a nuclear state.

Nuclear plants require constant management by trained staff. Minor oversights were responsible for the crises at Three Mile Island and Chernobyl. In 2003 cracks were found in 14 US reactors; "Every one has the disease," said Alex Marion, director of the Nuclear Energy Inspectorate, "it's just a matter of time before the symptoms appear." Only prompt action by an employee prevented a reactor at Forsmark in

Sweden getting out of control in July 2006, and this incident resulted in four of the country's ten reactors being shut down. Is it ethical to require this level of supervision for the indefinite future, when coastal reactors may be flooded and the stability of our civilisation is in question?

As well as nuclear fission there is nuclear fusion, which enthusiasts see as the energy of the future. The Experimental Reactor being built in France is planned to be operational by 2016, though the first commercial plant will not be complete until 2050. If successful, nuclear fusion will produce almost unlimited electricity with virtually no pollution. Each plant would produce so much

power that switching them off for maintenance would cause havoc. So the reactor might also be used to produce hydrogen for the separate production of electricity. But this has all the uncertainties of extremely high technology and will not feed the grid for at least 45 years. It is irrelevant, then, to the present energy crisis.

The cost of the experimental fusion reactor in France is estimated at $13 billion for construction and $13 billion for operation. Many scientists see it as an immensely exciting project for limitless and almost free electricity. Sceptics see it more as an immensely exciting job-creation scheme for plasma-physicists.

Twelve years after Chernobyl, Ukraine estimated that the disaster had cost over $120 billion.

Technicians standing by the old control board at the Chernobyl nuclear plant

Uranium

an abundant resource?

Uranium is ubiquitous in rocks and seawater.
The nuclear industry therefore claims that, at the
right price, limitless supplies are available. But
the proportion in granite is tiny: 0.000,04%U.
In seawater it is even less: 0.000,000,3%U.
The critical issue is not cost but the amount of
energy the uranium will produce against the
amount of energy needed to extract it.

High-grade uranium (2%U) is dug from open-
cast mines using fossil fuels, so its extraction
produces significant greenhouse gas emissions.
Hundreds of tonnes of sulphuric acid, nitric
acid, ammonia and other chemicals are injected
into the strata and left for several years to
dissolve the uranium. A thousand tonnes of
rock are then ground up to extract one tonne of
yellow uranium oxide, 'yellowcake'. Radioactive
waste from the mining process along with the
chemicals can blow into surrounding areas or
seep into the ground, poisoning drinking water.

Reserves of high-grade uranium have been less
researched than reserves of oil but the industry
accepts that it is a limited resource. At present,
recycled uranium makes up 40% of world
supplies, but this will decline as the stocks from
civil and military programmes run out.

On current projections the demand for high-
grade uranium will exceed supply within ten
years. But if all electricity, rather than the
present small proportion, were to come from
nuclear plants, demand would exceed supply
within just four years (the industry claims seven
years). Meanwhile, as the reserves deplete,
increasing amounts of fossil fuel will be needed

Uranium reserves

High-grade uranium reserves: 3.53mt
Present uranium use: 0.07mt/year
Supply, with no new reactors: 50 years
Supply, all electricity nuclear: 7 years

**Reasonably assured and inferred high-grade
uranium reserves:**

Australia	1.07mt	30%
Caspian area	0.87mt	24%
Africa	0.51mt	14%
Canada	0.44mt	12%
Brazil	0.14mt	4%
USA	0.10mt	3%

(mt = million tonnes)
Source: Uranium Information Centre Ltd

to mine them. The market is already reflecting
the difficulty of extraction: uranium prices rose
six-fold between 2001 and 2006.

As with oil, competition for what is left is likely
to induce new conflicts, particularly in Africa
and the Caspian zone. These two regions are
thought to contain 38% of high-grade reserves
between them. And the mining of lean ores
(0.1%U and less), in particular, will require
massive inputs of energy from fossil fuels.

Investment in new nuclear reactors would
therefore lock us into a technology that
stimulates conflict and increases emissions of
carbon dioxide. The emissions take place in
areas where the uranium is mined, not at power
stations in the west, allowing politicians in these
countries to claim that nuclear power generation
does not emit greenhouse gases.

Oceans
out of sight, out of mind

"Failure to cut CO_2 emissions may mean that there is no place in the oceans of the future for many of the species and ecosystems that we know today." The Royal Society, 2005

LIFE ORIGINATED IN the oceans some 3,600 million years ago. Beneath the sea's surface millions of species and numerous ecosystems flourish down to depths of 11 kilometres: coral forests, mountains, volcanoes, minerals, bacteria, algae, complex plants, mammals, fish, reptiles, crustaceans, molluscs, even birds, as well as thousands of other unknown life forms.

The earth's lungs are not just forests on land but also marine plants, phytoplankton and algae, which capture vast amounts of carbon dioxide and release oxygen. Water vapour rises from the oceans to form clouds and deposit salt-free water on land. Ozone rising from the surface protects us from ultraviolet-B rays. Oceans are where life began on earth and they are essential for its continued survival. Our existence depends on maintaining their health.

Throughout human history the oceans have been our rubbish dump. In the last couple of centuries this has started to take its toll. Many things the modern world throws away do not disintegrate. Persistent organic pollutants (POPs) are man-made and nature has not evolved ways to make them harmless. They are taken up by marine plants; small fish then eat the plants; big fish eat the small fish; larger mammals eat the big fish, and so on up the food chain. At each stage the POPs concentrate further in animals'

fat. In bottlenose dolphins the concentration can be up to 100 million times higher than the level found in the water itself. Heavy metals persist for thousands of years in the food chain, causing cancer, acute poisoning, and damage to the nervous system, muscles and bones of humans and other animals. The seas are also awash with radioactive nuclides, oil spills, billions of plastic bags, untreated sewage ... the list goes on.

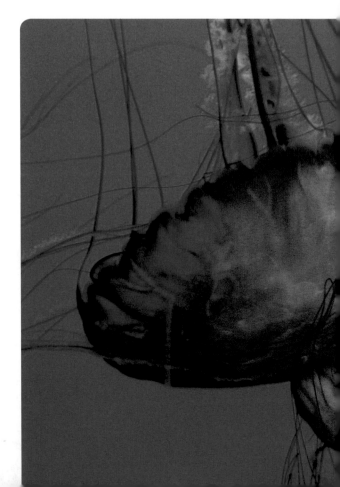

Mangroves are an essential marine ecosystem. They protect coastal areas from strong waves and currents and they are a vital breeding ground for fish. More than half the world's mangroves have been cut down for agriculture, development and shrimp farming. In East Asia, shrimp farms are rarely productive for more than five to ten years, and the land they leave behind is so polluted it is unusable.

Coral reefs are one of the world's richest and most bio-diverse ecosystems, believed to host several million species. In the tropics, up to two thirds of coral reefs have now been damaged, while in Europe and North America trawling and mining activities have destroyed at least half. Corals, like other marine species, are sensitive to temperature and many are dying due to global warming.

Fish populations are also dwindling year by year. There may be almost none left by 2050. The largest ever study of marine fisheries reported in November 2006 that fish stocks would collapse if the present rate of extraction continued. Currently up to 18% of stocks are over-fished, half are fished at maximum capacity and many fisheries have disappeared altogether. We know what action to take. The problem is not lack of knowledge but lack of political will.

Once a community activity, fishing is now big business. Half the catches worldwide are made from just 1% of fishing vessels. Imagine a kilometre-wide net being dragged across the plains of Africa, scooping up everything in its path – trees, bushes, lions, rhinos, warthogs, giraffes – then discarding most of its catch as worthless. This is what trawlers do every day

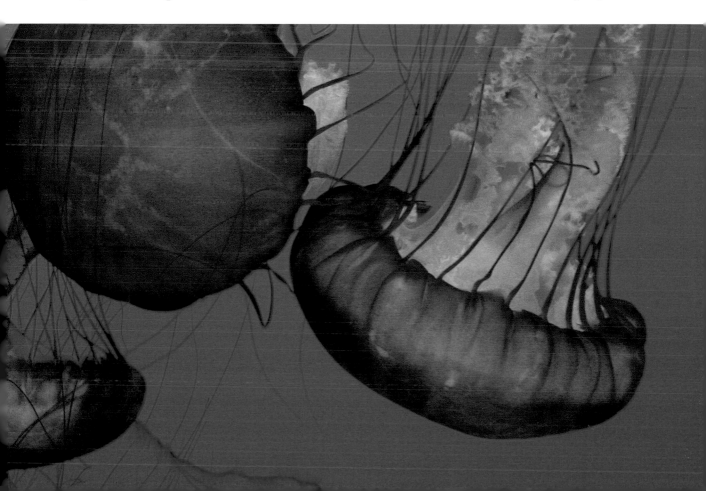

in oceans all over the planet. There are many species of deep-sea fish that live for 100 years and take as long as humans to breed; they will never recover from this invasion. And still, governments subsidise fishing fleets.

Most fish are found close to the shore, where countries can establish policies to preserve them. This is perhaps the one hope for the health of the oceans. The current state of the North Sea fisheries, however, shows once again that politicians will ignore scientific advice when it doesn't suit the commercial lobby.

Fish farming is on the increase but this too has severe problems. Interbreeding passes defective genes to wild fish; the farms act as hothouses for disease; their antibiotics and pesticides pollute coastal waters. The farms also need vast amounts of fish-food. It takes 10kg of trawled wild fish from the seas of countries like Peru to produce 2kg of farmed Atlantic salmon. Thus, in many areas the poor are being deprived of their staple diet to serve the tastes of the rich.

Krill, a Norwegian word for whale food, is the generic name for 85 species of tiny crustaceans that are at the base of the marine food chain. Their numbers determine the life of the oceans, so the recent banning of commercial krill fishing in the US is a real triumph.

However, global warming may be more harmful to this ecosystem than other human-induced hazards. The oceans are picking up excess atmospheric carbon and becoming acidic; with increased acidity, krill are unable to grow their protective shells. Their demise will have disastrous consequences for larger marine animals. "While climate change has uncertainty," said Dr Turley of the Plymouth

Marine Laboratory in the UK, "these geochemical changes are highly predictable."

It may be possible to restore the life of the oceans to normality if:

- the tens of billions of dollars given in subsidies for over-fishing are removed;
- the certification of seafood from well managed sources is promoted;
- coral reefs are effectively protected;
- chemical flows from fields to rivers to oceans are checked;
- a network of protected marine areas is enforced;
- a moratorium is imposed on unregulated fishing in marine ecosystem hotspots;
- bottom trawling is outlawed;
- local communities are given power over their local fisheries;
- levels of carbon dioxide in the air drop to a sustainable level.

Market-based economics in the fishing industry have failed. The growth of human capital (in the form of fishing vessels) is reducing nature's capital (fish).

Subsidies given to fishing fleets in 2005:

Japan $2,700 million
US $1,220 million
EU $1,280 million

Fresh water
a limited resource

WARS OVER WATER are not the stuff of history, but they are now considered inevitable. This is madness, for there is plenty of it – we just abuse it and waste it on a gargantuan scale. Water is far too precious to be fought over: we must learn to conserve it.

Flying over the prairies of the United States you will see clusters of dark circles in a desert landscape. Each circle is a cultivation, one kilometre in diameter, irrigated from a single drop-well and rotating arm. This land used to have thin grass and wandering herds of buffalo. Now it produces wheat with the highest yield in the world. The grain exports from this area feed much of the growing global population. It is a miracle of modern agriculture.

The biggest aquifer in the world, the Ogallala, lies beneath these prairies. It covers 26,000 square kilometres and stretches from Texas to the Dakotas. Millions of years ago, water from melting glaciers seeped into the gravel that washed down from the Rocky Mountains and settled here at an average depth of 60 metres. Before the 1940s the land was hardly cultivated, but new technologies for drilling deep wells have been able to extract the water. Since the 1960s, ten times more water has been removed for irrigation each year than has entered the aquifer.

No one knows how long this can continue. Farmers believed their grain production was so valuable to the US economy that the government would provide another massive water project, such as diverting the Mississippi, if their supply

ever ran out. So farmers have done nothing to economise on the use of water. The area's future is likely to be a return to the Dust Bowl conditions that devastated the area in the 1930s.

Most fresh water fell from the sky thousands of years ago and accumulated in aquifers that are now being depleted all over the world. Some of these are finite reservoirs that will never be replaced. Others are replenished by rain. Even these, however, have problems, as nitrates used in industrial farming, sewage from leaky pipes and other polluting chemicals gradually seep into the groundwater. Nitrates, benzene and arsenic take years to spread but may be impossible to remove. Already some aquifers in Britain are laced with benzene.

We know even less about our impact on groundwater than we know about our effect on the climate. How much pollution is already in the ground? Can we extract it? The cost of purifying water is escalating because of the increasing range of pollutants, but this is not charged to the polluters – that is, the farmers, oil companies, the sewerage system and numerous industries. "Let them drink bottled water," the politicians may say when it becomes too expensive for their people to drink tap water.

Thousands of rivers around the world have been dammed to provide power and irrigation. In the US there was an orgy of dam construction in the 1950s and 1960s to provide virtually free Federal-funded water. But dams don't last forever: they gradually silt up. Building finally stopped in the early 1980s and the US is now casting an envious eye on Canada's abundant free-flowing rivers. When the US gets desperate, its northern neighbour has reason to worry. Under NAFTA (North American Free Trade

Agreement) regulations Canada may not be able to protect its natural fresh water heritage.

The famous Yosemite National Park in the Sierra Nevada of California attracts three million visitors a year. Close to it lies Hetch Hetchy valley, ancestral home to the Paiute and Miwok tribes. The naturalist John Muir once described this valley in quasi-religious terms, so beautiful were its savannah oaks and giant sequoias, its waterfalls, huge cliffs and dramatic colours. He was horrified when, in 1908, he heard that it would be flooded: "One might as well dam the people's cathedrals and churches for water tanks, for no holier temple has ever been consecrated by the heart of man."

Hetch Hetchy valley has now been under 90 metres of water for over 80 years and people are wanting it back. Restoring the plants and animals, while preventing non-native species from overrunning the barren sludge, will be a huge learning experience. The knowledge acquired could be of use globally for restoring other areas flooded by dams.

Dams and aquifers provide water for irrigation, but irrigation has problems. If a field has an impervious substrate beneath it, the water cannot drain and salts are drawn to the roots of plants. Even if the land does drain, the salt may pass into rivers where it becomes concentrated in dam reservoirs as the water evaporates. By 1973 the salinity of the Colorado River, where it crossed the border into Mexico's most fertile region, was liquid death to plants, causing an international incident.

The benefits and dangers of irrigation are as old as history, so it is a depressing reflection on our species that we so often repeat our mistakes.

The Sardar Sarovar dam under construction on the Narmada River, India

Irrigation requires organisation and bureaucracy, and so the need to water fields brought the first civilisations into existence. Salt then destroyed them. Irrigated fields in Sumer, the earliest civilisation in the Middle East, produced 2,500 litres of barley per hectare in 2400 BCE, a respectable yield even by modern standards. By 1700 BCE the yield had fallen to 900 litres per hectare. Soon afterwards, crop failures began and Sumer came to an end. Most of the great civilisations that have depended on irrigation went the same way: salts came to the surface and destroyed their agriculture.

Egypt, however, was a glorious exception and managed irrigated farming satisfactorily for 7,000 years. Each year the Nile flooded the fields, deposited rich new silt and flushed surface salts out to sea. And then, in 1970, the Aswan dam was built. Now the silt no longer renews the land each year and salts are no longer washed way. The reservoir behind the

dam is filling with fertile soil that should be rejuvenating the fields. US experts, with their own disasters behind them, warned President Nasser of the dangers, but he refused to back down. This dam, affecting the country's entire population, may come to be seen as the worst technological mistake in human history.

Dams have also been disastrous in India. The Narmada river – Lord Shiva's pure, unmolested consort – has tragically been dammed at numerous points. The Bargi dam, completed in 1990, flooded 27,000 hectares of permanently fertile land and irrigates only 8,000. Work is proceeding on the infamous Sardar Sarovar dam – the largest on the Narmada river – which has become a political plaything between two states. Yet more thousands of villagers will be displaced with promises of land that does not exist. The development politics of dam construction is messy; a well balanced analysis of it comes in Dilip D'Souza's book, *The Narmada Dammed*.

India, however, has a long history of sophisticated water harvesting using bunds, channels, small-plot foot pumps and ancient community-managed tanka reservoirs for capturing monsoon rains. This kind of detailed, small-scale care is often more effective than the grandiose schemes beloved of politicians. In many places in India these traditional approaches, refined over millennia, are now being re-introduced. New techniques are also being added: large cisterns to collect monsoon run-off from roofs, for example, can store drinking water indefinitely when sealed from light. Urban wastewater, including sewage, is being organically treated for cultivation close to source, reducing the need for fresh water and the danger of flooding.

Glaciers store water in the winter and release it throughout the summer, thus keeping rivers continually flowing. They are releasing more water each year as the melting speeds up due to global warming. These full rivers are a fool's

Hybrid cash crops use large amounts of water and cause shortages for local communities. Traditional cultivation developed appropriate crops to suit local climate conditions. The replacement of millet by maize, for example, is responsible for much of the starvation in sub-Saharan Africa.

paradise. One sixth of the world's population – over a billion people – rely on water from glaciers that are disappearing. The great rivers of north India, which provide water for half the country's population, are fed by retreating Himalayan glaciers. Coastal Peru and many other parts of the world have the same problem. "Lima is built on a desert," said Adolfo Pena of the grassroots movement Peruanos Sin Agua, "and in 20 years there's going to be no water." The prospect is horrifying. The solution is immediate global action to halt the release of greenhouse gases.

Water is more valuable than gold. As King Midas found, gold does not quench your thirst, and so just as we are dependent on air to breathe so we are dependent on water to drink. But due to global warming droughts are increasing and half the world will soon suffer water shortages. Excitement among corporations is palpable: pipelines and tankers are being built to carry water from where it falls or lies in aquifers to where people can pay high prices for it. Conflicts for water may soon exceed conflicts for oil.

A bund irrigation system

The Amazon
our greatest biological treasure

"The one process that will take millions of years to correct is the loss of genetic and species diversity by the destruction of natural habitats. This is the folly that our descendents are least likely to forgive us for."

Edward O. Wilson, *The Diversity of Life* (1992)

THE AMAZON RAINFOREST covers a third of South America. Its beauty, majesty and timelessness are awe-inspiring. It is the earth's greatest biological treasure.

The origin of the rainforest is so remote – between 200 million and 500 million years ago – that its plants, animals and insects have had time to evolve intricate symbiotic relationships that are unparalleled elsewhere. Scientists have a better understanding of the number of stars in the galaxy than they do of the number of species in the Amazon. They have identified less than one per cent of them. One hectare may contain 750 types of tree and 1,500 types of other plants; a single tree was found to harbour 43 different ant species. The rainforest is an inexhaustible reservoir of molecules that could be of use to agricultural science and medicine. The soil, however, is relatively infertile because so little light penetrates to ground level: the forest's fragile, complex ecosystem occurs mainly up above in the canopy. When that is gone nothing of value is left.

The Amazon rainforest is the planet's most important set of lungs, recycling carbon dioxide, releasing a fifth of the earth's oxygen and influencing all the world's weather systems.

Rising hot air on the equator, having warmed the Gulf Stream, draws humid trade winds from the north and south towards Brazil's coast, where the moisture condenses as torrential rain. A quarter of the rain is caught by the canopy and never reaches the ground. Of the three quarters that does, half is drawn up by the trees' roots and evaporates through their leaves. The resulting clouds keep the land 10°C cooler. The damp air then moves westwards and repeats the process as many as seven times before it reaches the Andes. Here the damp air rises, condenses as snow and forms glaciers that feed the rivers of Peru, Ecuador and Colombia.

Over two thirds of all the fresh water on earth lies in the Amazon basin. Where the river enters the Atlantic it is over 300 kilometres across; 4,000 kilometres upstream it is deep enough to accommodate ocean liners. The number of fish species the river contains exceeds the number found in the entire Atlantic Ocean, and a single Amazonian lake can sustain a greater fish variety than that found in all of Europe's rivers.

It is estimated that ten million indigenous people lived in the Amazon forest before Europeans arrived. Most medicine men and shamans remaining in the forest today are over 70 years

The Iguaçu River, Brazil, divides dense forest from deforested farmland

old. When one of them dies without passing on his or her arts to the next generation, the community and the world loses thousands of years of irreplaceable knowledge about medicinal plants; it is like losing a library.

Three thousand species of fruit have been found in rainforests of which only 200 are now used in the western world. A quarter of western pharmaceuticals are derived from rainforest ingredients, including 70% of plants that are active against cancer cells. These figures come from analysing only a tiny fraction of what exists. Scientists and individuals can easily understand that the Amazon and other rainforests are the richest and most essential of all ecological systems on earth. Tragically, this understanding is not translated into effective action. Humanity has no collective intelligence.

Our generation is destroying, ever year, an area of the Amazon rainforest equal to the size of Belgium. If the destruction of tropical forests in central Africa and Southeast Asia is added to

this, the annual loss is the size of England and Wales combined. These figures double if we also include the areas affected when key individual trees are extracted, opening up the forest for others to exploit.

Much of the deforestation is happening close to the Atlantic and could damage the start of the process that recycles humidity across the continent. Rain from the trade winds of the Atlantic increasingly falls on bare ground and runs back into the ocean instead of evaporating back into the sky. The next part of the forest will then lose much of its rainfall. A tipping point may be reached when the remaining forest does not receive enough rain and the whole cyclical system collapses, turning the area into savannah or desert. In one generation we might destroy the most ancient biological system in the world and plunge global weather patterns into chaos.

Set against the workings of nature, the human preoccupation with money and competition seems strange and unrealistic. Brazil allows logging in order to export timber. Why? Because three quarters of Brazil's income goes to service external debt – not even to repay it. The interest has to be paid in dollars and, because the Brazilian real drops in value, export earnings must be constantly increased. Exporting ancient timber is a top earner. Others include beef and soya, produced in areas where the forest has been cleared. Because of the impoverished soil here, the yield of beef per hectare ranks among the lowest in the world. But due to the vast areas given over to cattle grazing Brazil exports more beef than any other country.

Seventy-nine major hydroelectric dams are planned for Brazil: they will flood an area half the size of the UK. The electricity produced will be responsible for more carbon dioxide emissions than coal-fired generators, if you include the gases that the rotting, flooded vegetation will give off. If the rainforest collapses, the dams will become towering monuments to folly in a waterless desert.

Greece cut down its extensive forests before the Classical period (4th century BCE) and they have never re-grown. Britain felled its oaks to build a navy in the 16th century. Some countries that have traditionally exported tropical hardwoods, such as the Philippines, Malaysia and Nigeria, will soon run out and become importers. The World Resources Institute says that the demand for timber will double by 2050.

Sustainable logging is possible in some places but not in the Amazon. Only shade-loving seeds germinate in this mature rainforest, so when the trees are cut down sun-loving plants flourish there instead. Once an area is cleared it will never, ever, grow back to what it was before. A complete ban on the sale and use of tropical hardwoods may well be necessary. Otherwise, the only hope for the Amazon would be a collapse of the global economy.

In December 2005 the Amazon suffered the worst drought since records began a century previously. Wildfires that are normally put out in time by rain, spread unhindered. Fish died on caked mud as streams and rivers dried up. People drove cars where previously they swam. Polluted water caused epidemics and communities were cut off from supplies when ships were unable to navigate upstream. It is thought that warm surface temperatures in the Atlantic were to blame. They caused air over the ocean to rise and air over the Amazon to descend, preventing cloud formation

and rainfall. It was the same warm surface temperatures in 2005 that caused the increased violence of hurricanes in the Gulf of Mexico and the first major hurricane south of the equator. Some scientists blame a normal climate cycle; others say it is a symptom of global warming. We will see who was right in due course.

Three reasons can be given for saving the Amazon. First, the moral one: it belongs to the planet, to all creatures, to the people that have lived in it for thousands of years, and to future generations. Morality, however, has little influence on world leaders. Second, the scientific logic: rainforests are essential for capturing greenhouse gases and maintaining the delicate balance of weather patterns. But inaction over global warming since 1985 demonstrates that politicians do not take science seriously. Third, greed: rainforest timber is worth $1,000 per hectare, a one-off income, and land converted to cattle yields $150 per hectare each year until the soil washes away. By leaving the rainforest intact and harvesting its many nuts, fruits, oil-producing and medicinal plants it will yield $6,000 per hectare annually on a perpetual basis. This argument may be the only way to delay destruction of the Amazon until morality and science play their part in world affairs.

The rainforest is a treasure for all of us. Please don't harm it!

Money

systems, ideas and community

THE GLOBAL ECONOMY is a fragile house of cards. No one can understand every part of it. The financial sector likes to keep it that way. It adds card after card to the crazy structure, making it more and more complicated and extracting ever bigger profits.

But the economy rests on a money system that is, by contrast, easy for anyone to understand. A cursory glance at this faulty foundation reveals that the superstructure is bound to collapse one day. We can have a stable economy only by changing the money system.

Environmental degradation, social inequality, wars and even over-population are all driven by a money system that requires constant growth. The rich loot both the poor and the world's resources in order to satisfy their ever-expanding 'needs'. But there were money systems in the past that did not require constant growth and flourished instead with on-going stability.

"Of all vile things current on earth, none is so vile as money."

Sophocles, *Antigone* (441 BCE)

Usury and greed

our economy

"If you advance money to any poor man amongst my people, you are not to act like a moneylender; you must not exact interest from him."

Exodus 22.25, the Bible

USURY AND GREED used to be seen as deadly sins. Nowadays they are the pillars of our economic life. 'Interest on debt', the modern phrase for usury, is how our economy works. Greed – encouraging the desire for more, more and yet more consumption – is the motor of our economic activity.

From the Pentateuch onwards, Jewish and Christian writers have condemned the charging of interest. The reason is obvious if you think beyond platitudes about communism. Look at it like this. If you have spare money you can lend it to someone who needs it. If you demand interest on the loan then that person has to work to pay back not only the money borrowed but some more as well. You, meanwhile, can watch your pile grow and lend more to someone else.

Interest means that money flows from the poor person, who needs to borrow, into the hands of the rich person who has spare money to lend. The same works for poor countries borrowing

from rich ones. **Interest is therefore responsible for the constant growth of inequality.**

If the interest rate stands at 5%, a company that starts with borrowed money has to have grown by 5% the following year in order to pay the interest. With compound interest it has to grow to twice the size in 14 years, and to four times the size in 28 years. It therefore has to grow continuously. Stability is not an option. But growth requires increasing use of resources.

Advanced economies claim to decouple economic growth from the consumption of resources. But this is usually because their

money comes from providing services that use few resources while their goods, which do require increased resources, are made abroad and therefore don't show on the resource ledger. **A second result of an economy based on charging interest is that global resources are depleted at an escalating rate.**

A growing economy cannot, within its borders, produce all its needs – in particular, most industrial countries have to secure energy supplies from abroad – so it has to buy, loot or fight for them in competition with other countries. **Conflict and war is therefore a third result of an interest-based economy.**

As the economy grows, more and more damage is done to the earth's flora, fauna and climate. Productive land is degraded, oceans are over-fished, ancient forests are cut down, biodiversity is depleted and mass extinctions follow.

The charging of interest is destroying the planet's ability to support life.

Leviticus, the third book of the Bible, describes a benign economy without interest, where debt is cancelled at the Jubilee every 50 years, those who fail in their enterprises are supported, and a surplus allows the land to rest and recuperate on a regular basis. Writing at the beginning of civilisation, Leviticus had a more realistic and humane grasp of how to regulate money without damaging society and the environment than our present economists do.

But Christians ignore their scriptures because usury is now so ingrained in their culture that

they cannot conceive that it might be the root of their problems. So the churches say that God made a slip of the tongue; what he really meant was to condemn excessive interest.

As a result of the interest-based money system the concept of value, which used to refer to the quality of social, artistic, intellectual and spiritual life, in most western societies is now measured mainly by money. The west is forcing this pernicious belief system on all countries and cultures throughout the world.

Many other cultures have totally different values. Buddhists reject acquisitive attitudes. Islam has a principled objection to interest: one of the five pillars of Islam is zakat, the duty to distribute wealth to the poor. Islamists have good reason to uphold their fundamental, often passionate, objection to the imposition of usury and greed as a value system. For Hindus, business is just one of the four stages of life, with the other three having little or nothing to do with money. These are just three examples: in all religions value is originally measured by qualities other than money.

Many indigenous societies work on a cooperative basis. To them, wealth is the community, and individual windfalls are shared with anyone in need. Being a member of the community gives you security in your old age. Many of these ethnic groups have survived for tens of thousands of years, though in today's capitalist world their enlightened practices are usually condemned as primitive.

Through the centuries, other civilisations and religions have explored ways of understanding and defining the concept of value. Usury and greed were not among them.

They make money
we owe it to them

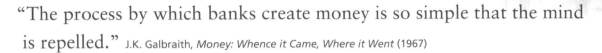

"The process by which banks create money is so simple that the mind is repelled." J.K. Galbraith, *Money: Whence it Came, Where it Went* (1967)

LULU HAS A REGULAR job and can therefore borrow money. If the bank loans her £100,000 to buy a house, she has to pay back that same sum as well as accumulated interest on it. Banks, however, do not have to borrow money from anyone, and so they do not have to pay interest either. When the bank makes a loan to Lulu it is simply creating the money she needs on a computer.

You and I are not allowed to create money by forging banknotes. If we did so we would end up in jail. But banks – private commercial institutions – are legally allowed to create almost as much money as they like. Not surprisingly then, they take every opportunity to give us loans – putting you and me into debt – and to milk us for interest payments. "The modern banking system manufactures money out of nothing," said Lord Josiah Stamp, former director of the Bank of England, in 1937. "The process is perhaps the most astounding piece of sleight of hand that was ever invented."

You can understand the system from your own experience. Peter goes to meet his bank manager. The manager thinks Peter looks a reliable guy and allows him to take out a loan of £100,000 to buy a flat or set up a business. The manager does not have to go into his vault to see if he actually has that amount of money, or ring someone else to ask for a loan. He simply keys the figures into his computer. The money is now in circulation and Peter can use it. (Banks do have to lodge a very small proportion of the money they create with the central bank, which is why the system is called 'fractional reserve banking'.)

Overnight, Peter changes his mind. He returns to the bank and says he does not want the loan after all. Fine, the bank manager says. He taps into his computer and the money is cancelled. The money existed – was 'in circulation' – for a brief period and then ceased to exist.

However, if Peter does use the money to buy a flat he will have to pay back the loan over, say, 15 years and pay interest as well. Once he has paid it back, the original £100,000 ceases to exist. But by this time the bank has made a profit of around £100,000 on the interest payments of Peter's loan.

Banks and building societies, with their stake in mortgages, own more than a third of UK housing. They insist that the interest is paid before the loan capital in order to retain a maximum stake in the houses. But houses are overvalued and when the bubble bursts it is the borrowers, not the banks, who bear the loss. If houses revert to half their present value, banks, through repossession, will be able to capture two-thirds of the housing stock. So never think that they are doing you a favour by lending you money: the more banks lend to the public, the more interest they receive, the more power they have over our lives, and the more they corner the wealth of the nation to award themselves vast salaries, large pensions, share options and annual bonuses.

Banks also fleece the British state. The government borrows money from private banks – the Public Sector Net Cash Requirement (PSNCR) – and has to pay them interest on the loans. The government services these interest payments by taxing its citizens: this, of course, is not popular, so it also cuts back on public services in order to pay the interest. Financing its expenditure in this way is mad, but the chancellor doesn't dare to challenge the financial world because it has so much power – and it is prepared to wield it ruthlessly.

The government has found a good wheeze, though, in the Private Finance Initiative (PFI), to please financiers and hoodwink the public into thinking it is providing public services. The PFI allows private companies to raise money to build hospitals and schools, then rent them to the government. This gives the companies a 20- to 30-year guaranteed income stream and with this they are able to refinance their borrowings at low rates of interest, boosting their profits to stratospheric levels.

The present UK government is thus providing health and education by mortgaging future generations in perpetuity. As a result, the final cost to taxpayers will be massively more than if the government had carried out the work itself. Even if it had to borrow money to build schools and hospitals – which, of course, it does not have to – the cost would work out as less

in the end than all the rent paid out to private companies through the PFI.

British monarchs used to create money by issuing coins bearing their portrait. These became the currency of the nation. Later on, rather than handing out coins or gold whenever a customer wanted to withdraw cash, the central bank gave out paper notes declaring, "I promise to pay the bearer on demand" the equivalent sum. Paper became the nation's main currency.

"The aspects of things that are most important to us are hidden because of their simplicity and familiarity. We fail to be struck by what, once seen, is most striking and most powerful."

Ludwig Wittgenstein, *Philosophical Investigations No. 125* (1953)

Nowadays, paper and coins minted by the British government account for less than 5% of the actual money in circulation. Computer entries have become the national currency. Neither the Queen, however, nor the government, nor even the central bank issues this money. Over 95% of what we use has been created by private institutions putting their customers into debt. These institutions own the nation's money and we pay them interest for using it, not just once, but year after year. If the government allowed the central bank, instead of commercial banks, to create the UK's currency it would be returning the country to a sane banking system – one that existed before it was hijacked by the commercial banks.

The banking casino

an asylum run by its inmates

"Speculators may do no harm as bubbles on a steady stream of enterprise. But the position is serious when enterprise becomes the bubble on a whirlpool of speculation. When the capital development of a country becomes a by-product of the activities of a casino, the job is likely to be ill-done."

John Maynard Keynes, *The General Theory of Employment, Interest and Money* (1936)

BANKS CREATE MONEY by putting their customers into debt. In the UK, house owners with two salaries use, on average, a fifth of their income to service mortgage payments. This is a new phenomenon. Rising property prices make people think they are getting richer as their houses increase in value. In fact, they only do so if they 'downsize'. The buoyant housing market is making banks richer but it's making home owners poorer.

A prosperous and well managed company will pay salaries that enable its employees to afford mortgage payments on a comfortable house. The estate agent sets the price of the house as high as possible, knowing how much people who work for such a firm can afford. Other employers are then under pressure to raise salaries to the same level, so that their employees are also able to afford reasonable accommodation. The first company then raises its salaries in order to maintain a differential, and so the estate agent can set house prices at an even higher level.

It is a circular process by which both salaries and house prices are continuously rising. The buyer, struggling to pay the mortgage on a house, becomes financially vulnerable. The seller finds that her next house has also gone up in price, so she too continues to struggle to cover her mortgage payments.

Banks and building societies are the only ones to benefit. As mortgages rise the banks receive ever-increasing interest for doing an unchanging type of transaction. If the value of a house increases by £100,000 between sales, the new owner takes out a mortgage from the bank to cover the raised price. At 5% interest she will be £5,000 poorer each year and the bank will be £5,000 richer. The term mortgage, incidentally, comes from the French word for 'death pledge'.

Businesses are also under pressure from the need for constant growth. Many pay more than a quarter of their income to service borrowings. As a result, they produce cheap, short-lived goods that have to be replaced regularly. Industrialised societies are aggressively competitive not because it is in our nature, but because we have to struggle to survive in a world where the financial sector creams off nearly half of all wealth.

And what does the financial sector do with the money it extracts? It runs a casino.

The largest global trade is currency gambling: $2 trillion slosh back and forth around the world every day. The risks are so great that they have to be spread through hedge funds, derivatives (slicing up and re-packaging securities such as corporate debt, mortgages and shares), private equity groups (the ultimate asset strippers), and collateral-debt-obligations. You and I may not understand what they're playing at. But nor do they, as even *The Economist* admits. It's an exciting game nonetheless.

Hedge funds, unlike most aspects of modern life, are unregulated, so they can make up their own rules. They were responsible for the notorious 1997 East Asian financial crisis that destroyed the economies of many nations. Ben Bernanke, chair of the US Federal Reserve, once said that he didn't understand how hedge funds worked but that he had confidence in "sophisticated financial institutions" that did.

Governments don't know how to regulate hedge funds because only insiders have any idea what is going on. The insiders, for obvious reasons, are reluctant to tell. The top 25 hedge fund managers in the world each earn an average

of $250 million a year. In the UK in 2005, 250 hedge fund managers who, by their own admission, create nothing, each received around $40 million. These financial mechanisms are meant to keep the global economy stable. In reality, such a concentration of money in so few unregulated hands makes the global economy resemble a fragile house of cards. It could collapse at any moment.

This nearly happened in 1998 when the bets of the hedge fund Long-Term Capital Management went wrong. The Federal Reserve said that its failure posed "unacceptable risks to the US economy." In panic, 14 major Wall Street banks gave $3.6 billion to bail the fund out. The banks would never donate that sort of money to save a country from debt or its people from starvation.

The global economy can be seen as an asylum run by the inmates. "To say the financial system is crazy is an understatement," says Michael Rowbotham in his book *The Grip of Death*. "The situation defies description, and it beggars belief that no one involved in the operation takes a long hard look at what they are doing and just bursts out laughing at the innate insanity of the whole process."

Monetary reform

the central bank should issue money

"It should be illegal for commercial banks to create money denominated in the national currency, just as it is illegal to forge coins or counterfeit banknotes." James Robertson, Simpol-UK Policy Forum, House of Commons, 2005

AMERICANS ARE GENERALLY admired for their facility with money, so it is surprising that the most damning criticism of the banking system has come from two of their most revered and intelligent presidents.

"If the American people ever allow the banks to control the issuance of their currency," said Thomas Jefferson (US president 1801–1809), "they will deprive the people of all property.

I sincerely believe that the banking institutions having the power of money are more dangerous to liberty than standing armies."

Abraham Lincoln (US president 1861–1865) forged America into one nation. Reconciliation between the northern and southern states was a truly great achievement, but had Lincoln lived longer he might have left an even greater legacy. A paper he wrote on monetary policy was a masterpiece of clarity and brevity that provided a vision for the country's monetary system. "The government should not borrow capital at interest as a means of financing government work and public enterprise," he wrote. "The government should create, issue and circulate all the currency and credit needed to satisfy the spending power of the government and the buying power of consumers."

Had Lincoln's policy been implemented, it would have led to the end of bank power in the US, and the rest of the world might have followed suit. He was assassinated shortly after publishing the document, which was quietly suppressed. The reason for his assassination has never been satisfactorily explained.

In his 2006 article, 'The Need For Monetary Reform', James Robertson, co-founder of the New Economics Foundation, defined how monetary reform could be introduced:

- "The central bank, independent of government, should bring into being as much money as it decides is needed for the money supply. Government should spend it into circulation like it does with its other revenue, such as money from taxes."

- "Commercial banks would then have to borrow money in order to make loans. They would become brokers charging a fee for their services. There would be no restriction on borrowing and lending except that the money must already exist. Banks would not be allowed to create money out of thin air as they do now – just as you and I are not allowed to forge banknotes and lend them to people at interest."

In the UK, these two measures would increase government revenue by up to £45 billion a year, allowing it to finance hospitals and schools without burdening future generations or increasing taxes. The banks would lose over £20 billion a year, which they now receive from creating money and charging interest on it.

Governments, of course, might wish to flood the market with money before an election in order to buy votes, and this would cause inflation. Therefore the central bank alone, independent of government, should create the money needed each year before handing it to government.

Thus the government, not commercial banks, would receive the benefits of issuing money. The advantages for the government and society are so obvious that it is difficult to understand why the measures are not adopted immediately. However, for equally obvious reasons, they are fiercely resisted by the financial sector together with their professional, academic, corporate and political associates. These bodies would rather see the whole financial edifice collapse than give up their privileges.

Thomas Jefferson and Abraham Lincoln got it right!

The bancor
proposed by Keynes

"The modern crises are, in fact, man-made and differ from many of their predecessors in that they can be dealt with."

Club of Rome, *Limits to Growth* (1972)

ABRAHAM LINCOLN SET out principles for an internal US currency that would have curbed banking excesses. The banks suppressed it.

John Maynard Keynes, who led the British delegation at the Bretton Woods Conference in 1944, was determined to avoid a repeat of policies that led to the Great Depression of the 1930s. As with Lincoln and his principles for a US currency, Keynes's ideas for the post-war world were revolutionary and would have prevented extreme concentration of wealth.

His proposals were based on the work of David Ricardo (1772–1823), one of the founders of classical economics. Ricardo had laid down four essential conditions for trade between nations:

- Capital should not cross borders from a high-wage to a low-wage country.
- There must be a balance of trade between participating countries.
- There should be full employment within participating countries.
- There should be no monopolies or near-monopolies.

Current trade regulations contravene all four conditions. Keynes wanted trade to be practised freely but without nations sinking into debt.

John Maynard Keynes (right) at the Bretton Woods Conference, 1944

When the US rejected his proposals he warned that the Bretton Woods measures would lead to endemic debt for poorer countries. He has been proved right beyond his worst fears.

Sixty years is too long to try patching up a treaty that has created such inequality, poverty and environmental destruction. Debt-cancellation puts sticking plaster on sores, aid salves uneasy consciences, fair trade relieves some desperation, but none of these measures changes a system that is structurally unfair.

Keynes's scheme is waiting in the wings and should be applied. He insisted that:

- the trade of every country should be in equilibrium. Creditor nations (those that export more than they import) and deficit nations (those that import more than they export) both disturb this balance;

- an International Clearing Union (ICU) should maintain the balance of trade between all countries;

- there should be an independent currency for trade between nations called the 'bancor'. It would be worthless except when used for buying and selling real things.

Within this system a country's excess or deficit would be taxed up to a defined limit each year. Above this limit, any further excess would be surrendered to the ICU. Each country would therefore have a powerful incentive to clear its bancor account by bringing it close to zero annually. A country with surplus income from trade would seek to spend the surplus back into deficit nations.

A careful study of his scheme shows that companies would be unable to extract mineral wealth except in return for goods and services. An individual would only be able to export money (in the form of bancors) if goods entering the country balanced this money. There would be no incentive for corrupt politicians to store money abroad because the bancor could only be used for international trade. A country would only want to import what it could not produce within its borders. Trade between neighbouring countries at similar levels of development would have advantages over trade with distant countries. And all countries would concentrate more on production for their own people than production for export.

Other measures would introduce regulation that encouraged elected governments to manage their own economies before giving access to overseas investors and corporations.

Keynes predicted the disasters that poor countries would suffer, but he did not appreciate the extent to which the Bretton Woods arrangements would also exhaust fossil energy supplies and destabilise the climate.

Why can Keynes's proposals not be adopted under the present regime? Because at Bretton Woods the US gave itself a veto on any change proposed to the neoliberal rules of the World Bank and the IMF. The proposals could, however, be taken up by the consortium of rapidly developing countries known as the BRICS (Brazil, Russia, India, China, South Africa), which represent half the world's population. Having established the International Clearing Union for their own affairs they would be able to invite other nations to join in.

Indebted countries should unite and repudiate debts that have no economic, legal or moral status. They could then give the World Bank the choice of either collapsing the global economy or progressing in an orderly manner towards a self-balancing international trading system.

This is, perhaps, the only way we can really make poverty history.

Global eco-currency
the four currency model

"The future is not some place we are going to, but one we are creating. The paths are not to be found, but made, and the activity of making them changes both the maker and the destination."

John Schaar, Professor of Politics, University of California-Santa Cruz

HEGEL POINTED OUT at the beginning of the 19th century that all economies unfold according to their own internal rules, in spite of the best or worst efforts of politicians. Once established, they run their course. The course of neoliberal economics is nearing its end. Inequality has reached horrific proportions and economic growth is destroying the planet's life-support systems.

Flat-earth economists have elaborate formulae for working with the present ludicrous economy that causes such problems. Few, however, seem to think about money itself – what actually is it? – or stop to consider that multiple currencies might be needed. A new money system is not just desirable; our survival will depend on it. Anyone who takes part in a baby-sitting circle uses a form of payment other than the national

currency; it may be IOU chits, entries in a diary or just a mental note. There is nothing odd about multiple currencies. What is odd is the use of just one currency for speculating on the international money market, buying cabbages, and saving for your old age.

Richard Douthwaite, an economist whose books include *The Growth Illusion* and *The Ecology of Money*, suggests that four currencies are necessary, each for a specific purpose:

- an international currency for trading between nations;
- a national-exchange currency for trading within a nation;
- various user-controlled currencies;
- a store-of-value currency for your savings.

The international currency

The international currency would prevent any single nation having the advantage of its own currency being used for global trade. Like Keynes's bancor, it could be designed to prevent nations sinking into debt. But since Keynes's time a new situation has arisen. Oil production is declining and carbon emissions from coal, oil and natural gas are changing the climate. Oil and gas extraction has always increased to feed the global economy. In future it will be the other way around: the economy will be dependent on the amount of fuel available. Energy, not money, will become the currency.

Douthwaite proposes a new international currency using the **emissions-backed-currency-unit** (ebcu). To get the new currency going, the regulator – the IMF or a new Issuing Agency – would issue ebcus to every central bank in proportion to its country's 1990 population. No more would ever be issued. A nation's existing wealth would remain in its other currencies.

Then the Cap and Share scheme would kick in, with Special Emission Rights (SERs) being traded in ebcus. The Regulator would distribute SERs to each country annually, on a per capita basis, to be handed out equally to all the country's residents. Producers and importers of coal, natural gas and oil would buy SERs from the residents through financial institutions. These coupons would confer the right to emit a limited amount of greenhouse gas and would be surrendered to the Regulator whenever the companies sold coal, natural gas or oil. Each year the number of SERs issued would fall, so that the total amount of greenhouse gas released by human activity would match the earth's capacity to absorb it.

SERs would form the basis of international trade. India would have a surplus to sell because its people would not need to use their full allocation. The US would need to use its full SER allocation internally and buy more on the international market, using ebcus in payment. It would have to export goods and services in order to acquire the ebcus. Trade would thus be limited to a level that would not harm the planet and would prevent the accumulation of excessive wealth in a few countries.

The effect of this international currency would be dramatic. The poor throughout the world would have a limited source of income, thus enabling local markets to function properly. Rich countries would purchase SERs from poor countries, making money flow from the rich to the poor – the reverse of the present system – and Third World debt would be eliminated. All countries would seek to increase the economic

value they can extract from a limited amount of coal, natural gas and oil. And all countries would have an overwhelming incentive to switch from fossil fuels to renewable energy sources. Since this currency would control the amount of fossil fuel extracted, and hence the amount of carbon dioxide emitted, there would be no need for the other currencies to address this issue.

National-exchange currency

The national-exchange currency would be used for buying and selling within a country. The central bank would only print more of this currency as trade increased. The government would spend it into circulation, such as by building schools and hospitals. It would not allow commercial banks to create money. This newly printed money might cause mild inflation and slightly devalue existing money but this is desirable for two reasons. First, it would allow

prices to adjust. Oil-based products (plastics, industrial food, transport) would rise in price while other goods, such as organic food, would remain stable. Second, we would want to spend the money before it loses value, thus encouraging trade and employment.

User-controlled currencies

The national-exchange currency would be supplemented by a wide range of user-controlled currencies such as Local Exchange Trading Schemes (LETS), locally created currencies known as scrip issues (see Wörgl, page 104), Time Dollars, and systems modelled on the Swiss Wirtschaftsing (Economic Circle) co-operative that has been running since 1934.

The store-of-value currency

The store-of-value currency would be a special form of money used only for purchasing and selling capital assets. For example, if more houses or shares were traded the need for this kind of money, and hence its value, would rise in relation to the national-exchange currency. People's savings would keep pace with the rising wealth of the country. If existing assets decayed and were not replaced, the wealth of the nation as a whole would reduce and the value of people's savings would match this reduction. Other thinkers believe that incremental change to the current money system would be more successful. But with the spiralling growth of money likely to lead to a global financial crash, it would be better to adopt Douthwaite's radical proposals than to patch up the perverse existing system. Douthwaite's ideas are no more radical than John Maynard Keynes's, but they also take into account oil depletion and global warming.

To summarise:

The international currency would keep the world economy within the 'carrying capacity' of the planet. It would ensure fair trade between nations and keep the use of fossil fuel down to sustainable levels.

The national-exchange currency and many user-controlled currencies would encourage economic activity within a nation.

The store-of-value currency would link your savings to the prosperity of the country – no more and no less.

Value added to property by local development ⟶ £600,000 ⟶ £700,000 ⟶

Land Value Tax
value to the community

"Landlords grow richer in their sleep without working, risking or economising. The increase in the value of land, arising as it does from the efforts of an entire community, should belong to the community and not to the individual who might hold title."

John Stuart Mill, *Principles of Political Economy* (1848)

WHO GAVE GOVERNMENTS the right to allow large companies to pollute the atmosphere? Who permitted them to trade these rights? "How dare they do this?" we may think. The sky is not for sale! But our attitude to land in Britain is equally short-sighted. Through the centuries we have come to accept that individuals can own vast swathes of it. Such an attidue is medieval.

Though individuals have a need for secure use of the land on which their houses or businesses stand, it is the community that gives it value. A hectare in the centre of a large city is worth vastly more than a hectare in the country. The community should benefit from the value that the community itself bestows.

"Location, location, location!" cry the estate agents. If your house overlooks Regents Park it may not have cost much to build but it's worth a fortune – not because of you, but because the community has cherished this London parkland. Part of the value of a building is in the bricks

and mortar and part is in the location. The bricks and mortar gradually reduce in value unless you spend money on keeping them in good repair. The value of the land on which it is built rises or falls depending on the quality of its environment, communications and shops. Often three quarters of the value is its location.

Our present council tax and business rates in the UK discourage investment in buildings. If you improve your property by adding rooms the tax rises. If you allow your building to become uninhabitable the tax may be zero and you pay nothing while you wait for community improvements to raise the value of the location. Property developers buy up agricultural land around a city and allow it to deteriorate in the hope that the council will then re-zone it for development – at which point they will make a fortune. The UK government has made three attempts to capture this enhanced value of land with a one-off development tax and each attempt has been abandoned.

£800,000   £900,000   £1,000,000   Underground station

Land Value Tax (LVT) is a serious alternative. It would encourage owners to improve their properties and allow the community to benefit from the raised value of the location. More like rent than a one-off payment, it taxes the land, not the buildings on it. If there are ten sites in a row, nine of which have buildings on them and one of which is derelict, all ten sites will have the same tax. The owner of the derelict site has an incentive to develop it or sell it. Or the planners can decide that the community needs it as a children's playground, in which case the LVT would be zero. Derelict brownfield sites, such as those where disused industrial buildings stand, would disappear. If all brownfield sites were developed for housing there would be no shortage of residential land in Britain.

LVT is ideal for local taxation since it gives each authority an incentive to increase the environmental qualities of its villages, towns and cities in order to attract residents, businesses and investment. It is held back in Britain by landed interests, and by the government's desire to control everything from the centre. But many countries, including the US, Denmark and Australia, do use LVT, often just for local taxes.

In 1982, Harrisburg was listed as the second most rundown city in the United States. It introduced a tax on land value at three times the tax on buildings. This proved so successful that the building tax was subsequently halved. Vacant sites have been cut by 85%, there are now five times as many businesses, unemployment has fallen by 20% and crime is down by 58%. In neighbouring Pittsburgh,

politicians tried to catch votes by reducing the partial LVT that was in place. But taxes then increased overall because the tax on buildings had to be raised instead. Within just two years construction fell by 20% and businesses started to move out of town.

Estate agents already have data on the value of different locations, so LVT would be easy to introduce. The taxing of buildings, by contrast, is immensely complicated as each has to be assessed individually. Most building valuations are appealed, creating a backlog that stretches to years. Where a split-tax system is in operation, typically 95% of staff is employed in valuing buildings and only 5% in valuing land.

The London Underground's Jubilee Line extension has cost the UK taxpayer £3 billion. The value of land and properties affected rose by £13 billion. Those lucky enough to own houses or offices near new underground stations received a free lunch, while the nation's taxpayers had to pay the cost of construction and inherited an ongoing liability for maintenance. A child might question the intelligence of a chancellor who gives away such huge sums to local property owners. The mayor of London, however, is struggling to move in the direction of LVT to enable future projects to pay for themselves out of increased land values.

Land Value Tax could replace all but high-income tax, it could form the basis for a Citizens' Income, it would encourage enterprise and empower local communities. In sum, it would allow land to serve the people.

Inequality
in the neoliberal world

THE REVEREND WILLIAM LEE, frustrated that his fiancée spent more time with her needles and wool than with him, invented a machine for knitting socks. The implications were not lost on his parishioners who forced him to flee to Paris, where he died of grief. That was in 1589. It was 200 years before new technologies were allowed free reign in England.

In the medieval period artisans' guilds imposed strict rules on their members. They regulated methods, quality standards, prices, hours of work and banned work on Sundays or holidays. They limited competition and prevented outside goods from being sold in their town except on market days. If a guild member obtained raw material at a bargain price he was expected to share his luck with fellow members.

This all changed at the end of the 18th century when James Hargreaves invented the spinning jenny and Edmund Cartwright introduced the power loom. Unemployment spread rapidly across the country. The Luddites, who destroyed industrial machinery in protest at the havoc caused by new technology, were widely supported. But while technology brought riches to the country's elite, many protestors were hanged or deported. Working conditions deteriorated alarmingly. Jobs that had allowed an individual to use initiative, abilities and skills were replaced by machines. The degradation that William Cobbett described in his *Rural Rides* at the beginning of the 19th century contrasts depressingly with the quality of life documented by Daniel Defoe a century earlier.

One can find a virus infecting economic thinking in a piece of doggerel written by Bernard de Mandeville as far back as 1704:

> *Millions endeavouring to supply*
> *Each other's lust and vanity.*
> *Thus every part was full of vice,*
> *Yet the whole mass a paradise.*

Adam Smith, founder of the science of political economy, was repulsed by de Mandeville's praise of avarice and in 1759 wrote *The Theory of Moral Sentiments* in response. But in a later book, *Wealth of Nations*, he used the phrase 'an invisible hand' – just once – and it became iconic in liberal economic thinking. It refers to de Mandeville's idea that selfish enterprise ultimately benefits all. Smith included many caveats to protect against exploitation by voracious bosses, but these passages were, and still are, conveniently forgotten.

 For every dollar of aid sent to poor countries, ten dollars are sent back as debt repayments.

David Ricardo, the other great pioneer of political economy and 50 years younger, also held Smith's reservations about uncontrolled markets destroying employment. He used the example of an improved machine for making stockings that enabled one person to do the work of four: if the demand for socks only doubled, some workers would lose their jobs.

However, the concept of an 'invisible hand' suited the ruling classes well. Even today, it continues to make life easy for neoconservative economists, who relentlessly claim that unrestricted commerce will benefit everyone in the long run. As each new generation in the west has enjoyed more prosperity than the last, they urge us to accept the wonderful benefits of technological innovation.

Or should we? Admittedly, some firms had, at first, an excellent record for creating new jobs, but only by destroying others. The ghastly social conditions of the poor in the 19th century (as seen in Gustave Doré's etchings) were the result of new productivity that crushed the role of rural labour and caused large-scale migration to the cities. The next logical step was to export job-destruction abroad. Industrialised European countries created colonies overseas where they bought cheap raw materials for their factories, and sold their surplus manufactured goods back to their colonial subjects. In the process, they annihilated the livelihoods of millions of artisans in these colonies, just as they had done at home.

Yes, the Industrial Revolution produced an unimaginable increase in wealth, but it is wealth that ignores people. Enterprising innovators no longer create jobs: the world's 200 largest corporations account for 28% of the world's economic activity but employ less than 0.25% of the global workforce. The new century sees the majority seething with an overwhelming sense of injustice. Perhaps Ned Ludd was right after all.

Nine tenths of the world's population has only 15% of the world's wealth. The rest is devoted to the rich minority's excessive consumption. The worse the standard of living becomes for people at the bottom, the more galactic are the sums extracted by people at the top. "These levels of inequality are grotesque," said Duncan Green of Oxfam, "It is impossible to justify such vast wealth when 800 million people go to bed hungry every night."

A perverse neoliberal framework of economics and trade, infected by a misreading of Smith and Ricardo, has systematically transferred real wealth – crops, old growth timber and minerals – from poor to rich countries. On top of this transfer of material wealth, the poor are said to owe the rich piles of money. "If you don't pay up," say the rich, "our economy will collapse and you will suffer too." Poor countries, in fear of reprisals from the rich, sell their dwindling resources and hand over essential services to western companies. In order to do so, they cut spending on health, education and welfare.

At the time that Smith and Ricardo were writing, Europeans considered it their God-given right to exploit and/or settle the rest of the world. Some of these occupations, such as in India, eventually came to an end. Some, as in North America and Australia, dispossessed

The capitalist liberation of the Soviet Union produced:

- 36 billionaires
- 88,000 millionaires
- an average wage of $3,300 a year

It is too dangerous for the children of the wealthy to roam free because of the danger of being kidnapped.

Russians who successfully exploited their country's new riches are now among Britain's wealthiest residents.

Average income

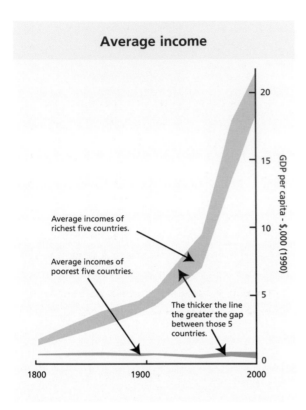

Average incomes of richest five countries.

Average incomes of poorest five countries.

The thicker the line the greater the gap between those 5 countries.

GDP per capita - $,000 (1990)

20

15

10

5

0

1800   1900   2000

Distribution of the world's wealth

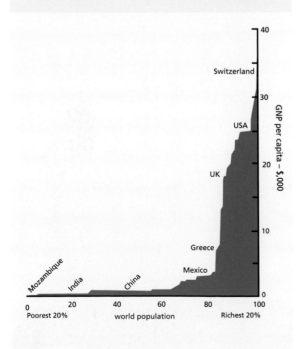

Switzerland

USA

UK

Greece

Mexico

China

India

Mozambique

GNP per capita – $,000

40

30

20

10

0

0   20   40   60   80   100
Poorest 20%   world population   Richest 20%

the original inhabitants altogether. Others, as in Latin America, achieved economic control but were challenged politically first by Simón Bolívar in the 1820s and later through the ballot box. Other western implants – cultural, economic, political – still remain alongside, if separate from, populations across the world, like a cancer eating at the guts of a region.

Military colonisation is now frowned upon, but economic regulations, usually imposed by the west, can achieve the same results. Rich nations, corporations and individuals use their wealth to manipulate public opinion, destroy opposition and buy politicians, scientists and the media. Military invasion is now only necessary in exceptional circumstances.

Karl Marx predicted that a global society based on the free movement of capital would result in the accumulation of wealth in fewer and fewer hands. He was right. However, the workers have not overthrown the bourgeoisie as he expected. Instead, global discontent has led to a growing threat from global terrorism.

There is obviously something structurally wrong with an economic system that allows these inequalities to increase. Yet economists say, against all the evidence, that further economic growth will relieve poverty. And politicians claim that debt and aid can solve the problems of poor countries – problems caused by an economic system that will inevitably continue to transfer wealth from the poor to the rich.

Some of the consequences
Wealth is not shared even within rich countries. The US, the wealthiest nation the world has ever seen, is at the bottom of the Human Poverty

Index for industrialised countries. It has the highest proportion of people who don't expect to reach the age of 60 (12.6%), the highest proportion that survives on less than half the average income (17%), and, along with the UK, the highest proportion that lacks functional literacy skills (over a fifth). A quarter of Americans suffer from a mental disorder – the highest proportion in the world. Ten per cent are dependent on private charity for food, while 47 million have no health cover and many others have huge health-related credit card debt.

In Britain, the top 1% of the population had 6% of the nation's wealth when Margaret Thatcher came to power in 1979. A decade later it had 9%. Under New Labour this has risen to 13%, the fastest hike for the mega-rich since the war. The poorer half had only 7% of the nation's wealth in 1996 and that has now dropped to below 5%.

Inequality is also rising in poor countries as increased prosperity benefits only the rich elite. When the Indian stock market and GDP reached record highs in 2005 and the government boasted of 'India shining', Karnataka state returns showed record poverty levels: 93% of people were living below the poverty line in Chamrajnagar, 88% and 77% in other districts.

Other consequences of global inequalities are the drugs trade and the violence that comes with it. Wealth in the west has created astronomic prices for narcotics. Drug barons exploit both these prices and the desperation of local farmers whose income from food crops has declined because of free-trade policies. To earn enough to survive, these farmers grow poppies and coca instead. The west then sends in its military to destroy this alternative livelihood – the only one

remaining to them. The fault lies not with the dealers or growers but with the system and its resulting inequality.

Economists love to do cost/benefit studies. When the IPCC was assessing the costs of climate change and its potential threat to human survival, the leading British economist David Pearce was asked how to evaluate human life. He insisted that one US life was the equivalent of 15 Indian lives. This did not please the Indians, but his calculation was correct in terms of neoliberal economics. A person in the US, however, is responsible for 15 times more damage to the atmosphere than an Indian, so an ecologist would have reversed the figures.

Every cow in Europe receives a subsidy of €2.62 per day – more than the daily income of half the people in the world.

Population

more or less?

"If current predictions of population growth prove accurate and patterns of human activity on the planet remain unchanged, science and technology may not be able to prevent either irreversible degradation of the environment or continued poverty for much of the world."

The Royal Society and the US National Academy of Sciences, *Population Growth, Resource Consumption and a Sustainable World* (1992)

IN 1798 THE REVEREND Robert Malthus declared that populations could only be held in check by wars, famine and disease. Without these they would rise exponentially, outstripping the ability of agriculture to support them. He advised against helping the poor in the seething slums of London because, he said, this would only enable them to breed like rabbits.

In the 20th century the analysis of population pressure was straightforward: western medicines had caused the death rate to fall worldwide while the fertility rate of so-called primitive peoples remained high. It was thought that industrialised development and enlightened attitudes would help these peoples change their traditional ways of life, raise them out of poverty and bring their birth rate down. But this didn't happen. As development spread, populations grew ever faster. At the same time, the analysis was being questioned by anthropologists who were finding more and more indigenous communities where population numbers were stable and people's lives were long and healthy, until disturbed by outside, particularly western, influences.

Kerala is one of the poorest and least developed states in India, yet its fertility rate – only 1.7 live births per woman – is similar to many western countries, well below replacement rate and the lowest in India. Female literacy and gender equality are seen as the main factors behind this. The economist Amartya Sen, studying India in general, found that where women have inferior status there is higher fertility, and that "gender inequality does not decline automatically with the process of economic growth."

The low birth rate in Kerala is the result of a programme set up by the local communist government in 1957 and pursued by subsequent governments. Literacy levels, at 91%, are the highest in India and considerably higher than in Britain – visitors are struck by the number of local people they see reading. Life expectancy, at 73 years for women, is also the highest in India, while child mortality, at 1.5%, is the lowest.

Literacy and security, regardless of a country's state of development, appear to be the prime factors that bring down population numbers. China has adopted more draconian measures.

Spectators watch a carnival procession in Goa, India

Chairman Mao's Great Leap Forward of the late 1950s was in part an attempt to relieve population problems by increasing cultivation in marginal areas in the Manchurian hinterland. However, disastrous agrarian policies degraded the farmland there and elsewhere. The government then introduced the single-child policy. The population is still increasing but the fertility rate has been below replacement for more than two decades and now stands at about 1.2 children per woman. In 20 years the population will start to fall, slowly at first and then more rapidly.

From now on, the number of Chinese turning 20 each year will decrease. This is unlikely to lead to a shortage of labour because overall population numbers remain so high. However, a different and more serious social problem may develop with the burgeoning population of young males. As parents are only allowed one child, they often abort or abandon daughters in favour of raising a son. In 15 years' time there will be 30 million more young men in China than young women – a recipe for potentially dramatic social upheaval.

The growth rate of the world's population is in the hands of three billion women. If, between now and 2050, every second woman has three children, the population will rise to 27 billion. It is more likely, however, that women will have an average of 2.1 children, so the population will stabilise at nine billion. If every second woman decides to have only one child, the world population will sink to 3.6 billion. Women's attitudes can have dramatic consequences.

The population of industrialised countries is dropping. Japan's fertility rate is now 1.25 live births per woman, well below replacement level. If this continues, its population will halve by the end of the century to the level it was in 1920. Governments in rich countries see their own reducing numbers as a threat, because our crazy economic system requires growth. However, it is the populations of rich countries, not poor ones, that are devastating the planet.

The global human population remained stable for thousands of years. Local communities developed their own forms of contraception – prolonged breast-feeding, abortion, restrictions on intercourse, removal to monasteries – which enabled them to live for millennia in balance with their environment. But with the industrial revolution the population in many parts of the world began to rise, and it rose even further with improved health care, education and the agrichemical revolution of the 20th century.

Rich countries should be welcoming the decline in their population numbers.

Since the 1970s, however, the growth rate has slowed. The global fertility rate has already dropped from an average of five children per woman in 1950 to 2.7 children today. Some predict that total population figures will rise further and then level off. Demographers can also apply a mathematical model to past trends and show a startlingly different outcome. The graph levels off in 20 years' time and then drops rapidly to pre-industrial levels.

This model ties in with the World Wildlife Fund for Nature's suggestion that we are overshooting the planet's bio-capacity by 20% to 40%. The figures imply that the earth can only support a little over two billion people. This number will, of course, decrease if we continue to inflict irreversible damage.

Two mechanisms could reduce population numbers to a sustainable level.

The first is to allow Malthus's wars, famine and disease to do the job for us. Neoliberal capitalism is already leading us along this path into runaway global warming, degradation of farmlands, over-fishing of the oceans, genetic mutation of animals and plants, chemically induced endocrine changes, vulnerability to pandemics, energy and water wars, insurgency, radioactive contamination and possible nuclear holocaust. These human-made disasters will probably be an effective combination.

The second is for industrialised countries to welcome their falling fertility rates as a painless way of reducing the world population. But they must also spread the conditions that would enable other countries to do the same. This means using the wealth-creating capacity of the modern world to reduce inequality. We should maintain the productivity of small farms in poor countries, since mothers earning an income prefer to have fewer children. Gender equality, and education for girls, must be pursued. Contraceptives must be universally available, and people must have control over their own lives. If we do these things, a benign decline in numbers to a sustainable level could happen throughout the world.

The choice is ours.

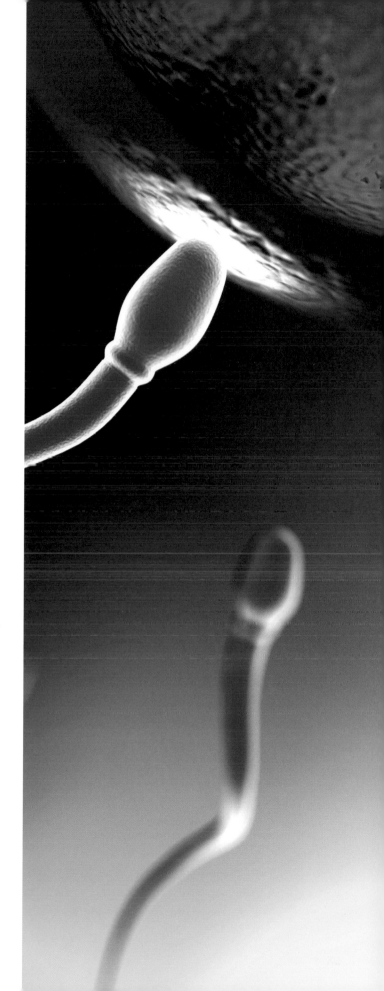

Economic growth
and the second law of thermodynamics

"If something can't go on forever, it will probably stop."

Herb Stein, President Nixon's economic adviser, 1980

FREDERICK SODDY FRS was a British pioneer atomic scientist who received the Nobel Prize in 1921. He was deeply concerned about the uses of atomic power: "If the discovery were made tomorrow," he wrote in 1926, "there is not a nation that would not throw itself heart and soul into the task of applying it to war." The Royal Society ridiculed him for criticising new advances in science. He in turn criticised the Royal Society's comfortable view that scientists have no responsibility for the uses to which their science is put.

Frederick Soddy, circa 1919

Soddy believed that the economic system, given power by science, contained built-in elements for conflict and the destruction of nature. So he tried to apply scientific thought to economics, only to be ridiculed by economists.

To understand Soddy, try thinking about this: a sack of grain is real and solid and represents material wealth. But grain does not last. It rots or is eaten by weevils or gradually turns into dust. This process of disintegration is known as the second law of thermodynamics. Now consider the idea of minus one sack of grain: this moves you away from a material concept to a mathematical one. The minus sack represents virtual wealth – in terms of debt – which can grow ad infinitum, unrestrained by material reality. According to Soddy, the ruling passion of economists is to convert real wealth into virtual wealth (debt), which has no limits to its growth.

Economists have turned the world on its head. You can save their virtual money and its worth will increase, but if you store something real it will decay and gradually lose value. Economists insist on making the real world of physical matter conform to a purely mathematical concept of growth; then they add interest and compound interest and the growth reproduces itself forever. This is logical nonsense, said

Soddy, which can only lead to catastrophe in nature and the breakdown of society. To illustrate its absurdity he pointed out that if Jesus Christ had invested $1 in our economic system it would now be worth $1,000 trillion trillion trillion. Soddy believed that the outcome of this non-scientific thinking must inevitably be debt cancellation, revolution or war.

Development since the Industrial Revolution has, in Soddy's view, been the flamboyant period of history, when humans have been using up the limited capital stock of coal. This can only be a passing phase, he warned, after which we will have to live by sunshine. There is therefore a finite limit to growth.

"The earth has finite limits – a difficult idea for Americans to adjust to."

John D. Rockefeller III (1906–1978)

Looking back after 75 years, has Soddy been proved right? Economists might say: "He was an amateur who knew little about our discipline. There has been steady economic growth, wealth has multiplied and our standard of living has increased out of all recognition. Our scientific achievements have been spectacular and the whole world is now open to markets, communication and tourism. Through our wealth we have gained the knowledge to deal with whatever problems of health and the environment may arise. There are, admittedly, still pockets of need but the way to fill them is to ensure further economic growth.
Is Soddy saying that all our politicians, economists and businessmen are misguided?"

Soddy, if still alive, might reply: "Yes. Precisely. The Wealth of Nature, real wealth such as fisheries, topsoil and oil, has been eroded. We have already passed the limit of growth and any further economic growth may reduce nature's ability to provide us with adequate energy, food and clothing. Agriculture has had to adopt unnatural practices that conflict with nature's processes. Individual problems with health and the environment are being swamped by pandemics and general degradation. Virtual wealth, concentrating power in the hands of a few, has now reached unimaginable levels and is causing endemic conflict and the breakdown of society. Economists have created a make-believe world that has nothing to do with reality. To aim at yet further economic growth is suicidal."

Who is closer to the truth? Take your pick.

Nature provides the model for a stable economy without net growth. It has infinite variety, and its complexity increases with time. When things go wrong it finds new alternatives. It gradually turns dust into things of value, which, in turn, die and feed the cycle of life. It captures pollution and lays it down in the earth's crust. But nature has no net growth. It is stable. It provides wonders on a finite planet. To say that a stable no-growth economy is impossible simply shows the poverty of our imagination.

A paradox
the history of growth in the UK

The UK has experienced a period of record growth in the new century. The astronomical remuneration of directors is a regular media topic, London has the highest property values in the world, shareholders pocket gains as our companies are sold abroad, first-time buyers can't get on the property ladder, stress at work increases, couples put off having babies, and our children are subjected to tests more frequently than anywhere else in the world. The government's obsession with economic growth even leads it to condone corporate corruption.

But a look at history indicates that, far from improving the well-being of all citizens, growth has the reverse effect.

The Index of Sustainable Economic Welfare (ISEW) shows a gradual reduction in the quality of life in Britain over the past 25 years, though the gross domestic product, which measures all economic activity, rose by 50%. Richard Douthwaite analyses this paradox in his book *The Growth Illusion*, devoting a chapter to each of the themes in the following paragraphs. If you instinctively question these provocative statements, try reading his arguments in full.

Capitalism, being based on debt and the charging of interest, cannot survive without growth. Firms must expand to avoid collapse. The compulsion for an increasing supply of raw materials and new markets fuelled the British Empire, destroyed indigenous cultures all over the world, and finally led to world war.

Growth in Britain during the Agricultural and Industrial Revolutions made life progressively worse for ordinary people until about 1850. Conditions then began to improve – as a result of depression, not growth. By the beginning of the First World War living conditions had, just, returned to their level of 200 years previously. Major improvement in living conditions followed the two world wars and the redistributive policies of the 1945 Labour government. Whenever growth appeared, however, life for the majority got worse.

Governments saw their role as the proper management of society. It was not until 1955 that accelerating the growth rate became the major British economic obsession. Since then, the methods used to generate higher levels of output have caused a large increase in chronic illness. All indicators of the quality of life show that it deteriorated in Britain between 1955 and 1988. Unemployment, for example, soared and crime increased eightfold.

Because the Thatcher government sought to accelerate growth by improving investors' returns, it engineered a major shift in the distribution of incomes and wealth in favour of the better-off. Economic power was concentrated and an ever-higher share of the nation's income had to be spent by the state. The need for growth forced firms to adopt new technologies before their impact could be assessed, and environmental disasters such as the large-scale release of dangerous chemicals – for example, CFCs that deplete the ozone layer and PCBs that harm the central nervous system – were inevitable.

Douthwaite concludes that a sustainable society requires a stable economy – history and logic show that there is no such thing as sustainable growth. Morality lost all control over the direction of economic change after Smith's concept of 'the invisible hand' gained acceptance. If the world is to have a bright future, morality must govern our actions again.

Wörgl

money not worth keeping

HAVE YOU EVER wondered at the beauty of buildings from the 12th and 13th centuries in southern Europe? In this period, hundreds of new towns were constructed with solid stone houses that have survived to this day. Ironically, it was not a politically stable time. The many wars waged by the Church on the Cathars – partly about religion but more about the Pope's loss of power – were hugely destructive.

Inadvertently, in the period following these wars, a rather strange system of money was developed that brought about the impressive rebuilding of the towns that give us so much pleasure today.

In the Holy Roman Empire, rulers of the numerous small independent states issued thin silver coins called bracteates, which were reclaimed by the state at three quarters of their value when the ruler died. Realising the benefits of this system, rulers started reclaiming and reissuing the coins more frequently. Holding on to this money therefore became risky. As the coins did not store value it was better to use them straight away to build houses, which could keep their worth. This led to a high demand for construction labour, which led to an improvement in wages and working hours – reduced to about six hours a day – and at least 90 religious holidays a year. People enjoyed a better quality of life thanks to the strength of their dynamic local economies.

But when gold coins were introduced in the 15th century it was suddenly worth saving money because of the amount of precious metal the coins contained. So demand for labour dropped, wages fell, unemployment appeared, and many businesses closed down as traders earned more from lending money than from buying and selling goods. To cap it all, rulers had to find new means of taxation.

The idea of issuing money that is not worth storing has often cropped up since the days of the Holy Roman Empire. Take, for example, the small Austrian town of Wörgl. During the Depression of the 1930s a third of the town's workforce was unemployed and local taxes were badly in arrears, crippling the work of the council. The mayor negotiated a loan from a credit union bank and printed scrip notes. These were guaranteed against the national currency but only to 98% of their value. Everyone had to go into the council office each month and stamp notes in their possession, paying one per cent of their value. This encouraged people to use them as quickly as possible. Council staff received half their wages in scrip notes and local taxes could be paid with them, so businesses and shops were also prepared to accept them as payment.

The effect was dramatic. Local trade was stimulated again, tax arrears were paid off and there was full employment. The council was able to take on 50 extra people to repair and surface streets, and to extend the sewerage system. They even built a ski jump and a reservoir without incurring any debt. As the scrip notes were used for local trade, people's livelihoods were not harmed by the rapidly inflating national currency. Not surprisingly, other towns started to copy the scheme. The central bank, alarmed

that it was losing control of the money system, took out legal proceedings and closed it down soon after it started.

Many similar schemes were tried in the US, with the same response from the banks. In March 1933 Roosevelt forbade the issue of any further scrips, having been advised that the financial system was slipping through the government's hands – and into those of the people.

Economic activity using a local currency

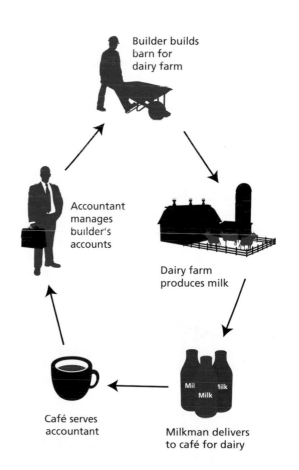

Builder builds barn for dairy farm

Accountant manages builder's accounts

Dairy farm produces milk

Café serves accountant

Milkman delivers to café for dairy

Interest-free banking
and demurrage currencies

THE SWEDISH MEMBER-OWNED JAK Bank has over 30,000 customers who neither pay nor receive interest; they are only charged administration fees.

The trick is in 'savings points'. These represent not just the amount of money in your account but also the time it has been there. Savings points are therefore measured as pound-months (krona-months in Sweden). Normally, you can only borrow up to the number of pound-months that you have managed to save. But you can borrow up to eight times more if you continue to save while paying back the loan. The pound-months you save must equal the pound-months you pay back; in this way you build up a nest egg that cannot be withdrawn until the loan is paid off. The savings of its members finance the bank's loans, so both members and bank are secure and insulated from the interest rate changes of the money market.

The usual response is: "Why would I want to invest my money in a bank that doesn't pay me interest?" Well, look at the long-term view: most people, over their lives, pay a lot more interest on money that they borrow than they receive on money that they invest. Members of the JAK bank therefore benefit from paying no interest and receiving none. Imagine taking out a mortgage of £100,000 and paying it off over 15 years without the burden of interest as well. At the end of this time you have the house plus the sum of money – potentially another £100,000 – that you would have lost by covering 15 years' worth of interest payments.

The JAK movement (Jord Arbete Kapital is Swedish for Land Labour Capital) originally started in Denmark in the 1920s and wherever JAK banks were established they increased prosperity in the local area. Official banks took every opportunity to crush them, as they threatened the extraordinary concession that society usually gives banks to create money and cream off interest. The Swedish JAK bank has at last found a formula that the establishment cannot easily put a stop to.

What about the bigger picture? Bernard Lietaer, the world's top currency trader before he was overtaken by George Soros, suggests that a currency with negative interest – not just zero interest – is necessary and might even be welcomed by big business.

Our interest-bearing currency forces most companies into short-term investment. If they don't need to sell a product until next year then they don't make it now because money grows faster than inflation. Expenditure in ten years' time needs only half the money at today's value. This difference is called 'discounted cash flow' and financial planners use it as a standard technique. Even if a company decides to be conscientious by investing for the future, an asset-stripping predator may well come along and gobble it up. Currency growth therefore directly favours currency speculation in preference to investment in real assets.

However, if a currency is constantly losing value – what is called a 'demurrage currency'

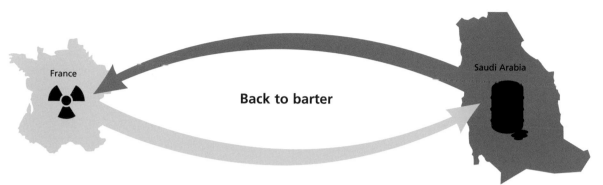

Back to barter

– the reverse applies. For example, if you are convinced that solar photovoltaics will have a big market in ten years' time, the sooner you build a factory the better. It will cost you a lot more to build it in a few years when your money has dropped in value. So a demurrage currency favours long-term planning, not speculation.

The current money system used to serve the trading needs of big companies. Not any more. Less than five per cent of trade relates to the real world of goods and services. Currency speculation has taken over: it is growing at 15% a year, and is unregulated and untaxed. The Tobin Tax has been proposed in the UK as a small levy on money transactions – 0.1% to 0.25% – but even this is fiercely resisted by the financial community. With a demurrage currency or a global eco-currency, however, the Tobin Tax would be unnecessary.

States, corporations and banks are helpless in the face of currency speculation. It is like a demolition ball swinging from a crane and wreaking havoc in its path. Not surprisingly, big companies don't like trading with such an unstable commodity, so a quarter of world trade has already gone back to barter. Pepsi, for example, takes its profits from Russia as vodka; France builds nuclear power stations in Saudi Arabia in exchange for oil. This return to barter is surely an admission of defeat for flat-earth economists. It is time they started thinking about financial mechanisms that serve the real world.

Demurrage currencies have served prosperous civilisations well in the past – the Ming Dynasty, ancient Egypt, 10th to 13th century Europe (the age of cathedrals). It is now quite possible that companies will turn to the stability of a demurrage currency to escape the demolition ball of the speculators.

Not all currencies, however, are the result of long-term financial planning. Jaime Lerner, mayor of the Brazilian town of Curitiba during the early 1980s, created a local currency almost by accident. He had a headache over rubbish. The city had grown to over a million residents and there were tens of thousands of squatters living in its chaotic favelas. The town's rubbish trucks couldn't enter the favelas because the streets were too narrow, so the rubbish piled up, rats invaded and disease became rife.

Many mayors would have bulldozed wider streets through the shanty towns but Lerner, even if he had wanted to, did not have the funds. Instead, he positioned large bins at the edges of the neighbourhoods, each labelled for glass, paper, plastics or biodegradable material. Anyone arriving with a bag of pre-sorted rubbish was given a bus token. Soon, the neighbourhoods were picked clean by thousands of children, and their parents used the tokens to catch the bus to their jobs in the city centre.

As well as having to clear rubbish, the local council had a duty to provide food to poor

neighbourhoods and notebooks to schools. So, following the initial success of the rubbish-for-bus tickets scheme, it was extended to include tokens for food and school materials. The tokens gradually became a currency used by two thirds of households in the city. But unlike ordinary money, this currency was an integral part of local social life and the day-to-day functioning of the city.

The Talent Exchange website, set up by the South African New Economics Foundation (SANE) in 2003, is another example of a non-monetary economy. In this system, interest, by definition, has no place.

'Talents' are a currency that you acquire when you create a trade record on the Exchange website. If you are able to offer something that other people want you can access other people's goods in return. You can borrow from the Exchange by going into deficit in your account, and you can hold reserves in it by going into credit. If your deficit becomes too deep, members will not sell to you. If you stay in credit too long, you are asked to start spending to keep the system lively. You can trade health services, furniture, accountancy, gardening, home cleaning, repairs, car services, anything. A network of community workers equipped with laptops enables even those living in townships – who can offer home-grown food, for example – to join in. It is not limited by geography so it has some members outside South Africa too.

Talents only exist in terms of computer entries that go briefly into debt or surplus but resolve around the zero line, where they cease to exist. They are simply a record of exchange and people with no money can still use the system.

There are many ways in which society can be creative with money in order to serve the needs of exchange. Interest is the most destructive aspect of our present system and we could manage perfectly well without it.

Fresh fruit is exchanged for sorted rubbish in Curitiba, Brazil

Citizens' Income
make poverty history

"The time has come for us to civilise ourselves by the total, direct and immediate abolition of poverty." Martin Luther King, *Where Do We Go From Here?* (1967)

THE IDEA OF a Citizens' Income was pioneered in the 1930s, but it was overtaken by the welfare state. It is now under consideration again, and was even mentioned in the Queen's October 2006 speech: "My government will take forward legislation to reform the welfare system and to reduce poverty. A Citizens' Income would make it easier for many families to earn their way out of poverty." The Basic Income Earth Network (BIEN) is championing a similar idea; in New Zealand, they call it the Universal Income; in South Africa, the Basic Income Grant (BIG); in Canada, the Guaranteed Annual Income; in the US, the Citizens' Dividend.

The Citizens' Income would work like this: the government would distribute an equal amount of money to every man and woman, rich and poor, every month. It is not pay, welfare or charity. It is a right. It is every citizen's share of the nation's inherent wealth. Attempts to alleviate poverty up until now, such as welfare payments, have been indirect and often demeaning, requiring a huge bureaucracy and giving rise to fraud. Why not abolish poverty itself? The change would be dramatic. It would do away with the iniquitous benefits trap – 'marginal withdrawal rates' – and it would give purchasing power to millions who at present have none. There would be an explosion of local economic activity and the crippling stress of modern life would be reduced.

But can it be afforded? Clive Lord, in his book *A Citizens' Income*, showed that in the UK a Citizens' Income of £320 per month (£420 for pensioners) would require a 7% increase in income tax. But all taxpayers with an income below £30,000 would be better off, as the Citizens' Income would offset the tax increase.

The BIG idea

Unemployment among South Africans runs at almost 50%. Means-tested welfare payments, if attempted, would be too expensive to administer with any pretence at fairness, and would encourage corruption.

Instead, the South African government is considering the BIG idea, the Basic Income Grant. The grant would be given to all citizens equally and would be clawed back through tax from people with an income. No change is necessary to the tax regime and it overcomes the horrendous difficulty of assessing the need for welfare. To promote the idea, a BIG coalition has been formed by labour unions, church bodies and NGOs.

This figure of £320 is low but it could be raised if, for example, government also taxed environmentally damaging activities; it could be doubled if the Bank of England, not private banks, issued the country's currency. A Citizens' Income would simplify the bureaucracy of benefits and tax returns, save government money and reduce its involvement in people's private affairs.

It sounds too good to be true. Alaska, however, already runs a citizens' dividend by distributing equal royalties from oil companies to all its citizens. This is only about $1,200 a year per person, but it has boosted local economies and reduced child poverty significantly. Though small-scale, it demonstrates how the principle of a Citizens' Income can work.

Our civilisation is wealthier than any previous civilisation. Who created this wealth? Not the corporate executives who make millions in the financial sector. It was the work and imagination of farmers, industrialists and countless individuals who produced Britain's wealth over many generations. It is an inheritance from which all should expect to benefit.

A Citizens' Income would profoundly change the basis of our economy, which makes it hard to imagine. But could anyone have seriously imagined, or wanted, the world we have created today? It is a world in which just 220 people own more than the joint income of half the world's population. The wealth of these few people – already breath-taking – doubled in the last four years. Soon, if business continues as usual, much of the planet, all humanity's inheritance built up over millennia, will become the private property of a few individuals.

The rest of the population live in fear of losing their jobs, of being unable to pay a mortgage, of falling ill, of penury in old age. People are driven to aggression or theft to gain illusive security. A billion people around the world already live with the threat of starvation. We have achieved a world of hatred, terrorism and cut-throat competition that drives businesses to expand, regardless of sweatshops and environmental destruction. To repeat: could anyone have seriously imagined, or wanted, this kind of world?

It is possible to develop a humane world without poverty because global society has a greater ability to create wealth than ever before.

A Citizens' Income, if fully applied, could free people to improve their lives.

- It would provide them with a financial platform from which to choose the life they want to lead.
- It would give them the independence to demand proper wages and conditions.
- They would be able to leave a job that is unsatisfying, making way for others who want it instead.
- They could avoid work that harms the environment.

Why do they give the country's inherited wealth only to the rich?

- Small-scale farmers could better survive.
- Local shops within a community would become more viable.
- The centralisation of economic activity would be reversed, making it possible to curb the excesses of corporations.
- Small-scale employers would only need to top up the Citizens' Income and could therefore employ more staff.
- There would be no need to produce unnecessary or short-lived products just in order to generate employment.
- People would not need to amass excessive wealth for their old age or even to pass it all on to their children.

"People who don't need to work for their living will become antisocial layabouts," say the rich. But some people in society have always benefited from unearned income – those with inherited wealth or with partners who earn large salaries. A Citizens' Income would simply extend this benefit in a small way to others. This is a less divisive route to social justice than provoking the dispossessed to call for revolution, and it would remove the plight of those who have no option but to beg. Most people would want to work to earn more than the Citizens' Income, though some, content with low earnings, might choose to write a book, build their own home or grow their own food instead.

A Citizens' Income would do more than anything else to give us a humane and civilised society. Its time has come.

Bhutan
gross national happiness

"There is no wealth but life. Life, including all its powers of love, of joy, and of admiration. That country is the richest which nourishes the greatest number of noble and happy human beings."

John Ruskin, *Unto This Last* (1862)

ICE-BLUE WATER tumbles over rocks, men in flowing robes practise archery by the willows, paddy fields spread out beneath the forested hillsides and vast tzong monasteries, with their battered walls and wide, overhanging roofs, look down over the valleys below. Floating above everything, snow-capped peaks merge with the clouds and the sky. Bhutan is a small kingdom where Mahayana Buddhism, interwoven with Bonism, infuses all aspects of life.

Until 1998, Bhutan was an absolute monarchy, but the National Assembly can now force the king to abdicate by a two-thirds majority vote. Ironically, this measure was forced through by the king. Gradually, the Assembly has delegated appropriate powers to the districts and the districts are in turn delegating powers to the geogs, the village groups. These powers include the control of a budget, and each geog has a representative in the annual National Assembly. Bhutan may be an absolute monarchy but this arrangement seems closer to participatory democracy than Britain's elective oligarchy.

Bhutan is one of the world's ten 'least developed countries', according to the United Nations. Yet it has little sign of malnutrition, people are well clothed and there are no slums or shanty towns.

Having only recently opened its borders, the country is determined to avoid the pitfalls of development that plague other small nations. It has rejected the mad rush for an increase in growth and competitiveness, and struggles instead to identify and measure policies that maximise GNH (Gross National Happiness).

From macro to micro, decisions are tested against their effect on the environment and society. The profitable timber export trade, for instance, was closed down because it was seen to be causing erosion of the hillsides; no one may own more than ten per cent of a business; plastic bags are forbidden, not least because of the dioxins released by their incineration. This last measure encourages local paper production – not from trees but from the regeneration of edgeworthia bushes.

Bhutan's buildings are exquisitely decorated. New monasteries and temples are built on rocky outcrops high in the mountains. Down below, houses are continually being constructed since all Bhutanese, at some point in their lives, build their own home. These large three-storey dwellings are built along the edges of the valleys, to avoid wasting farmland. House construction is not a commercial activity but a part of community life. Trees are selected by a forester (three new ones are planted to replace each one taken), then adzed into shape and slid down the hillside. The walls of the houses are made of clay, dug from the adjacent ground and tamped into wooden shutters by teams of singing women. The houses are then decorated with intricate patterns. The cost, in terms of money, is minimal. The massive mud walls of abandoned houses gradually meld back into the ground from which they were built. A family house belongs to the wife and children and is inherited by the eldest daughter.

Bhutan is so small that the effects of change can be observed and modified. It has its problems, of course, but it is a crucible for testing how a society can select the best of modern life without being destroyed by global commercialism. In Britain, the government's roadmap is GDP

(Gross Domestic Product), a measure of economic activity where the road simply leads uphill with ever more growth. Ultimately the road must reach the peak – then where?

GDP is a strange map to use. A disaster, even a terrorist's bomb, adds to economic activity because it produces extra work for police and for hospitals. Nurturing a child, by contrast, cannot be measured as economic activity and therefore isn't shown on the map. All that matters is competition. To achieve success, children are put through constant testing, while the unemployed are considered 'jobseekers'. Competition must determine business, social services, health provision and academia.

By using the wrong map we are, inevitably, arriving at an unintended and thoroughly undesirable destination.

World map colour coded according to the Happy Planet Index

The New Economics Foundation (NEF) has prepared a better map, called the Happy Planet Index (HPI). It measures the efficiency with which a country uses its ecology to deliver human well-being, and incorporates life satisfaction (only partially subjective), life expectancy and ecological footprint.

This parallel way of thinking about economics – as if people and the planet mattered – has a long history that includes Jefferson, Ruskin, Morris, Gandhi, Keynes and Schumacher. The NEF is now assessing the damage inflicted on the planet and suggesting how to prevent further disasters.

It identified one of Britain's most visible failures as our city centres – 'clone town Britain' – where universal choice means no choice, where there is little life outside shopping hours and where even old buildings are gutted and given a new corporate uniformity. Remote bureaucrats regulate how we live, and boardrooms decide what we buy. But decisions taken like this, far from the people and places they concern, are ineffective: communities and neighbourhoods unravel, crime rises, social cohesion collapses and the vital work of looking after old people, guiding young people and mediating disputes is ignored or forgotten. Money never did measure what really matters.

The G8 countries, whose leaders determine the world's economy, are all near the bottom of the Happy Planet Index: the US is 150th out of 178, Britain lies at 108th. These politicians fail to understand the real needs of their people. Perhaps the King of Bhutan, Jigme Singye Wangchuck, when he abdicates in 2008 at the age of 51, should lead a new G8 of leaders from countries at the top of the HPI.

Happy Planet Index – how it works

The HPI indicates the efficiency with which a country converts the earth's finite resources into the well-being of its citizens. The three components of the Index are life satisfaction, life expectancy and ecological footprint.

Countries with differing footprints vary: The Netherlands (70th), with half the footprint of the US (150th), is nearly twice as efficient at achieving long happy lives.

Countries with similar footprints vary: Jamaicans (53rd) live on average 27 years longer and experience greater happiness than Equatorial Guineans (170th), although their footprints are identical.

Map key

■	All 3 components good
■	2 good and 1 medium
■	1 good and 2 medium
■	3 medium
■	Any with 1 poor
■	2 poor, or any with a blood red footprint

Basic needs

isn't everyone as happy as we are?

"Not everything that counts can be counted, and not everything that can be counted, counts." Attributed to Albert Einstein (1879–1955)

SINCE 1974, THE activist Helena Norberg-Hodge has had close contact with the people of Ladakh, a region in the Indian Himalayas with one of the harshest climates in the world. For eight months of the year it has temperatures below freezing and during summer it is scorched by the harsh sun. Norberg-Hodge has noted the immense care that Ladakhis take over the use of their minimal resources, relying on the outside world only for salt and tea. There is literally no

waste in their communities. They work hard in the summer but at their own rate, accompanied by laughter and song. The distinction between work and play is fluid. Winter is a time for festivals, parties and storytelling. They understand their own needs – and these do not relate to western-style development.

Having visited this region for more than 16 years, Norberg-Hodge wrote: "Their sense

New Year's celebrations in Phuktal monastery, Ladakh

of joy seems so firmly anchored within them that circumstances cannot change it. At first I couldn't believe that the Ladakhis could be as happy as they appeared. It took a long time to accept that the smiles I saw were real." Is this romanticism or does it suggest that we need to re-define human needs?

Manfred Max-Neef, the Chilean economist and ecologist, has spent much of his life among poor communities, trying to understand development from their perspective. He believes that there are nine basic human needs:

- Subsistence – health, food, shelter
- Protection – security, society
- Affection – friendship, family, love
- Understanding – curiosity, education
- Participation – responsibilities, interaction, community
- Leisure – play, fantasy, intimacy, privacy
- Creation – skills, work, feedback
- Identity – belonging, groups, recognition
- Freedom – autonomy, rights, dissent

These basic human needs can be satisfied in very different ways by different cultures. When changes are proposed to the economic system of a country the proposals should be checked against all nine of them. To facilitate this, Max-Neef discusses each need against four aspects of living: what we are, what we have, what we do and how we interact.

Severe deprivation in one area may undercut all other considerations of human development. This is particularly the case with hunger, which paralyses an eighth of the world population. But it is true of other needs too. In an affluent society with little community participation, social exclusion may lead to criminality. Total

lack of affection or loss of identity may lead even wealthy people, who can satisfy all other needs, to severe depression and suicide.

For politicians and bureaucrats the concept of basic human needs is usually limited to food, health and education – to be met in the poorest communities through aid and advice from international agencies. These take account only of economic goods, which represent a fraction of real needs. Yet the donors are surprised when these solutions, imposed with the best of intentions, cause havoc in countries with a strong spiritual and traditional culture.

> Many indigenous communities have satisfied their basic needs without consumerist competition.

For Max-Neef, human-scale development comes from the grass roots. Successful strategies enable those in need to decide how they will develop. An economic strategy may satisfy one need but not another, and if it causes extreme deprivation to any of the nine it should be abandoned, however beneficial it appears in other respects. Development will be destructive unless those involved decide what their real needs are and how they can be met.

Back to Ladakh. Globalisation may bring additional income to the region, but the influx of money and consumer perishables will not necessarily bring greater happiness. It will allow Ladakhis to focus for the first time on the deprivations of their extreme climate, and it may encourage them to turn their backs on a culture that has long succeeded in satisfying all their fundamental human needs.

Them or us
a Gandhian approach

"Civil disobedience is the storehouse of power."

Mahatma Gandhi, *Constructive Programme* (1941)

KING HENRY VIII is widely credited with creating Britain's centralised state, a system that Thomas Jefferson tried to reject for the New World and Gandhi did reject for India. Various projects are now applying Gandhi's alternative 'panchyat raj' approach, in which the local community forms the basic unit of government.

Seventy-five villages in Lathur, south India, were recently identified as below the poverty line and in need of aid. The government gave the money to the local authority without specifying how it should be spent; that was the job of the villages. Under panchyat raj, it is the village that decides which individuals are in need and how the aid

should be distributed. The village councils of 20 men and 20 women are elected annually and the post of headperson rotates.

Mr Rajamani, for example, realises that he could double his income if his well were deeper, so he applies to his village council for a loan. The council checks that his proposal is realistic and approves the loan (which comes from the local authority). Having deepened the well and increased his income he repays the loan, plus interest, to the village council (not to the authority). This is how government aid accumulates to the village community. Ninety-eight per cent of loans are satisfactorily repaid through this scheme. The occasional failures are usually for a reason that can be appreciated by the village council.

In this way, a village builds up a fund that it handles through a community bank controlled by a group of village councils. Once the fund reaches a certain size the authority withdraws and the village itself continues with the same process using its own accumulated income. Now, after five years, 35 of the villages no longer require further aid.

Each village must, of course, keep to the system and not be bullied by a few individuals or taken over by a party-political group. This is

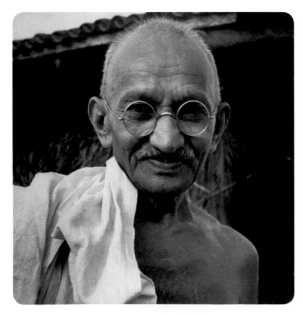

Mahatma Ghandi in 1942

ensured not by the authority, but at an annual two-day gathering of all the villages. The gathering also becomes a festival, providing a place of contact and even a marriage market. It is the lowest tier of the state electoral system that Gandhi recommended, where each tier takes responsibility for its own affairs and aims to determine the policy of higher tiers of authority. The higher authority must be the servant of the lower. In other words, through their chosen representatives the villagers are their own legislators and the makers of their own destinies. Should the authorities fail to respect this devolution of responsibilities, they can resort to non-violent civil disobedience.

In Britain, even more than in the US, power is now in the hands of a small clique in Downing Street, which is subject only to occasional elections. You might vote for a member of parliament because of her policies, but she can exert little influence on the rulers. This is a system we still call democracy, though political analysts call it elective oligarchy: rule by a small elite group. Indeed, the centralisation and personalisation, the withholding of information, the rejection of scrutiny or collegiate decision-making – for example, in going to war in Iraq – have led some to describe our system as an elective dictatorship.

Margaret Thatcher's government appointed administrators to control bodies they knew little about – a policy doggedly pursued by New Labour. Applied to the National Health Service this policy has reduced morale among doctors and nurses to an all-time low, in spite of high funding. The NHS now compares unfavourably with the community-based health service of Cuba, which receives only a tiny fraction of our funding.

Each tier of British government distrusts the one below, so rules and regulations abound. The lowest tier does not represent communities since it controls several thousand people. Local authorities protect their powers jealously and will never allow a street community to decide how its road might be allocated between children and cars, nor to decide on the design of new buildings, nor to run its own recycling of waste and water, nor to combine with other communities to provide its own school or clinic. A street community in Hull secretly grassed its road overnight for the Jubilee in 1977 and had it ripped up by the authority the following week. It took 20 years for the community to get the road back to grass through official channels.

"Freedom is to be attained by educating the people to a sense of their capacity to regulate and control authority."

Mahatma Gandhi, *Young India* (1925)

Citizens only really feel involved when they themselves make the decisions that vitally affect their lives. There is a fundamental difference between decisions made by 'them' and decisions made by 'us'.

It is no wonder that social exclusion has become a major issue in Britain. When people cannot determine their own destiny, the community falls apart. The vital step is from mere consultation to full participation. Budgets should be managed by communities that are small enough for all to be involved – street-scale communities. This is democracy. We have much to learn from Gandhi's ideas for India.

Wealth in poverty
adivasi attitudes

"The world's most primitive people have few possessions, but they are not poor." Marshall Sahlins, *Stone Age Economics: The Original Affluent Society* (1972)

THERE IS A STRANGE and very old story. Two brothers come together and make offerings to their Lord. The Lord is pleased with the offering from Abel, the free-ranging nomadic brother, but displeased with that from Cain. Cain is so furious he murders Abel. Many years later, he is found tilling fields and building cities.

This story was, perhaps, first told by hunter-gatherers to explain the erosion of their lifestyle and later found its way into the Bible. It records the greatest turning point of human history. For hundreds of thousands of years humans lived with nature and then, only five thousand years ago, they began developing agriculture, cities and settled civilisations.

The old animosity between Cain and Abel remains. Civilised man despises the freedom of indigenous peoples. He takes their rich and diverse land by force, leaving only the inhospitable margins. He attacks them when they get in the way, or condescendingly offers them clothes, houses and education. The 17th century philosopher Thomas Hobbes's conviction that the life of pre-civilised humanity was nasty, brutish and short is deeply ingrained and constantly reinforced in books and films.

Anthropologists have recorded very different views. The !Kung Bushmen, in spite of living in the most marginal habitats of southern Africa, spend only three to five hours looking for their food each day. And their life is not necessarily short: ten per cent of Bushmen of the Kalahari in the 1960s were over 60 years old. For most hunter-gatherers, particularly before they were forced off fertile land, nature was bountiful. A report by the World Conservation Union (IUCN) in 2007 found that pastoralists make the best use of natural resources, can be ten times as productive as commercial ranching, increase biodiversity and retain more carbon in the soil than when it is ploughed.

Co-operation was an essential part of hunter-gatherers' community life. A single hunter might have a one-in-four chance of making a successful kill, but four hunters working together would have a reliable food supply. Years of anthropological research have found that indigenous peoples tend to live in egalitarian, consensus-based societies. A few hours are spent working, often with friends, and the rest of the day is for eating, telling stories, making music, dancing, philosophising, playing with children, relaxing and sleeping. Only the elite in civilised society enjoys this amount of leisure.

The advance of settled agricultural societies brought with it new diseases: the common cold, measles, chickenpox, influenza. It also brought new power hierarchies. Agricultural surplus led to greater inequalities. In today's world, we have sedentary office workers working eight or more hours a day in a job that is usually boring and often followed by a long commute, ready-made meals and a slump in front of the television.

The adivasi indigenous communities in Gudalur, south India, have developed a very different way of life in the modern world. They used to live deep in the forest where there was no need to prove ownership of any land – indeed, where there was no concept of land ownership. Land, water and air were regarded as commons, available for all to use.

The British–Indian government sold the forests in which the adivasis lived, assuming that the land was empty. An international

tea corporation acquired large tracts of it for plantations. Adivasis continued to live on the edges of the land but how could they secure their rights? The only way was to plant permanent crops. But when they did so, the forest rangers pulled them up and destroyed their homes.

In 1984, Stan and Mari Thekaekara, Indian social activists, persuaded five adivasi tribes, totalling nearly 2,000 families, to act together. When individuals were threatened, the whole community gathered to protest. They secured land for some families, but ownership of individual plots did not help them as a group.

The adivasis decided that the only way to strengthen the community was to have a project of their own. They prepared a business plan and obtained a 'soft' loan, guaranteed by a community in Germany, to buy a tea plantation. The yield soon doubled. Their tea fetched high prices because of the care with which it was picked. However, rather than dividing the profits among the group working on the plantation, the pickers said that any extra earnings should go to the community. They said that if they became wealthy while others remained poor their community would fall apart.

No wonder the Lord was displeased with Cain.

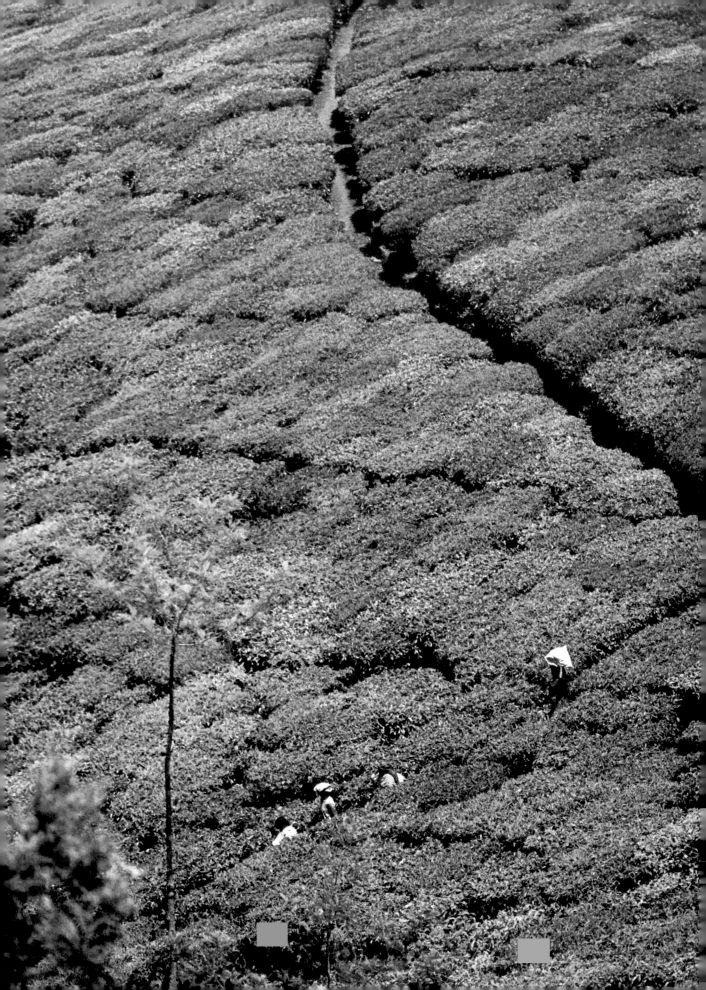

Mari Thekaekara once sat in on an adivasi group discussion about their assets. Afterwards she commented: "They were clear about their wealth. 'It is our community, our children, our unity, our culture and the forest.' Money was not mentioned. We, the non-adivasis, were stunned. As we discussed concepts of poverty further, we realised that they didn't see themselves as poor. They saw themselves as people without money."

As part of a North–South exchange, Stan and Mari were invited to visit the deprived Easterhouse estate in Glasgow. Here, they were faced with a different kind of poverty. They noticed that in Glasgow everyone had a television, running water, heating and benefit payments. The adivasis would regard these things as inconceivable luxuries. "But most of the men in Easterhouse hadn't had a job in 20 years," Mari said. "They were dispirited, depressed, often alcoholic. Their self-esteem had gone. Emotionally and mentally they were far worse off than the poor at Gudalur, though the physical trappings of poverty were less stark."

On another occasion, Stan and Mari brought a group of adivasis to Germany. The gift the adivasis valued most from their hosts was being treated as equals – something they did not experience at home in India. But they were speechless when they saw an old people's home. "How can children send their old parents to live alone?" they asked. "We must ensure that such things never happen in our society."

Back in India, when a group was next threatened with eviction by an international tea trader, the adivasis' contact with friends in Germany persuaded the corporation to concede, realising that its image was at stake. The adivasis had found that an empowered community like theirs could extend across the world.

Kariyan, of the Kattunayakan adivasi tribe, made a clearing in the jungle one year and planted ginger. As luck would have it the price of ginger then shot up from Rs60 to Rs160 and he made a large profit. By the end of the year, however, he had none of it left; when people asked him for money he had given it to them without asking questions. Does he need lessons in money management?

Kariyan values the community. He shares what he has with others and vice versa. He did not calculate his gifts but acted instinctively as he and others had always acted. If he had taken off on his own, the money would have run out eventually, leaving him destitute. He has security as long as the tribe has security. Kattunayakanis do not need to store money for their old age, they do not consume more than they need, they move their houses every few years to preserve the soil, and they do not harm the forest or its animals. They depend on their surroundings.

The Kattunayakan tribe has facial features like those of Australian Aborigines, and anthropologists have confirmed the connection. This indicates an extraordinary continuity in the Kattunayakan gene pool since the time when humans migrated to Australia 50,000 years ago. It would seem that, deep in the forest, the Kattunayakans have maintained an isolated, sustainable way of living over millennia.

Is this just a story about a remote community, or does it touch on human values deeper and more lasting than those of modern western capitalism?

A tea field in Tamil Nadu, India

Just Change

beyond fair trade

Co-operative trade has evolved in many places and in many different ways.

When a group of adivasi indigenous people from India visited Germany, their hosts explained the 'fair trade' movement to them, expecting them to be pleased and impressed. Quite the reverse. Bomman, an elder of the adivasi Bettakurumba tribe, thought that inducing people to pay more for their product was a kind of exploitation. Was it not possible for both producer and consumer to benefit?

This question started them thinking. Then, the devastating impact of global free trade policies on their tea plantation focussed their minds even more. "One of the most unfortunate issues has been the drop in price of both tea and coffee," wrote Ramdas, who runs the adivasi school, in July 2000. "The government has opened up the Indian market and large imports are being allowed in. This has created a fall in the price for producers, while the price in shops remains the same." The wholesale price of tea continued to fall. When the business plan for their tea plantation was first prepared in the 1980s the price for leaf tea had never dropped below Rs12/kilo. But now it was down to Rs4/kilo. The adivasis faced bankruptcy.

They contacted other local communities that produced things essential to the adivasi way of life – lentils, rice, fish, textiles, umbrellas (needed in the monsoon) – and set up an exchange co-operative. All members can now buy essential products below market price and are paid a fair wage for their work.

Surplus income is not divided on a proportional basis in the adivasi co-operative: the group gets together and discusses how it should be used. As a result, they have established a school and a hospital. Two doctors, Nandakumar and Shyla, who used to work in the US, now work in the hospital. Their American colleagues regarded them as saints for moving to India and accepting such a drop in income, but after visiting them in Gudalur they saw the benefits. The doctors are treating real needs rather than, for example, the results of obesity. They have escaped the rat race, they are unlikely to be sued, and they have built themselves a beautiful house just ten minutes' walk from the hospital.

"The economy of the future is based on relationships rather than possessions."

John Perry Barlow, *The Economy of Ideas* (1993)

When the adivasis first owned their plantations they followed normal practice: picking leaf tea and selling it to the factory, thus losing control of their product. Later on, they persuaded the factory to become a member of the project so that the tea leaving the factory would still belong to them, and they could then trade it within and beyond the co-operative. The factory has now become an enthusiastic participant: with the market becoming more unreliable it has assured work through the co-operative. If the organic market in Europe can be tapped, the demand will rise further. Gradually, more and more of the chain have begun to join in – the financier, the pickers, the middlemen, the lorry drivers, the shopkeepers, even the consumers. Women's groups have joined up also and made an income by selling tea to their communities.

Adivasi tea pickers in Assam

The network of exchange now touches the lives of two million people. The group have created a new way of trading. They call it Just Change.

Just Change shipped tea to a co-operative of workers running a wholefood shop in Manchester. The tea-packaging was initially contracted out to specialist firms in England, but is now done within the project in India, adding value where people are most in need. Stan, Mari and some of the adivasis know their European contacts personally. This is not normal business practice – only one person would usually make deals – but Just Change regard trade as co-operation between friends, and this requires meeting each other as a group. Their produce is now spreading to community groups, schools and local authorities in Britain and Germany.

Just Change enables Europeans to buy commodities below market price – because there is no need for retailers' profits, advertising and expensive packaging – and to the direct advantage of the producers. However, its greatest benefit is in the distribution of essential commodities among poor communities in India. In due course, Just Change may even develop a currency of its own, which would allow it to avoid the instability and vicissitudes of the national currency.

Stan Thekaekara sums up their objectives: "The challenge for us today is to create a radically new structure, which will directly link consumer and producer communities, and measure the economy not just by the profits generated but by how equitably this profit has been distributed."

Mosques and churches
how to live

IMAGINE PASSING FROM a noisy, bustling suq in Damascus through a small door and into a large, calm, colonnaded courtyard. Groups of men and women sit on carpets in the shade and talk, read or sleep. Mosques are enclosures for the community and fill for prayers five times a day. Churches have different qualities. In Gothic cathedrals, holy rites are performed at the altar and the architecture soars towards heaven. Orthodox churches embody mysteries shrouded in incense. Protestant churches, chapels and assemblies encourage the congregation to focus on the preacher.

Muhammad was both prophet and head of his community, in which there was no separation between religion and state. The Qur'an, revealed to him over a period of 23 years, insists that a Muslim's first duty is to create a just, egalitarian society where poor and vulnerable people should be treated with respect.

Muslims are supposed to lead their lives according to the 'five pillars of Islam'. First, is the declaration of the unity of God, who is given no attributes, especially not human ones. The other four pillars – prayer, zakat, ramadan and al-hajj – emphasise social equity and community. Everyone should pray five times a day alongside others, not just think or say the prayers on their own. Zakat almsgiving, based on a proportion of one's income, encourages the fair distribution of wealth in the community.

The ramadan fast serves as a vivid reminder of the privations suffered by the poor. For the fifth pillar of Islam, al-hajj, pilgrims have to wear a standard white garment that allows no difference of rank or standing.

With its care for the community, Islam appeals to the poor and is embraced by a sixth of the world population. The Muslim is a social being in the body of Islam, the ummah, which transcends nationality. When a Muslim nation is ravaged, the hurt and shame is felt universally and by each Muslim individually.

Muhammad did not believe that he was creating a new religion but rather that he was bringing the primordial religion of humanity to his Arabian tribe. God had sent messengers to every people on earth to tell them how to live. When they disregarded these basic laws, creating tyrannical societies that oppressed the weak and refused to share their wealth fairly, their civilisations collapsed. This required jihad, struggle, for the right way of living.

Seventh-century Arabia was a land of warring clans, which may explain some harsh phrases in the Qur'an. But these are always followed by injunctions such as, "If they let you be, and do not make war on you, and offer you peace, God does not allow you to harm them." War is only permissible in self-defence and is always evil.

Southern Spain was, for hundreds of years, a Muslim country that embraced thriving Christian and Jewish communities. Córdoba was the centre of western civilisation and scholars from all over the west visited its libraries to consult ancient Greek manuscripts. Its intelligentsia was the forerunner of the Enlightenment in the rest of Europe. In the 11th and 12th centuries, the Moorish Córdoban philosophers Avicenna and Averroes argued against conflict between religion and reason, and were a fundamental influence on Christian thinkers such as St Thomas Aquinas. They held that it was only possible to talk about the indescribable God in terms of signs and symbols, so every story in the Qur'an is called an aya, a parable. This freedom from literal interpretation explains why Islam has had little trouble with the science of evolution.

In 1492, Ferdinand and Isabella, King of Aragon and Queen of Castile, made their first conquest in the name of a united Catholic Spain. Muslims and Jews were forcibly converted, massacred or expelled, and many Jews fled to the Ottoman Empire, where they were welcomed.

Just as the west's aggression and weapons of mass destruction are in total violation of the Bible's Sermon on the Mount, so al-Qaeda's terrorism is a gross perversion of the teachings of the Qur'an. But thinking more carefully about the social and egalitarian aspects of Islam's five pillars may help us to understand why it is the fastest growing religion in the world. With a rejection of the destructive forces of fundamentalist Islamism, a denial of fanatical imams of the Wahhabi sect from Saudi Arabia, and a return to the enlightened and inclusive culture that it once extolled, Islam could become the model for how all of us should live after the collapse of consumerism.

In Santarém, Portugal, the mosque is being restored after 700 years of disuse. The local synagogue and the monastery of São Francisco are also being repaired. Might this town soon experience the intellectual and cultural dynamism that it had once before?

Power
trade, war, corporate and empire

"**WHAT IS HATEFUL** to you, do not do to your fellow men. That is the entire law, all the rest is commentary." The Talmud.

"Do nothing to others which, if done to you, would cause you pain." The Mahabharata.

"What you do not want others to do to you, do not do to others." Confucius.

"Always treat others as you would like them to treat you." Jesus.

The Golden Rule spans all cultures. In the neoliberal world, however, it reads like this: "He who has the gold makes the rules."

This rule has consigned four fifths of humanity to poverty and debt. Tiny groups of the elite in several nations fight to protect their privilege and their access to the dwindling resources of the planet. The rule enables them to do so with weapons of ultra sophistication and mass destruction.

The concentration of power in the hands of the rich, and the impoverishment of millions of others, flow from rules that regulate money and trade. These rules can be changed.

The first rule
oil for dollars

"We trade little pieces of paper (our currency, in the form of a trade deficit) for Asia's amazing array of products and services. This is patently an unfair deal unless we also offer something of great value, such as a strong US Pacific fleet. This squares the transaction nicely."

Professor Thomas Barnett, US Naval War College, *Asia Energy: A Globalization Decalogue* (2002)

MONEY IS AMERICA'S single biggest export. It sends billions of dollars, which cost nothing to make, around the world every day. Poor countries need these dollars and get them by sending crops and minerals to the US. In return, many receive a US military presence. Big deal!

Sixty-three years ago, at the Bretton Woods Conference, John Maynard Keynes said there should be a currency for trade between nations that is independent of any national currency. He was overruled. The US insisted that national currencies could be used for trade but that oil should be sold only in dollars: petrodollars. Keynes objected. President de Gaulle called it "an exorbitant privilege". The value of this privilege was limited as long as the dollar was linked to gold, but in 1971 President Nixon broke this link and the supply of dollars multiplied. The petrodollar is still in place.

Money is not real wealth. People grow food and flowers, mine minerals and refine them, design and make things, create art and music, run businesses and do everything that satisfies people's needs and makes a country tick. These things flow in and out of countries and can be defined as real wealth. But the US imports many

more of these things than it exports. Instead, it exports vast amounts of dollars.

A sheikh in the Middle East sells oil to the US for dollars. He might buy a skyscraper in Sydney with the money as an investment. The Australian, in turn, may buy goods from Japan using the dollars. The Japanese may set up a factory in the US. And so the money circulates. The more trade there is, the better for the US because people will need more dollars. The more dollars it exports, the more goods it receives. Countries also need a cushion, so there are dollars held in central banks, in businesses and in private accounts all around the world.

The amount of dollars held by foreigners is huge: perhaps $11 trillion. This is, in effect, an interest-free loan from the poor to the most opulent country on earth. While the system continues it can be regarded as a gift. It is the basis of US wealth.

In order to support its standard of living the US must export two billion dollars every day. It therefore needs global trade to increase so that people will need more dollars. It is annoyed with Japan for failing to get its economy going. It is

How the dollar works:

"A German company, say BMW, gets dollars for its car sales in the US. It turns the dollars over to the European Central Bank in exchange for Euros it can use. The ECB buys US Treasury bonds. In effect, German workers build the cars and give the money away free."

William Engdhal, *Crisis of the US Dollar System* (2003)

annoyed with Europe for not growing fast enough. It wants poor nations to cultivate cash crops for export rather than for local consumption. And it insists that heavily indebted poor countries will only have their debts cancelled if they open their markets to global free trade.

How does the petrodollar affect developing countries?

• A poor country needs oil and has to pay for it using dollars. Most of its trade with other countries is in dollars because they also need to buy oil with dollars. And it has to keep a reserve in case of need. How does it get all these dollars? It sends the crops that it grows and minerals that it mines to the US. Poor

countries lose their produce this way because they need dollars so badly – they are, in effect, the dispossessed rather than the poor – while the US remains flush with everything it wants.

- An oil-producing country sells its oil to other countries, including the US, and accumulates a huge stack of dollars. It invests many of them in bonds, property and companies back in the US. The foreign-owned bonds enable the US to spend as much on armaments as the rest of the world put together. Wealthy Arab countries, among others, effectively fund the US war machine and receive protection regardless of their human rights record and lack of democracy. If an oil-rich country threatened to sell its oil for currencies other than the dollar, or withdraw its investments, the US would take every opportunity to demonise it, seize its assets, and bomb it into the Stone Age.

In September 2000, Iraq started selling its oil for euros. The US invaded – along with its non-euro accomplice, the UK – and after occupation changed the trade back to dollars. It nullified Iraq's contracts with France, Russia and China, and transferred Iraqi assets worth $1.7 billion that had been invested in the US to the Federal Reserve. Iraq's oil installations were the only assets that the aggressors took care to protect.

In 2005, Iran went one stage further and said it was planning to establish an oil bourse using euros and other currencies in competition with NYMEX (New York) and IPE (London), the only existing oil-trading markets, both of which require the use of dollars.

If people no longer need dollars to buy oil they will cease to be the main international currency.

Dollars will continue to flow into the US in exchange for goods and services. But with fewer dollars flowing back out, the Federal Reserve will have to destroy them in large numbers to prevent hyperinflation. The value of the dollar will, of course, continue to drop. This could benefit the US because its debt would lose value (a privilege denied poor countries that are not allowed to retain debt in their own currencies), its exports would become competitive and its internal economy would flourish as Americans had to start making the things they could no longer import. The US as a whole, like every other country, would have to work for its living instead of bleeding the poor.

Poverty, violent disaffection and seething anger around the world can be traced back to the dollar being privileged as an international currency. It is difficult to understand how such an iniquitous arrangement has been allowed to run on for so long.

The US dollar

- $33 trillion are created by internal debt (official, corporate and personal).
- $11 trillion are held by foreigners (China's central bank alone has $1.2 trillion reserves, enough to buy a controlling interest in all US Dow companies).
- $2.7 trillion (deficit) are in the net international investment position (NIIP) – the excess of US assets owned by foreigners above foreign assets owned by the US.
- $805 billion: 2005 record annual balance of payments deficit.

Source: Economic Policy Institute 06/06 and Loren Goldner, *The Dollar Crisis and Us* (2005).

The second rule
free trade ideology

"Free trade principles have become, verily, a religious question."

John Bright MP, 1846

A LAW THAT prevents free trade, said Richard Cobden in the House of Commons in 1843, is a "law that interferes with the wisdom of the Divine Providence. We have a principle established now which is eternal in its truth and universal in its application, and must be applied to all nations and throughout all times, and not applied simply to commerce, but to every item of the tariffs of the world."

Cobden and his colleagues of the Enlightenment wanted to bring an end to the ancien régime in Britain and break down the old alliance between monarch, church and state. They saw the role that commerce – as a mutual interest crossing borders – could play in undermining nationalist sentiments for war.

However, this first attempt to establish free trade principles at the end of the 19th century resulted in a famine across India in which ten million people starved to death. Foreign trade imperatives and market discipline were given precedence over the distribution of grain for poverty relief. This attempt at global free trade collapsed with the First World War.

After the Second World War there was a respite. The economies of poor countries gradually improved and Britain introduced the welfare state. But free trade principles were re-introduced by Margaret Thatcher in 1970 with the quasi-religious zeal of TINA, 'There Is No Alternative'. Politicians flocked to the World Economics Forum at Davos to hear words of wisdom from corporate leaders. But only true believers could be blind to the effects of the creed.

In Britain, with the imposition of competition as the only regulator, the welfare state was taken apart, the country's industrial base collapsed, fat-cats got fatter and poverty deepened. Long-term unemployment, crime, bankruptcies, family breakdown and infant mortality all rose. The income gap is now at its highest since the 1880s. Following TINA, Britain converted its arms production from national defence into a

In 2000, Thames Water was sold to the German RWE Group for £4.3 billion. The Germans raised £1.4 billion in loans against their assets and deposited the money in Germany; but that debt has to be repaid by Thames Water's customers in London.

In 2006, the managers paid themselves £10 million in bonuses, raised tariffs for consumers and sold the company to an Australian firm for £8 billion. China is now awarding huge contracts for water projects. These will be picked up by Australia, not Britain.

commercial enterprise, laying the groundwork for the violence and insecurity that has taken centre stage in world affairs.

With the imposition of free trade, poor countries have taken a nosedive. Their politicians no longer have the freedom or the means to carry out the policies for which some of them were elected. Half the world lives on or below the poverty line. Since 1980, Africa's GDP, which had previously been rising, has fallen 6.2%. The debt of these poor countries is out of hand. Many of their rural areas are experiencing suicide epidemics as the price of basic farm produce is cut drastically by competition between multinational corporations.

The high point of laissez-faire free trade was the creation of the World Trade Organization (WTO) in 1995. Regulation is usually necessary in order to prevent the strong from oppressing the weak, but the WTO – deliberately – ensures that the weak cannot protect themselves against the strong. Food is no longer something people eat to stay alive but the stuff of market competition. Poor countries might wish to promote their infant industries but the WTO calls this protectionist interference. Scientists say that society is causing catastrophic damage to the environment but, incredibly, the WTO sets maximum, not minimum, standards for environmental protection.

Compare these two comments made nearly 150 years apart. In 1864, Edwards Lester, an American living under colonial rule, wrote: "Yes, England preaches to us Free Trade, which means for us to buy everything from her and she takes nothing from us in return but breadstuffs, provisions and raw materials. She makes money by taking the raw material from other nations,

manufacturing it and selling it back. She has therefore always endeavoured to suppress the development of manufactures in other nations."

In 2006, the European trade commissioner, Peter Mandelson, made it "crystal clear" to Latin American delegates that this remained the policy of industrial nations: "We can make moves to offer greater prospects for agricultural trade for efficient Latin American producers only if you in turn open your markets in those areas where we seek new market access. If that does not happen in industrial goods and services, let me be crystal clear, there will be no deal on agriculture." Colonialism remains alive and well.

"I sympathise with those who would minimise entanglement between nations. Ideas, knowledge, art, hospitality, travel – these are the things that should by their nature be international. But let goods be homespun whenever reasonably possible and, above all, let finance be primarily national."

John Maynard Keynes, *National Self Sufficiency* (1933)

This second attempt at establishing global free trade started to collapse in 2000, having generated intense anger outside the luxury world of the elite.

The UK has demonstrated the crass stupidity of abandoning its strategic assets to the free market. We extracted North Sea oil and gas

at breakneck speed when prices were low, and now we are forced to import our energy, just as supplies become increasingly insecure and prices spiral out of control.

The biggest disaster of free trade ideology has been to treat money as a commodity and allow it to cross borders without restriction. Money traders who move huge sums from one country to another overnight have destroyed national economies – overnight. Foreign companies can buy up Britain's assets and pay tax abroad. Sixty per cent of trade takes place between different parts of the same corporation, allowing transfer pricing to avoid tax. Corporations now move their money to whichever country has the lowest tax. In one year, 20 major UK non-oil companies with a turnover of £100,000 million paid taxes of just £350 million – 0.35%. *The Economist* suggests that governments may have to abandon corporation tax altogether.

Without revenue from the wealthiest companies, the chancellor has to get his money from small- and medium-sized enterprises, and from individuals like you and me. As a result, our health, education and security services are constantly strapped for cash.

One way the UK government has extracted cash from the poor without raising taxes is through the National Lottery. But as this has proved inadequate the government is now promoting casinos in areas that need regeneration (thus, by definition, targeting lower income groups). The stake value of gambling under New Labour soared from £7 billion in 1997 to £48 billion in 2005. Between April 2005 and December 2006 the government approved 90 new casinos and said it wanted 40 supercasinos – though this was reduced to one, for the time being – as well as

Poppy cultivation in Afghanistan

online gambling. Its adviser, Peter Collins, runs a university department that receives £100,000 a year from casino corporations. Police say that this new gambling policy will increase addiction (excellent, as that will raise government revenue) and will increase crime (not so good, as our prisons are already full).

Compare this with the 19th century Opium Wars, one of the most disgraceful episodes in British colonial history. China was forced to open its ports to receive opium grown in British India in order to pay for Britain's luxury imports of porcelain, silk and tea. Yes, it did wonders for our economy, among other things giving us Hong Kong for 100 years. Our politicians were concerned only for these financial gains, even though they knew that their policy would turn millions of Chinese into opium addicts. New Labour will likewise be judged by history: it seems to care more about increased revenue

from these temples of 24-hour gambling, than about the damage it will do to thousands of families and their communities.

Britain has become the world's largest tax haven for the mega-rich due to chancellor Gordon Brown's non-domestic tax rules. The accountancy firm Grant Thornton worked out that in 2006, the UK's 54 billionaires paid income tax totalling just £14.7 million on their £126 billion combined fortunes – 0.01%. This explains why the most expensive properties in the world are in London. Margaret Thatcher's dictum, "a rising tide raises all boats," has worked in one respect: all property prices have risen and first-time buyers find it nearly impossible to get on the property ladder.

Globalised free trade, like the Soviet system, is not failing because of a rival ideology. It is failing because it doesn't work.

Free trade in practice
poverty and starvation

"To prohibit a great people from making all that they can of every part of their own produce, or from employing their stock and industry in the way that they judge most advantageous to themselves, is a manifest violation of the most sacred right of mankind."

Adam Smith, *Wealth of Nations* (1776)

THE COST OF the beans that make a £2 cup of coffee in the UK is hardly measurable. It is, perhaps, 0.01p.

Tatu Museyni cultivates coffee in Tanzania. The price she receives for her harvest has been driven down year after year by free trade regulations. Her annual income is now only $20. Her children can no longer go to school and the family face starvation. Worse is in store. Corporate researchers in Hawaii have recently developed genetically modified coffee plants whose beans all ripen at the same time. This makes it possible to pick them by machine. When machines replace pickers, Tatu and 25 million other small-scale coffee growers may have no income at all.

Nestlé, meanwhile, boasted in its annual report that, "thanks to favourable commodity prices profits have reached a record high." A coffee trader buys beans from wherever they are cheapest – if Brazil is cheap one year it will buy there; if Tanzania drops its price it will move here; if Indonesia is prepared to accept a lower price, it will go there. It is a race to the bottom in which the income of the poor continually drops and the wealth of the shareholders rises. That is free trade in action.

The corporation adds the monetary value to Tatu's cheap beans. Why doesn't she do this herself? She tried. She and her colleagues would like to process their coffee. They know how to do it, they negotiated micro bank loans to

invest in machinery and they understood the trade procedures. But their project never got off the ground. 'Tariff escalation' was imposed: the more value added to a basic commodity, the higher the import tariff charged by industrial countries. It is the means by which the rich protect their companies and ensure that the poor cannot add value within their own borders – "a manifest violation of the most sacred right of mankind." But even without tariffs, Tatu would never break the stranglehold that companies such as Nestlé have over marketing.

Free trade regulations, imposed by wealthy nations, prevent the poor "from making all that they can from every part of their own produce, or from employing their stock and industry in the way that they judge most advantageous to themselves." Free trade is contrary to the principles set out by Adam Smith, who is often misquoted as the founder of neoliberal economics. Free trade makes the poor poorer.

David Ricardo, the other founder of classical economics, established the theory of comparative advantage in 1817. One country is good at making hats, the theory goes; another grows oranges. Each country benefits from selling what it grows or makes better or cheaper than another country. This is no longer the case.

Now that capital and investment are mobile, a corporation can buy up any profitable land or business in a poor country and the country loses its only advantage. The law of comparative advantage now reads: "Multinational corporations benefit by taking over anything a country grows or makes better or more cheaply than other countries."

Consider a company that buys land in Kenya to grow flowers for sale in England. Self-respecting farmers become dependent labourers, and land that once fed the rural community now provides luxuries for the rich. But the company may suddenly transfer its operations to Uganda if labour there is cheaper. So, rich countries get cheap luxuries; the company makes a hefty profit, GDP in Africa rises and their business elites benefit. But in Africa, the poor become even poorer, and in England, flower-growers lose their business. Free trade harms people in rich countries as well as in poor ones.

"In the 1970s, Kenya was largely self-sufficient in food. Now we are a net food-importing country," says Oduor Ong'wen, a Kenyan analyst. "Most of the productive land where people were growing food for local consumption has been turned over to land growing food for export." In countries where the poor go hungry,

land is being monopolised to produce food for rich countries, where people eat too much and fertile land has been taken out of production.

Meanwhile, the prices received for these food exports have been plummeting. In the mid 1990s, a coffee farmer in Ethiopia was paid about £1.95 per kilo for her beans. At the turn of the millennium this was down to 12p. Other commodities are the same. Between 1980 and 2001 the price of sugar was down 75%, cocoa 66%, rice 65%, and cotton 58%.

Two more examples of free trade in action:

- 500 export factories in Mexico were closed in 2004, sacking 218,000 workers. Their $1.26 an hour wage was considered too high. Alcoa, one of these factories, now produces auto parts for the US in Nicaragua, where workers receive 40 cents an hour. These workers have been told to work for even less money or else their jobs will go to China where workers will get 16 cents an hour, work 16 hours a day, 7 days a week, with no health insurance and no pension.

 Hollow manufacturers are companies that design and market brands but use sweatshops to make their products.

- The US and Britain do not train enough health staff to meet their needs, so they use policies of selective immigration to poach those with training from poor countries. The poor countries train doctors and nurses and we offer them jobs. Over 60% of all doctors trained in Ghana have emigrated, and in one year alone it lost 3,000 nurses.

The transport of goods around the world will be curtailed when the availability of oil declines. It is short-sighted of the west to rely on basic necessities from distant countries, and for poor countries to base their survival on selling produce to rich countries at a distance.

Ships account for 4.5% of global carbon emissions and the shipping trade is growing at 15% a year. Aeroplanes, because of the height at which they fly, account for 6% of the damage caused by carbon emissions.

The west has used free trade theory to open markets in poor countries while subsidising and providing export incentives for its own producers. The US, for example, is the world's largest exporter of cotton because its cotton farmers receive $4 billion in subsidies for producing only $3 billion-worth of cotton. As a result the world price for cotton has been dropping, destroying the livelihoods of cotton farmers in poor countries.

In India, the government's guaranteed price for cotton dropped 13% due to the low international rate. In the north-eastern corner of Maharashtra, a cotton-growing area prone to drought, farmers gave in to pressure from multinational companies to buy genetically modified plants that require irrigation. However, the high cost of seed, fertiliser and fuel, combined with the lack of water and a drop in international cotton prices, spelled disaster for them. In the 18 months leading up to the end of 2006 more than 1,200 farmers in this area alone committed suicide.

Global free trade is forever associated with the laissez-faire policies of Thatcher and Reagan. It is now championed by New Labour too. Its 25 years have been a period of social disintegration, alienation, violent insurgency, breakdown of democracy, environmental degradation, new diseases and scene-setting for pandemics. A third of the world will soon be living in city slums and more people are hungry than ever before.

Ten thousand babies under a month old die every day: most could be saved with low-cost treatments that are not available due to rules that protect corporate patents. Life expectancy in many countries has plummeted.

The 2005 UN Human Development Report found that the world's poorest were worse off in many ways than they were when it first started the report 16 years ago. Throughout the world there is an epidemic of suicides among people who have had their livelihoods destroyed.

"Only one per cent of the price of a cotton shirt goes to the farmer."

Vijay Jawandhia, *New Internationalist*, April 2007

The neoliberal free trade agenda is akin to genocide. World leaders should open their eyes to the ghastly results of their ideological fanaticism, but all they can offer is, "hold tight, it will be alright in the end." This was Stalin's story about communism. In the end, the oppressive regimes collapse, leaving social and financial chaos behind them.

Oxymoron
sustainable development

"It is much too late for sustainable development; what is needed is a sustainable retreat." James Lovelock, *The Revenge of Gaia* (2006)

IN BALI, LIFE once revolved around music and festivals. In Ladakh, society flourished in an extreme climate. In Kenya, the Maasai lived in harmony with migrating herds. In China, most of the west's inventions were discovered, including gunpowder, but they weren't used. The word 'idiot' originated in Greece to describe anyone who did not spend much of his time in public debate. Islam showed how a classless society was possible; it developed philosophy and built beautiful buildings, like the Taj Mahal and the Alhambra. Cultures have grown in response to regional conditions, and excess time and wealth have been used for making buildings, art, jewellery and ceremonies.

During 4,000 years of civilisation human consumption hardly increased, but still we are left with evidence of wonderful cultural riches.

Then, on 20 January 1949, in his inauguration speech, US President Truman defined most of the world as "underdeveloped areas" where "greater production is the key to prosperity and peace." Set against this was Gandhi's previous warning in 1908 that "should India ever resolve to imitate England, it would be the ruin of the nation." Gandhi lost and Truman won.

Poor nations took up the idea of development with enthusiasm. Rich countries cut slices from their cake-of-wealth to feed to the poor,

believing that the magic cake would continue to grow forever and that they, the rich, would never need to reduce their own share. In the end, they thought, everyone would be satisfied.

Within a few years, however, it became apparent that economic development was not producing jobs. 'Manpower development' became the new theme. Then, ten years later, as hardship still persisted, 'social development' emerged as the key phrase at international conferences. This was followed by the 'basic needs approach', and then by 'equitable development'. Eventually, as the magic cake failed to grow, 'sustainable development' and the Millennium Development Goals were introduced as the solution. This moved the focus from global wealth to human well-being and poverty reduction. Eight goals were set out and 18 targets to be achieved at some point in the future. Throughout these numerous shifts in terminology the one thing that has never been questioned is the concept of development itself.

There is now an army of ecocrats drawing up papers – and emitting greenhouse gases as they fly from conference to conference – busily working out how to achieve more development with fewer resources. Light bulbs become more efficient, cars are shared, oil companies plant trees to absorb their fumes and cities find all sorts of ways to call themselves sustainable. The ecocrats strive

to bring appropriate technology and justice to the poor. Even nature itself has been renamed 'natural capital' so that it can be included in the sums. It is all very comforting.

The driving force behind sustainable development is the promise that we can achieve social justice while an ever-increasing proportion of global production flows to the rich elite. But after nearly 60 years of development, over half the world is still desperately poor and many cultures that used to sustain low levels of consumption have been destroyed.

There is a law of economics called 'the agricultural treadmill'. An Indian village manages with centuries-old technology that has been refined to its limit. A development agency then comes along and provides the villagers with new 'expert' advice. With a simple pump,

it says, a farmer can achieve a more constant supply of water and more income from his land. Jothi, one of the farmers, borrows money, buys a pump and bore-well, succeeds in growing a thirsty crop that commands a high price, and becomes sufficiently prosperous to pay off the loan. Success. The agency uses his achievement as a model for development and others follow suit. But two things happen.

First, as other farmers transfer to the new technology and produce the valuable crop as well as a greater quantity of ordinary crops, their prices drop. Jothi had his place in the sun for a short while, but the others had no such advantage. Instead, they had to adopt the same technology simply to keep up, or their output would have dropped in value; and unlike Jothi they would not be able to pay off their debt. The 'agricultural treadmill' has demonstrated its

meaning: as new technologies are found, a few people benefit for a short time while others go into debt or give up.

Second, the water table drops, hand-dug wells lose their water and those without pumps who depend on hand-dug wells either starve, commit suicide or have to migrate to the city, where they end up living penniless and unemployed in the slums. As more pumps are added the water table drops further, so more powerful pumps are necessary, and the water table drops further. The agricultural treadmill destroys lives and depletes natural resources.

Politicians love to solve problems with grand projects. China has built the Three Gorges Dam, the largest dam in the world, to be fully operational in 2009. It will divert water from the Yangtze River to the north of China. India has a grand project to link all its rivers. The scheme is so expensive that it can only be carried out with private capital, which means that India's water supply is handed over to the control of multinational corporations.

Development, with its requirement for ever-increasing exploitation of the planet's limited resources, is ruining the natural world on which we depend. A retreat from the belief in growth and consumption is desperately needed.

> Perhaps 4,000 years of culture were rather more nourishing than 50 years of development.

Odious debt
a humane US initiative

YOU ARE NOT liable for your parents' debts. This is a humane aspect of our legal system in Britain today. If it were not so, life would be slavery for many people. A similar concept exists in international law.

'Odious debt' is a legal concept established by the United States in 1898. The US had invaded Cuba only to find that its new colony had large

outstanding debts to Spanish banks. Washington refused to pay the debts, arguing that they had been "imposed upon the people of Cuba without their consent and by force of arms." Thus the doctrine was established that neither the people of a country nor its new government should be held responsible for the odious debts of a previous regime.

It is a humane and sensible doctrine. It means that the new regime, having thrown off the burden of its previous rulers, can use its resources to grow out of poverty. It also means that those who lend money are careful to check that they are not lending to a corrupt regime, just as a bank is careful not to lend to someone likely to become bankrupt.

But the policy of odious debt has fallen into disuse because it does not suit today's rich and powerful nations. Ironically, the US is now its fiercest opponent.

South African apartheid was defined by the United Nations as a crime against humanity. When Nelson Mandela became president in 1994, he and the people of South Africa inherited more than $18 billion in debts. Surely no debts could be described as more odious. But the International Monetary Fund warned that unless the debts were repaid, South Africa would be isolated by the international community. Money that should have been used locally to build schools and homes, to create jobs and to repair the environment, was sent to US, UK and Swiss banks that had financed apartheid.

In 1986, President Thomas Sankara of Burkino Faso urged the Organization of African Unity (OAU) to club together and repudiate their debt. "If we do not pay, the money-lenders certainly will not die of it; if, on the other hand, we do pay, we shall, with equal certainty, die," he said. "If Burkino Faso is alone in refusing to pay the debt, I will not be present at the next conference." The OAU did not act together. Later that year, Sankara was assassinated. Since then, not a single African head of state has dared to urge the repudiation of debt.

"One legacy of socialism is that most people continue to believe the state has a fundamental role in providing social services."

World Bank report, referring to Tanzania in 1999, indicating the bank's belief that neoliberalism should take precedence over democracy

Joseph Mobuto, dictator of Zaire from 1965 to 1997, had many friends in the west and received extensive loans from western banks and governments. He was known as the 'kleptocrat' because of his lavish palaces and his spending sprees in Europe. When he died in 1998 he left debts of $13 billion. Zaire became the Democratic Republic of Congo and the west called in its loans. The new government should have been spending every penny on rebuilding the shattered country. But instead it had to pay the equivalent of $260 for each man, woman and child in debt repayments.

A private company can buy a country's debt from its lenders. Zambia, for example, had a specific debt of $30 million, which the lender reduced to $4 million. Donegal International, a vulture trust, bought the debt for $4 million and then proceeded to sue Zambia for the original figure. In February 2007, Donegal was awarded $55 million – the original sum, plus costs, plus interest – by a British judge who ordered Zambia's assets in Britain to be frozen until it was paid. It must be difficult for Zambians and the people of other deeply indebted nations to understand western concepts of justice.

Poor countries are required to pay their debts, however odious they may be. But Long Term Capital Management, a US-based hedge fund, was treated with concerned sympathy when it mismanaged its investments and found itself with a $3.6 billion deficit. The Federal Reserve organised its bail out immediately.

The neoliberal requirement that capital must be free to cross borders has enabled speculators to gamble on currency values. Previously viable countries were plunged into debt as the value of their currency dropped; local companies were bankrupted and became rich pickings for multinational corporations. Dealing with the Asian crisis, the IMF declared, "Reducing expectation of bailouts must be the first step in restructuring Asia's financial markets." The IMF later changed its mind and agreed a $120 billion fund to pay off Asian debts, but who received these payments? The western investors, of course, who had benefited from the collapse. Banks were reimbursed for lending rashly and western companies acquired Asian businesses at knockdown prices.

The guiding principle for the IMF and the World Bank appears to be this: whatever happens, whoever is at fault, the wealth of western creditors must always be protected.

Third World debt
make poverty permanent

"The notion that for the Jubileum someone can come along and forgive that debt is whimsical. If you have a society based on debt forgiveness, who's going to invest in debt anymore? You really screw up the market." James Wolfensohn, President, World Bank, 2000

THIRD WORLD DEBT should be cancelled, totally, and poor countries should be compensated for the destruction of their economies. The stated intention of the World Bank, however, is to make debt permanent. Borrow – invest – export – repay. This is the policy for loans to developing countries. It has been a disaster from the start.

The first failure: the World Bank lent money for development projects in dollars, to be repaid in dollars. With the devaluation of local currencies, debts increased relative to a nation's economy. When a project's loan could not be repaid, it did not follow normal bankruptcy procedures: instead, the country had to pay by gearing its whole economy towards earning more dollars.

Over three million people faced starvation in Malawi when the country was forced to sell 28,000 tonnes of maize to repay debts.

The second failure: the International Monetary Fund (IMF) made further loans to countries so they could pay the interest, which pushed them further into debt. It made no suggestions for other income-generating projects.

The third failure: in the 1970s recession, the US could not find buyers for its produce so it convinced poor countries to accept tied loans, saying, in effect, "we will lend you $10 million provided you buy $10 million worth of goods from us."

The IMF was set up at the Bretton Woods Conference in 1944 to provide funds that poor nations could borrow in order to pay for imports. This was a gift for corrupt rulers who could then amass more wealth without having to attend to their debts.

The World Bank and IMF insist that failing company debts in developing countries should be converted into government debts, a procedure that has no basis in law. At the same time, they give every country the same advice on producing goods for export. The inevitable result is glut, falling prices, less income for poor countries and cheaper imports for rich countries.

These institutions have also insisted on financial deregulation, which allows money to slosh around the world in a gambling spree that outweighs real trade 20 to one, and causes the collapse of currencies that were once strong. Due to the debt produced by IMF policies,

Mexico has done everything the neoliberals asked for. Having a long border with the richest country in the world, its people find work across the border, while it receives massive inward investment. It signed up to NAFTA in 1992 and it is a member of the WTO.

Vietnam was subject to a US trade embargo until 1994. In return, it imposed tariffs and quotas on imports, it was not a member of the WTO and it carried out none of the policies that the IMF and World Bank dictated to other countries.

Which prospered? Since it signed up to free trade, Mexico's growth rate has been barely 1% and its wages have progressively fallen. Vietnam has grown at 5% a year and poverty has decreased dramatically.

the reformist leaders of the 1960s and 1970s – such as Lumumba in the Congo, Sukarno in Indonesia and Allende in Chile – were unable to implement their policies for wealth distribution (policies regarded as 'communist' by the US). Washington then supported military coups against these governments staged by corrupt but 'loyal' despots, including Mobutu, Suharto and Pinochet. This pernicious process continues to this day, with the US funding opposition against leaders who use their country's wealth for social reform (for example, Chávez, Morales and Correa in Latin America) and supporting instead countries that are prepared to hand their resources over to multinational corporations.

Since 1960, the total of Third World debt has at no point decreased. Between 1980 and 1996 the nations of sub-Saharan Africa paid twice the amount of their total debt in the form of compound interest, and ended the period owing three times more than at the beginning.

It is a cause of bitter mirth among poor countries that the IMF and the World Bank demand democracy and good governance while dictating policies to their governments. Their insistence that debts are repaid through structural adjustment programmes causes havoc to countries' health, education and other essential services. Typically, an African country spends only 7% of its budget on basic social services and 40% on servicing debt.

Multinational corporations working in Africa move 30% of sub-Saharan annual GDP – $145 billion a year – to tax havens, many under the jurisdiction of the British government. The soaring production and price of copper, gold, nickel and platinum has failed to benefit African governments. Tanzania's revenue from gold, for example, fell by a third in 2006 in spite of increased production. Meanwhile pressure from the IMF and World Bank to reduce corporate taxes has forced these governments to raise taxes on petrol instead, immediately raising the cost of living in every area of daily life.

Such comprehensive economic failure suggests that fault lies with those who gave financial advice more than with those who received it; yet only the recipients are blamed. This is an indulgent way of seeing the antics of these secretive, unaccountable institutions. The reality is more sinister and concerns the financial needs of the rich, not the poor.

All countries are in debt. Debt is how money is created. Poor countries have been forced to take loans of dollars in order to serve the liquidity of the international financial system, not the liquidity of their own country. Rich country debts are allowed to remain in their own currencies; if they were not, the IMF could treat the rich as it treats the poor and dictate fiscal measures to reduce US debt, which is the largest the world has ever seen. This is a system the rich have chosen to impose, deliberately, because it benefits them. It is not inevitable.

"IMF rescue packages are intended only to rescue western creditors."

Ellen Frank, Professor of Economics, Emmanuel College, Boston

Money is an abstract entity subject to arbitrary banking rules, and accountants are wonderfully creative when it comes to protecting the rich. The US Treasury, for example, holds records of 70-year-old British, French and Italian defaulted debts for accountancy purposes, without any expectation of them ever being paid. If these debts can be ignored ad infinitum then poor country debts could be similarly cancelled or ignored. Alternatively, the World Bank could simply create the money and pay off their debts, in the way that commercial banks create monetary wealth every day for rich customers.

The reason why such measures are not adopted has nothing to do with the stability of the global financial system – developing country debt is a mere 3% of global lending. Instead, it has everything to do with wealthy nations retaining power over poor countries that are rich in basic commodities and cheap labour.

This is made abundantly clear by the seven conditions attached to IMF and World Bank loans. At Gleneagles in 2005, following public demand for debt cancellation, the two institutions said they would help poor countries reduce their debts on condition that they:

- open their markets for trade and investment,
- phase out subsidies on domestic products,
- deregulate finance,
- allow free entry and exit of capital,
- float exchange rates,
- privatise to attract foreign investment,
- remove regulation of commerce.

Every single condition follows the agenda of western corporations who aim to extract resources from Asia, Africa and Latin America at rock bottom prices and sell them, having added value, to rich customers.

The World Bank has borrowed a word from the green movement, saying it will reduce debt to 'sustainable' levels. Sustainable debt, of course, means permanent debt. Dollar debt ensures that the poor country exports goods to earn dollars rather than to feed its people or trade with its neighbours. Significantly, roads funded by the Bank invariably lead from the interior of a country to the coast, not to neighbouring states.

Leaders in rich countries welcome Drop the Debt campaigns because they can make a show of 'forgiving' some debt and increasing aid. They spin public outrage into a public relations exercise saying, "Don't protest, celebrate!" But they refuse to acknowledge that Third World debt has no legitimacy, and they continue to promote a neoliberal agenda that requires the poor to be permanently indebted to enable western economies to grow.

Third World debt has been the greatest economic, cultural and humanitarian disaster of the 20th century, outstripping the two great wars for the sheer scale and depth of unrelenting tragedy. But it need not have been so. Back in 1960 Africa, Asia and Latin America, with their tremendous wealth of natural resources, were predicted to have prosperous futures. Yet they have lost these resources, foreign companies have appropriated their best assets, their essential services are crippled by debt, and poverty has destroyed millions – more accurately billions – of lives and livelihoods.

The effects of this diabolical system are so horrific that it is tempting for protestors just to focus on the symptoms – starvation, lack of education and health care – and fail to expose the root causes.

Between 1503 and 1660, 185,000 kilos of gold and 16 million kilograms of silver were transferred from Central America to Europe. One would hesitate to accuse Europe of looting or stealing; it was surely a loan.

Even if Central American nations only ask for modest interest, perhaps half of what we now charge poor countries, the amount we now owe them would run to an unpayable 300 digits.

Vibrant city regions
creators of prosperity

"Cities grow and become economically versatile by replacing goods that they once imported with goods that they make themselves. Blindness to this common, ordinary reality is the source of much confusion in how we think of economics." Jane Jacobs, *Cities and the Wealth of Nations* (1984)

BACK IN 1950 Taiwan had a rural economy with low wages, which attracted companies from North America looking for cheap labour. Their factories provided some employment locally but overall did little to stimulate the economy. Taiwan might have remained a supply region, like so many poor countries today, but instead it turned its economy round. What was the secret of its success?

The government distributed land to peasants and required landlords to invest part of their compensation in local light industry. The government also used training grants, tariffs, quotas and export subsidies to protect and stimulate the emerging local industries. People learnt skills from the foreign firms operating in Taiwan, and they worked for them as subcontractors. The Taiwanese slowly replaced imports with locally made goods, invented new products and financed their new businesses with the money that former landowners invested locally. The city of Taipei and its region became a hive of activity, operating first locally, then trading in the Pacific Rim, then globally. Having established a strong economy of its own it was able to relax tariffs and quotas. All these policies were the precise reverse of those forced on poor countries by the IMF and WTO.

A 'supply region', whether it produces minerals, food or oil, does well economically as long as its resources last, or as long as someone else wants them enough to pay good money for them. During this period the region may receive sufficient income to import all the goods it needs for a diverse and prosperous lifestyle. But when its goods run out, when other regions no longer want to buy them, or when their price has been driven down by corporations, it can no longer afford imports and has no money to invest in setting up factories to make these things itself. The region slips back into poverty. If, however, during the prosperous period, it replaces imports with locally made goods and focusses its economic activity in cities – where businesses and manufacturing support each other – it can build an economy that retains prosperity.

Jane Jacobs, in her book *Cities and the Wealth of Nations*, analysed this process in depth. She identified key conditions that have brought cities prosperity in the past. Ports, for example, had a natural advantage when ships were the main international transport. Cities near coal mines prospered until oil and electricity arrived.

Tariffs, import quotas and protection against takeover by foreign investment are essential tools for poor countries. And a network of city regions at a similar stage of development and with fluctuating currencies is their best environment. Above all, they must avoid selling only basic commodities for other countries to manufacture, or crops for others to process. They should manufacture their own frying pans, computers and pencils. These regions are referred to as 'import replacement economies' because their vitality comes from replacing imports with increasingly sophisticated local products. Rural areas need to be part of one of these vital city regions in order to receive good prices for their more basic produce.

This policy was used by the American Founders in their struggle against the tyranny of British companies, and it led to Alexander Hamilton's 'infant industry protection' policy that regulated US trade from 1789.

Received wisdom claims that a single currency increases prosperity by helping countries to trade with each other. The opposite may be true.

An analysis of history shows that regions prosper when cities with different, fluctuating currencies interact with each other. Wealthy European cities during the Holy Roman Empire each had their own currencies, which rose and fell to encourage exports or allow imports. Singapore, Taipei and Hong Kong likewise have separate currencies, which partly explains the spectacular success of the Pacific Rim.

Cities in the west no longer have their own currencies. Instead, the needs of one dominant city region determine the fluctuation of a national currency, and areas far from the dominant centre often suffer. London, for example, flourishes while most of the north of

Britain declines. The lira benefited Milan but not the south of Italy. Each Scandinavian country retains a prosperous city region, but only one. Following the same pattern, the single European currency may produce one dominant city region in Europe while outlying areas decline.

Indians have a genius for improvisation and import replacement, but the country's large size and single currency leaves most rural areas as supply regions. They have no possibility of being integrated into areas of prosperity, and no chance of competing with cheap imports from abroad. India has a sixth of the world's population – equal to the total world population of 1850 – with a market large enough for a full diversity of internal trading. Each of its great city regions could adopt a separate currency and, by trading with each other using fluctuating exchange rates, spread prosperity. The country's external tariffs and quotas should be set to encourage trade between the city regions within its borders.

Modern history, from the founding of the US onwards, has many examples to show how successful economies have developed. Among the most effective has been the encouragement of infant industries along with the use of fluctuating currencies for city regions that regulate trade.

Poor countries should be encouraged to help their infant industries.

The arms trade
disreputable and deluded

"Few of us can easily surrender our belief that society must somehow make sense. The thought that the State has lost its mind is intolerable, and so the evidence has to be denied."

Arthur Miller, *Why I Wrote The Crucible* (1996)

THE UN SECURITY Council was established in 1946 to preserve peace. Ninety per cent of arms bought by poor countries, however, come from four permanent members of this same Council – the US, Britain, Russia and France – along with Germany. Britain is the largest per capita exporter of military equipment. The US is the largest total exporter. A woman in Darfur pointedly reminded western aid donors of this situation: "It's very kind of you to offer to feed us," she told them, "but we've always known a degree of hunger. What would really help is if you'd take the guns away."

The Security Council should be re-constituted as the Peace Council and countries that export arms should be excluded from membership. To describe the arms industry as defence is an abuse of language.

The trade in death and destruction used to be easier to understand. Arms manufacturers were little more than workshops for national armed forces, providing each nation with the means of aggression or defence, and selling weapons to any country that lacked an industry of its own. Up to a point this is still the public perception. It is wrong. Following neoliberal free trade principles the west has converted arms production into commerce. Arms traders are now multinational corporations.

Take BAE-S. Is it a US or a British company? It started life as British Aerospace but dropped the British for just the B (like BT, BA and BP). It owns former US companies and claims to be "the only European arms company that is truly big in the US and the only US arms company that is truly big in Europe." At the same time BAE-S wants the UK government to believe it is British. This way it can continue to receive millions of pounds of taxpayers' money and UK prime ministers can promote it around the world. But the US accounts for over half of the world's arms expenditure, and so, in commercial logic, BAE-S will become a fully American company if the US continues its massive investment in death and destruction. The aim of the arms trade is not to serve any national interest but to maximise shareholder value.

Why should the government support an industry making products that, rather than being useful, wreak havoc? It would be more profitable and less damaging to support cocaine or cigarette companies.

Employment would not suffer if we stopped exporting arms: "The economic costs of reducing defence exports are relatively small and largely one-off," said the UK government's Defence Sales Committee in its 2002 report, adding that the loss would lead to an increase in civilian jobs over a five-year period if the factories were converted to manufacture civilian goods.

The G8 – the self-selected group of eight world leaders – exempts military production from free trade regulations, making it the only industry they can subsidise without offending the WTO. This leaves the leaders with a dilemma: should they promote peace? Or should they promote conflict and corruption? The UK government has 600 staff with a £16 million budget exclusively to market arms exports.

In February 2005, when there was friction between India and Pakistan, the US made a creative business plan. It sold Pakistan a fleet of F-16 aircraft and at the same time sold India an anti-missile system to shoot them down. Key members of the UK cabinet, meanwhile, visited both countries to promote

Annual military expenditure

US	$522.0 billion
UK	$79.3 billion
China	$70.5 billion
Germany	$57.5 billion
France	$45.0 billion
Japan	$44.3 billion
Russia	$32.4 billion
Italy	$28.2 billion
Saudi Arabia	$25.4 billion
South Korea	$21.0 billion
India	$19.0 billion
Australia	$12.2 billion

Source: CIA, *The World Factbook* (2005)

arms sales. In the past, the US has armed the Vietnamese (against Japan), Japan (against China), Iraq (against Iran), Iran (against Iraq) and Osama bin Laden (against Russia). Arms sales to poor countries are encouraged with export guarantees and loans: one fifth of Third World debt is due to past arms sales.

In 2002, the UK government approved the sale of a £28 million military air control system to Tanzania, which the World Bank said was out of date and unsuited to the country's needs. A civilian system could have been purchased at an eighth of the price, but a third of the contract value had already been secretly transferred to a Swiss bank account. "Number 10 insisted on letting this go ahead, when it stank," Clare Short, secretary of state for international development at the time, told *The Guardian* in 2007. "It was always obvious that this useless project was corrupt."

The UK's Serious Fraud Office (SFO) has been investigating BAE-S for bribery connected with deals in Saudi Arabia, South Africa, Chile, Czech Republic, Romania and Tanzania. Tony Blair personally ordered the SFO to drop its enquiry into a £40 billion Saudi contract, and the SFO may be disbanded.

A language of euphemism has replaced the horrors of war. Those who profit from selling weapons, along with leaders who encourage the trade, are detached from the results of their actions. They don't hear the screams of a child having her leg amputated without anaesthetic. How can 'decent' people and 'civilised' nations engage in such a disreputable activity with an end product of mutilation and destruction?

Among the officials that the UK Ministry of Defence invited to the September 2005 arms fair in London were delegates from seven countries listed by the Foreign Office for their record of human-rights abuses.

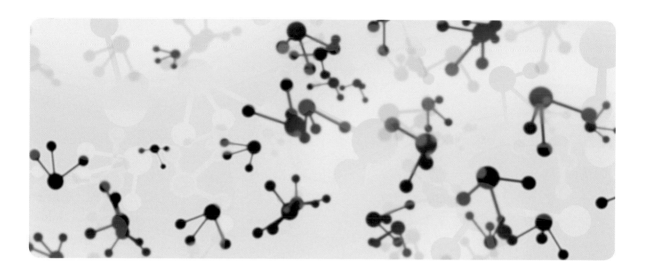

Weapons of war
unintended outcomes

"The American who first discovered Columbus made a bad discovery."

Georg Lichtenberg (1742–1799), scientist with a penchant for aphorisms

"NINE OUT OF ten Americans exterminated!" This would be a dramatic headline if any television or newspaper carried it today.

In 1527, there was death almost on this scale in Latin America. A troop of 170 Spaniards walked into an army of 100,000 Andean Indians. Pizarro captured the Inca leader, Atahuallpa, routed his army and proceeded to send galleys laden with gold back to Europe. The Spaniards' initial conquest was achieved using sharp steel weapons, horses, helmets, body armour and deception, but the destruction of the native population that followed was due to germs. Jared Diamond, in his book *Guns, Germs and Steel*, points out that smallpox was new to America and Americans had evolved no resistance to the virus.

In the mid 20th century, poor countries were young nations with a bright future. Now the west sees them as risk-prone zones suffering from epidemics, over-population, desertification, violence and corruption: breeding grounds for terrorism. But they hold coveted minerals, crops, genetic riches and large potential markets. This is a recipe for conflict. The rich now use trade regulations and legal frameworks instead of military hardware to extract this wealth.

However, the illogical belief in hardware persists. Vast sums are spent on nuclear weapons. 'Shock and awe' can destroy a city. A cluster bomb can spread 600 bomblets over two square kilometres. But Osama bin Laden, or an individual carrying a handbag with some polonium-210, remain elusive targets.

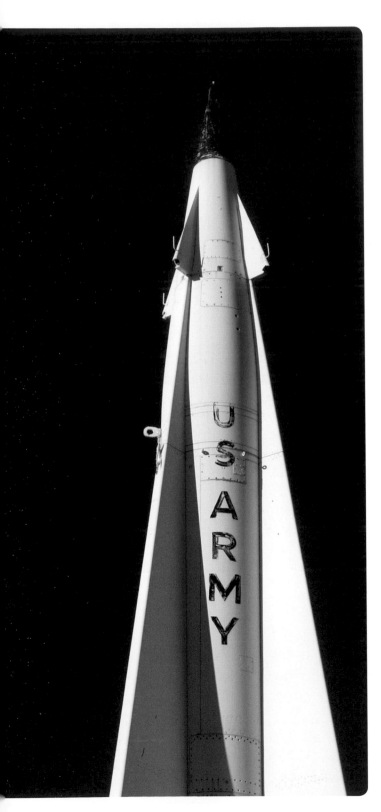

Commercial incentives make the development of further horrors inevitable; the frangible bullet, for example, explodes inside the body. The manufacturers of such weapons effectively say to a country, "Pay us to kill your enemies or we'll help your enemies kill you."

The obsession with hardware backfires. The way in which US star-war bases are edging ever closer to Russia could lead to a return to the Cold War. Poor countries, non-state groups and individuals can obtain plutonium and other lethal chemicals developed by the rich. The internet disseminates information that enables thousands of laboratories to create new viruses that could once again decimate a whole population. In a scientific conference a delegate held up a child-size talcum powder tin and explained that if this amount of TCCD, a product developed by Monsanto to defoliate parts of Vietnam, were dropped into the water supply of a city the size of New York, it could kill the entire population.

Scientific advance could also introduce biological weapons unintentionally. It has recently been established that the planet Mars has signs of water, which means that it may also have viruses. If a soil sample is brought back from Mars, as has been suggested, it might contain a virus that has not been part of the earth's evolutionary history; no one knows whether this could have a similar effect to the germs we took to America in the 16th century.

War in an electronic, nuclear, chemical and biological age does not bear thinking about. For if war is to remain part of our consciousness, we face catastrophe. Nothing less than a new way of thinking is required.

Tools of peace
alternatives to violence

"War appears to be as old as mankind, but peace is a modern invention."

Henry Maine, lecture series on international law, Cambridge University, 1888

WOMEN FROM WAJIR, a town in northeastern Kenya, have succeeded in ending clan warfare among their people. They formed an association, which new members could only join after answering this question: "If my clan were to kill your relatives, would you still work with me for peace? If you cannot say yes, then don't join the group." One of the women's innovations was the Rapid Response Team, consisting of elders, young people and women who intervened wherever there was a violent incident. After many stormy meetings, peaceful life has been restored in their region. An elder commented, "Most of what was accomplished was done by people with a heart for peace."

The Oxford Research Group has collected stories of numerous individuals, groups and organisations that have found techniques to avoid violence. Political leaders the world over have much to learn from them.

In 1992, when militant Hindus destroyed the Babri mosque and violence spread throughout India, Lucknow avoided bloodshed because school pupils, following the teachings of Gandhi, encouraged religious leaders to work together. The students took to the streets in their thousands using loudspeakers to appeal to the people, asking them to refrain from violence. They carried posters with slogans such as, "The name of God is both Hindu and Muslim."

In El Salvador, a group of businessmen started a 'guns-for-goods' scheme, offering $100 vouchers for goods in local shops in return for each weapon turned in. By the end of the second week, hundreds of weapons had been collected. They then called on the president to support their scheme and soon 10,000 weapons had been handed over.

In Belgrade, in 1998, a few hundred students were trained in techniques of non-violent action. They in turn trained 20,000 election monitors, two for every polling station. When the elections eventually took place it proved impossible for President Milosevic to rig the results. Some cases of conflict resolution may seem insignificant in relation to global wars, but one never knows when breaking the cycle of violence on a small scale might stop more major incidents.

Apartheid was not ended by invasion, and chaos was prevented in the post-apartheid era by the Truth and Reconciliation process.

There is a tendency to wait too long before intervening in conflict, so the use of military hardware often becomes inevitable. But there are usually reliable signs of impending violence: the denial of the right to vote, to speak a language or to practise a religion; theft or

diversion of resources; occupation of territory; arms build-up; warlords making threats. If recognised early enough, conflict can often be resolved through dialogue, mediation, bridge-building, promotion of democracy, protection of human rights, dispute resolution, election monitoring, confidence building and restorative justice. These are tools that can be studied and applied systematically. And, as with the women of Wajir, they can be rushed to a site at the first signs of confrontation.

The aim should not be to avoid conflict; conflict is inevitable and is often a stimulus to creativity. The aim must be to prevent it slipping into a cycle of violence.

"Religious differences do not cause conflict. Religion comes in only once the lines of conflict have been drawn."

Zaki Badawi, BBC Interfaith Dialogue, 2003

An atrocity inevitably induces horror, then grief and then anger. Left to itself, the anger often leads to hatred and revenge. Further atrocities will set the cycle of violence rolling faster. But the cycle can be broken. Intervention can channel anger into seeking justice through law rather than through retaliation. This is better, but it still cannot ensure that the original atrocity will go unrepeated.

Intervention can be taken a step further by analysing the causes of a conflict with a view to removing them and bringing about long-term reconciliation. This requires a combination of determined, powerful leadership, imaginative action and resolute adherence to key principles. It is a systematic and economical process. NATO countries spend 200,000 times more on defence than on the main regional body devoted to conflict resolution, the Organization for Security and Co-operation in Europe (OSCE).

Tony Blair gave a lecture about 'defence' on board HMS Albion in January 2007. In response, the Clun Valley Quaker Meeting commented, "Let us wage peace with the same professionalism as we wage war. Let us train mediators and peacemakers and study alternatives to violence seriously. No worthwhile resources have ever been devoted to this. It is a difficult option which would demand real courage and vision."

The UN Security Council should be replaced by a Peace Council, with members like Nelson Mandela, Jimmy Carter, the Dalai Lama and others who have proven experience of bringing about reconciliation. Each national government should have a Peace Department as well as a Defence Department. 'Security' and 'defence' are euphemisms for war. Each country should have peace academies and university departments devoted to disseminating techniques for resolving conflict. The first duty of all these bodies should be to look critically at their own governments before intervening elsewhere.

There are some signs of hope. The British government recently allocated £110 million for conflict resolution, and there are currently 50 institutes in Britain studying small-scale, non-violent intervention, such as at the military college of Sandhurst and Bradford University's Department of Peace Studies. Given the example of Costa Rica (opposite) it is not so fanciful to imagine more countries following suit.

Costa Rica

In 1948, José Figueres, president of Costa Rica, disbanded the national army. The military budget was given to the education and health sectors. The banks, insurance, railways and all utilities were nationalised. A wealth tax and a social security system were introduced, and women and Caribbean immigrants were given the right to vote.

Making these wide-ranging reforms was not an easy ride, however. Costa Rica was in the middle of a murderous region wracked by war and outside meddling. The US tried to overthrow Figueres in 1950 and twice attempted to assassinate him. It is the only country in the region that has not been invaded or used as a military base by the US.

Costa Rica is now democratic, relatively rich, and regularly makes the top 50 in the UN Human Development Index. The educated populace makes it an attractive country for investment. But 'economic violence' may yet destroy the dream. Privatisations, following pressure from the IMF, recently caused widespread rioting.

"Costa Ricans have cultivated a civilised spirit," a former president said, "a spirit antithetical to militarisation and violence, capable of finding peaceful solutions to conflicts and respectful of the rights of others. In the absence of weapons with which to impose an idea, the only weapon left is reason. Today, people such as myself have become fully convinced that a country that organises an army becomes its own jailer."

The terrorist
more of the same

"Nothing creates a sense of national identity so quickly as having foreign soldiers quartered in your village."

Michael Howard, *The Invention of Peace and the Reinvention of War* (2001)

SHINTOISM DID NOT motivate the Japanese Kamikaze pilots of the Second World War. Catholicism did not inspire IRA terrorist acts. Tamil Tigers are not defending Hinduism. Judaism should not be blamed for Zionist atrocities. Orthodox Christianity was not the reason for suicide bombers in Lebanon. But xenophobes on all sides make these connections.

In al-Qaeda's 1996 'Declaration of War Against the Americans,' Osama bin Laden announced that its grievances were not cultural or religious, but very specifically political – it was fighting to oppose US support for the House of Saud and Israel. In 2003, after 9/11, he said: "America and its allies are massacring us in Palestine, Chechnya and Iraq. The Muslims have a right to attack America in reprisal ... The targets [the Pentagon and the World Trade Centre] were icons of US military and economic power."

Al-Qaeda trains and coordinates fighters who are personally motivated to the extent that they will give their lives for a cause. This makes them an invincible underground force to match the west's invincible hi-tech force. Fundamentalist and selective interpretation of their religious texts can shift the war into jihad.

Ariel Merari, a psychologist, has traced the background of every suicide bomber in the Middle East since 1983. Not all have been Muslims, very few have shown symptoms of mental illness or drug abuse, and none have been pathologically suicidal. Most bombers were relatively wealthy, well educated young men. Virtually every suicide attack has been conceived and managed by militants who find people sympathetic to their cause. These recruits are formed into a group in which they can share their anger and develop a sense of mission and the nobility of self-sacrifice. The members then make a pact, declaring their commitment to what they are about to do. Beyond this point it becomes psychologically very difficult for them to back out. According to Merari, the sense of duty to a small group of peers can turn just about anyone into a suicide bomber.

It is not difficult to imagine how hatred builds up. People in the Middle East are angered by 50 years of humiliation, by the death of half a million children as a result of the sanctions against Iraq, and by the airborne 'shock and awe' inflicted on Baghdad. They are angered by US and UK support for Israel's occupation of Palestine and destruction of Lebanon; by the murder of thousands of civilians through indiscriminate use of cluster bombs, depleted uranium and phosphorus; by the horrific destruction of the city of Falluja; by Guantánamo, Abu Ghraib, and 'rendition'

to torture camps; by 'Christian' military occupation of Muslim lands, and by decades of looting the region's resources.

Reports from captured terrorists confirm this analysis. One group bonded while whitewater rafting in north Wales. "Rather than praying we had discussions about work, politics and the war in Iraq ... We always had new films of the war ... more than anything else those in which you could see Iraqi women and children who had been killed by US and UK soldiers, mothers and daughters crying ... There was a feeling of hatred and a conviction that it was necessary to give a signal – to do something."

"The war on Iraq," admitted the UK Ministry of Defence, "has acted as a recruiting sergeant for extremists across the Muslim world. Iraq has served to radicalise an already disillusioned youth and al-Qaeda has given them the will, intent, purpose and ideology to act." Scotland Yard came to a similar conclusion: "Iraq has had a huge impact ... what western foreign policy does provide is justification for violence."

Whatever we think of terrorists, we must accept that their actions are based on ideas. Critical to their self-identity is the conviction that they are engaged in a just war. Only by engaging with these ideas, exposing false premises, conceding truths and disentangling conclusions, can we hope to reduce this violence in the short term. In the longer term, the stark and extreme global inequalities must also be addressed.

The UK government has proclaimed that we are waging a war on terrorism. However, Sir Ken Macdonald QC, director of public prosecutions, has questioned whether this is in fact a war, and has called for a "culture of legislative restraint" in passing laws to deal with terrorism. He warned of the pernicious risk that a "fear-driven and inappropriate" response to the terrorist threat could lead Britain to abandon respect for fair trials and the due process of law.

"London is not a battlefield," Sir Ken said in January 2007. "Those innocents who were murdered on 7 July 2005 were not victims of war. And the men who killed them were not ... 'soldiers'. They were deluded, narcissistic inadequates. They were criminals." The fight against terrorism on the streets of Britain is not a war, he insisted, but the prevention of crime. Whether an imam preaches the mutilation of offenders and infidels, a Christian evangelist calls for political assassination, or a historian denies the holocaust, all should be judged by the laws of the land, not by political rhetoric.

Nuclear war
join the club

"US forces are determined to employ nuclear weapons if necessary to prevent or retaliate against WMD use."

The Pentagon, Doctrine of Joint Nuclear Operations, 2005

THE SECOND WORLD War degenerated largely into killing civilians. The British firebombed most of Germany's cities and the US did the same in Japan. The uranium bomb dropped on Hiroshima, followed by the plutonium bomb on Nagasaki, were intended to bring the war to an end – some say. Others say these were dropped to test two types of nuclear weapon on human populations before the opportunity was lost – and to frighten Russia.

The Soviet Union, duly frightened, developed its own bomb and a balance of terror ensued.

The Non-Proliferation Treaty (NPT) in 1968 committed nuclear states to "general and complete disarmament under strict and effective international control." Other states undertook not to acquire nuclear weapons themselves in return for being helped with nuclear reactors for peaceful purposes. Disarmament and non-proliferation were complementary, not separate, goals.

Proliferation began when the west assisted the development of nuclear weapons in the most politically volatile region on earth. France

provided the reactors, Britain the heavy water, the US turned a blind eye, and thus Israel was able to produce plutonium in an underground building below a power plant in the Negev Desert, keeping it hidden – even to this day – from the International Atomic Energy Agency (IAEA) inspectors. By 1973, Israel had 13 bombs: now it has between 100 and 200.

Nuclear states have betrayed the NPT treaty in relation to their own facilities. The US, Russia and France are all developing new nuclear weapons and Britain is part of a US programme for six new types of bomb. India developed and tested the bomb on its own. China provided Pakistan with knowledge and materials. Pakistan sold this information to others.

At an NPT conference in 2000, the US promised to take 13 specific steps towards disarmament, but it has failed to implement a single one. Instead, the Los Alamos and Livermore weapons laboratories are now receiving more funding than during the Cold War. The US is developing a new generation of warheads, such as mini-nukes and bunker-busters, supposedly for tactical use – which means that, in due course, they are likely to become part of the military's normal armoury.

Washington's 2002 Nuclear Posture Review named no fewer than seven countries as primary targets for pre-emptive nuclear strikes. Its 2005 guidelines envisioned using nuclear weapons against those the US thought might have, or might be developing, similar weapons, and required US troops to be prepared to fight in heavily radioactive conditions. The guidelines also recommended that the US use tactical nuclear weapons to win a conventional conflict it is losing.

Like Russia after Hiroshima, other countries feel threatened and want to develop their own bombs. We cannot blame them.

And Britain? Every minute of every day a British submarine armed with 48 nuclear warheads – each eight times more powerful than the Hiroshima bomb – is on patrol somewhere in the world. The UK defence secretary said that we are prepared to use small nukes in pre-emptive strikes against non-nuclear states. The government is investing £6 billion in the atomic weapons establishment at Aldermaston; the purpose is secret, though it is known to include test facilities for highly enriched uranium. When he was foreign secretary, Jack Straw's justification for the UK decision to renege on the NPT was that "we might have a nuclear enemy in 15 years' time." So might every other country. Join the club.

However, our government regards nuclear weapons primarily as political chess pieces. "A decision to leave the club of nuclear powers," it says, "would diminish Britain's international standing and influence." Is this a lesson we want others to learn?

The Trident system

- Four nuclear-powered submarines.
- Each submarine has up to 16 US Trident missiles.
- Each missile carries up to 48 nuclear warheads.
- Each warhead is equivalent to eight Hiroshima bombs.

Renewing of Trident would be illegal under the Non-Proliferation Treaty.

Britain's Trident submarine missiles are bought from the US, loaded from US bases, guided by US GPS satellites and can be disabled by the US at any time. Trident links Britain inextricably to US foreign policy and makes us an obvious target for terrorism. However, the Scottish Parliament could ban nuclear weapons, which would leave nowhere on the British Isles for Trident to be based. It could also ask the International Court to prosecute those responsible for breaking the NPT.

The US has 480 'tactical' nuclear weapons in Europe, including 110 at Lakenheath in East Anglia.

India was shunned for a short while after testing its bomb, but now it is welcomed by the other nuclear powers. It has been offered nuclear co-operation and is likely to gain a place on the UN Security Council, demonstrating the benefits of having nuclear status.

Iran is surrounded by nukes in Pakistan, Israel and Russia as well as on US warships; it is not surprising that the west thinks it wants to develop a bomb. The NPT allows countries "the inalienable right to develop nuclear energy for peaceful purposes." This is what Iran claims to be doing. Should it be the only country in the world not allowed to develop nuclear power?

Meanwhile, six Arab states – Algeria, Egypt, Morocco, Saudi Arabia, Tunisia and the United Arab Emirates – have expressed an interest in developing nuclear power, primarily for desalination purposes. But this has fuelled fears that the Middle East could be on the brink of a nuclear arms race.

There are now 30,000 nuclear weapons in the world, deployed and ready for use by intention, miscalculation or accident. However, an even more frightening scenario than further proliferation is the opposite: for one nation to feel invulnerable. This was the case with the US in 1945 – the only time nuclear weapons have been used for mass extermination. The willingness by the US and Britain to use tactical nuclear weapons pre-emptively has introduced an era in which nuclear proliferation is assured and nuclear exchange, somewhere, sometime, is almost inevitable.

The confrontation with Iran is based on the belief that civil nuclear research can lead to the procurement of nuclear weapons. If this is the case, the only logical conclusion is for nuclear technology, even for peaceful purposes, to be banned, totally, from the earth.

"How do I go to country X and say, 'you should keep your obligation not to develop nuclear weapons,' when the big powers are making no progress towards their obligations for disarmament? Britain cannot modernise its Trident submarines and then tell everyone else that nuclear weapons are not needed in the future."

Mohamed ElBaradei, Director General of the International Atomic Energy Agency, 2007

Depleted uranium

Depleted uranium (DU) is considerably harder than most metals. This means it can be used for armour-penetrating ammunition, cluster-bombs and bunker-busters. It burns on impact, releasing radioactive dust particles. US army manuals warn that contamination from DU "will make food and water unsafe for consumption." Children in Iraq play on destroyed tanks that UK survey teams will only touch in full-body protective suits.

Half the US veterans of the 1991 Gulf War are either dead or sick, and some of their children have been born without arms, with swollen torsos and shrivelled legs, just like many children in Iraq, the Balkans and Afghanistan where DU has been used. Lebanon and Gaza await its effects. These countries are contaminated forever. The UN describes DU as a weapon of indiscriminate use that continues to kill long after hostilities are over and therefore infringes the Geneva Conventions.

Iraq has become a toxic wasteland where 7,500 Iraqis develop cancer every year and horrific birth defects are common. An Iraqi mother's first agonising question about her newborn child is most likely to be: "Is it all right?"

War
no longer an option

"War is the continuation of politics by other means."

Carl von Clausewitz (1780–1831), Prussian soldier and military theorist

ROBERT McNAMARA was US secretary of defence during the Vietnam War. Responding to questions put to him 20 years later, in 1995, he provided revealing insights into how decisions at the time were made. The same questions could just as well be asked of politicians in the US and UK today about their current strategies in Iraq and Iran.

How good was your background knowledge? MacNamara: "We found ourselves setting policy for a region that was terra incognita."

Did the US understand countries with which it had no diplomatic ties? "We – certainly I – badly misread China's objectives and mistook its bellicose rhetoric to imply a drive for regional hegemony."

What about insurgency in surrounding countries? "We viewed these conflicts not as nationalistic movements – as they largely appear in hindsight – but as signs of a unified Communist drive for hegemony in Asia."

Was a military solution appropriate? "US commanders indulged, to some extent, in wishful thinking. Moreover, they – as I did – misunderstood the nature of the conflict. They viewed it primarily as a military operation when in fact it was a highly complex nationalistic and internecine struggle."

Who advocated military intervention? "The secretary of state was looking to a solution through military means and I, secretary of defence, was looking to negotiations."

Was the outcome assessed? "We never carefully debated what US forces would ultimately be required to do, what our chances of success would be, or what the political, military, financial and human costs would be. Indeed these basic questions were unexamined."

And strategy? "Data and analysis showed that air attacks would not work, but there was such determination to do something, anything, to stop the Communists that discouraging reports were often ignored."

Were the dangers of escalation considered? "The president and I were shocked by the almost cavalier way the chiefs and their associates accepted risk, possibly use, of nuclear weapons."

Could the conflict have been successful? "It became clear then, and I believe it is clear today, that military force – especially when wielded by an outside power – just cannot bring order to a country that cannot govern itself."

(From *In Retrospect: The Tragedy and Lessons of Vietnam* by Robert McNamara and Brian Van de Mark, 1995.)

Hmong women and children, Vietnam

IN MEMORY OF
ALL WHO HAVE GIVEN
THEIR LIVES IN THE
SERVICE OF THEIR
COUNTRY

Quakers have always been conscientiously opposed to the use of violence as a means to settle disputes – never more so than now. Westmorland General Quaker Meeting felt that the technology of war had become so horrific that it would be interesting to hear the views of acknowledged experts. Between 2000 and 2004, the Meeting invited 25 eminent judges, generals, historians, diplomats and scientists to give public lectures on the subject, 'Preparing for Peace'. The central conclusion that emerged can be simply stated: war cannot be used as a continuation of politics in the 21st century.

The institutions of slavery, segregation, apartheid and child labour – once thought of as inevitable – have been outlawed. War must also be outlawed. This is not to say that acts of violence will be extinguished, but that the solution to conflict must be found within social, economic and political frameworks.

Once violence has started it can escalate until there is a danger that weapons of mass destruction – nuclear, chemical or biological – will be used. There are several flashpoints at present: India and Pakistan with nuclear capability and a dispute over Kashmir; North Korea's provocative development of a nuclear bomb; Israel's friction with its neighbours; Iran's development of fissile material; and the nuclear powers' willingness to use tactical nuclear weapons. War in one area spreads; this is demonstrated by the Iraq war spawning global terrorism in many western countries. One of the contributors to the Quaker lecture series accepted the need for war as a last resort, but pointed out that the 'War on Terror' is using violence as the first option.

Some positive developments emerged in the later 20th century. Reconciliation and institution-building have now made war inconceivable in Europe in spite of its war-drenched history. The barbaric apartheid regime in South Africa was eventually overcome without military intervention from outside. New communication technologies have changed public involvement

in wars fought abroad and made leaders more accountable for its impact. In the 19th century, conflicts were over before information about them leaked out to the public: if soldiers in the First World War trenches had had mobile phones, could the slaughter have continued?

War crimes tribunals are making western leaders and their military think twice about their role in initiating war. Actions taken today might be re-classified as war crimes tomorrow. As the Pinochet case showed, leaders cannot assume that there is a time limit to the threat of prosecution under domestic or international law.

In 2004, Margaret Jones and Paul Milling, two peace protestors, were tried for causing damage to a B52 bomber at the US Fairford base in Gloucestershire. The bomber was headed for Iraq carrying cluster-bombs and uranium-tipped munitions. At the end of a long trial the judge advised the jurors that using weapons "with an adverse effect on civilian populations which is disproportionate to the need to achieve the military objective," is a war crime.

A German army major, meanwhile, refused to obey an order that, he believed, would implicate him in the invasion of Iraq. The judges acquitted him and re-stated that the UN charter permits a state to go to war in only two circumstances: in self-defence, and when it has been authorised to do so by the UN Security Council. The states attacking Iraq, they ruled, had no such licence. Resolution 1441, which was used by the British and US governments to justify the invasion, contained no authorisation. It is unlikely that members of the UK cabinet will be put on trial for war crimes in Britain, but they might have to be careful when going abroad. These and future rulings could deter further acts of aggression.

Who is the lawbreaker?

Is it the eight Quakers who locked themselves to the gate of the ammunitions area of the US Air Force base at Lakenheath and were charged under the new Serious Organised Crime & Police Act? Or is it the British government, for allowing a foreign country to locate 110 weapons of mass destruction on this base?

"I am here," explained one of the protesters, Lesley Grahame, "to enforce the law, not to break it. Weapons that cannot discriminate to protect civilians are illegal."

One hundred and sixty million people were slaughtered in the wars of the 20th century. Eighty-five per cent of those killed were civilians. Apart from the death and mutilation, there is a legacy of civilian populations suffering displacement, break-up of families, sexual violence, torture, disease, hunger, unemployment, and disruption of education and health care. There is also the loss of personal belongings, relationships and occupations – those parts of life that signify stability and identity. Environmental degradation, landmines, cluster-bombs and nuclear contamination accompany these human tragedies and last much longer than do the wars.

Recently, wars have not ended in victory or surrender. Instead, phrases like 'cessation of hostilities' have been used, leaving resentment to feed future conflict.

Water distribution
everyone must drink

PORTO ALEGRE IN Brazil has introduced a smart meter for water.

The first draw of water costs almost nothing. The rate goes up as you use more, so there is an incentive to conserve. For those who fill swimming pools the cost becomes astronomical. Retail stores, industry and other big users also pay the high rate. This little piece of technology gives the poor enough water for basic needs and avoids the need to subsidise water distribution. On the contrary, the utility has a surplus of 15% to 25% annually for new projects.

The water utility is municipally owned but independent of government. It has offices

throughout the city where local committees make the decisions. Residents report on faults and present their demands. These are discussed and voted on by the committee and, after technical evaluation, the cost is included in the following year's budget. During installation a group of local citizens supervises the contractors. The utility provides training, education and scholarships for its employees. It is a complete exercise in control by society. During a recent cholera outbreak in Brazil not one case was reported in Porto Alegre and infant mortality in the city is five times lower than the country average.

Porto Alegre is providing the model for the social control of water utilities, both public and private, throughout Brazil. Loan offers to other cities and districts are now conditional on adopting this approach.

But this is not the only model for an efficient and affordable water supply. An organisation called Corporate Europe Observatory (CEO) has collected many examples from around the world. It has found that the common theme of successful schemes is participation by the societies served.

In one part of Kerala, south India, for instance, the government tried installing house connections to public taps. Two out of three, however, never worked. Local politicians made promises to fix them but then forgot once they were elected. One hamlet, in frustration, galvanised its panchayat (village government)

Coke and Pepsi have cornered 80% of the soft drink and bottled water market in India. When a Coca Cola plant in south India dug bore-wells, the local farmers claimed that their wells dried up and they had to walk eight kilometres to collect clean water.

Poisonous metals like cadmium, present in the plant's waste – which the company had distributed as fertiliser – caused birth defects and kidney failure. The plant was closed and farmers trashed Coke's offices. Coca-Cola is now banned in the state and the national government has removed it from its canteens.

and marched on the district collector, brandishing empty pots and water vessels. Eventually, the village was allotted funds. It formed a committee and one person donated land for a well, and another for a tank. They pooled their expertise and labour and soon all the taps were working.

The left-leaning Keralan government, realising the benefits of local control, then empowered other districts to do the same by devolving 40% of the state budget for this and other services. The planning, estimates and implementation of the water projects are now done by locals who employ technical experts only when essential – so far, this has not been necessary. This social involvement over water distribution has brought government and people closer together.

Surely every individual in the world has a right to affordable drinking water? Not according to the World Trade Organization. In response to pressure from multinational corporations, it ruled that water is a 'need', not a 'right'. Is this just a semantic quibble? No. A need, in WTO parlance, can be traded, and corporations must be given the opportunity to manage it. The IMF and World Bank only offer financial assistance to countries if they privatise.

In the past, the distribution of drinking water has always been seen as a part of the state's responsibility to its citizens. But in poor countries this responsibility is often hampered by money shortages, the corrosion of old pipes and endemic corruption. If water is free, it also often gets wasted. State control can acquire a bad name, then, and corporations seize on these failures to highlight the advantages of privatising water distribution. But when this takes place, the corporations invariably prioritise supplying people who can pay over those who cannot. Water privatisation in Puerto Rico, for example, left poor people entirely without water while US military bases and tourist resorts remained well supplied.

In 1999, the Bolivian government was pressurised into privatising its water distribution by the World Bank. Water rates rocketed. In Cochabamba, streets were barricaded, 30,000 protestors seized the central square and police fired on the crowd. The crowd swelled to 80,000. Bechtel, the private water company, left the country. A few days later, World Bank president James Wolfensohn appeared to have learned nothing from the experience. He claimed that Bolivia still needed "a proper system of charging," and that there was no option but to pay international prices for a valuable resource.

Throughout the world there have been riots where poor countries have been forced to privatise their water distribution. However, many multinational companies, having found that they cannot make sufficient profit, are withdrawing, leaving financial and technical mayhem behind them.

Among European countries, only in Britain and France is water distribution carried out mostly by private companies. Studies by PSI Research Unit found that UK water prices are two to three times higher than elsewhere in Europe and environmental standards are lower. Shareholders in Severn Trent, Britain's second largest water company, have received £2.2 billion in dividends since privatisation. In 2005 to 2006, while its profits tripled, it leaked 540 million litres a day. In 2006, it raised its water rates by 8.5%.

There is no single blueprint on how public water utilities can deliver affordable clean water for all. However, removal of the ideological obsession with privatisation together with new approaches for 'public–public' participation give hope that public services, which still serve 95% of the world population, can be transformed.

Shareholders
and the divine right of capital

"Civil government, so far as it is instituted for the security of property, is in reality instituted for the defence of the rich against the poor, or of those who have some property against those who have none."

Adam Smith, *Wealth of Nations* (1776)

CORPORATIONS ARE, SURELY, communities of people who bring together their work, talent and enterprise to provide society with what it needs. Right? No. In law, neither these hard-working people nor their bosses are a corporation.

In law, a corporation is a group of people who do nothing for society. They extract wealth from the company. They are not liable for its debts. They don't bear responsibility for its crimes. Nor do they have to exert themselves in any way. They will sell the company abroad if this will make them money. They have no loyalty to it and can leave on a whim. They simply use it as a tool for gambling.

Shareholders own the corporation. In law, shareholders in effect are the corporation.

Back in seafaring days, a group of wealthy people would raise money together for a trading venture. Their ships might sink, in which case they would lose everything, or their ships might complete the voyage, at which point the investors could collect their profits. People who risk their money to help a new enterprise still provide a valuable service.

During the past 20 years, corporations have been buying back more shares than the number they have issued. In buying their own shares, then, they are putting more money into the stock market. Shareholders are mistaken if they think that they are helping a company by buying its shares: they too are just putting money into the stock market in order to gamble on which shares might rise in value.

Share values, on average, have been rising well above inflation for 50 years. Those who have money to invest benefit disproportionately compared with those who don't. Their winnings have to go somewhere, so they are tipped back into the game. It is strange that the central purpose of 21st century financial activity is to make money for gamblers rather than for wealth creators, or schools, hospitals, trains or all the other things that we value as a society. It is stranger still that governments look to this casino as a measure of their countries' success.

A chief executive used to behave like a king. This stopped when shareholders realised that, in law, they had the power to sack him or reward him with a vast bonus. He is now the shareholders' servant. His duty is only to make money for them.

Employees – those that create the wealth – are serfs, to whom the shareholders – the corporation – owe no loyalty. Employees are an expense that must be kept to a minimum at all times. They have no decision-making rights, they can be sacked at will, they can be replaced by sweatshops abroad, and the company to which they have devoted their lives can be sold without their being consulted. "Employees are our greatest asset," comments an enlightened CEO, little realising what he is saying. Assets are property that is owned. We are back to the days of feudalism.

In France, aristocrats had to supply the king with soldiers, so they were exempt from tax. They were later allowed to shed this military responsibility but they retained their tax-exempt privilege. The serfs eventually woke up to the fact that the aristocrats were allowed to amass wealth without having any responsibilities and they reacted by cutting off their heads. Shareholders have similarly retained privilege but shed responsibility; the divine right of kings has been replaced by the divine right of capital. Those without this privilege will one day wake up to the ludicrous situation.

The fault is not with the minor aristocracy – who jump on the bandwagon hoping to increase their savings – nor with the mega-rich, who are simply playing by the rules to multiply their millions. Most of us would do the same given the chance. The fault is with our collective mindset that remains blind to the absurd way in which we manage the economy.

> Tesco, pursuing a policy of minimum payment for produce, made record profits in 2006.

The UK chancellor, who is responsible for company law, allows shareholders to do what they like with the inherited wealth of our country. Consider, for example, Pilkington Glass. For 175 years it was a world leader in glass technology and cared for the welfare of its workers. It is now a Japanese company. Why should the Japanese nurture education and skills in Liverpool? Enquiries for glass technology, such as from China and India, are no longer sent to Britain but to Japan. A national asset has been lost and Britain is the poorer.

Great British institutions are being flogged off to foreign companies at an unprecedented rate. P&O has gone to Dubai, British Airports Authority to Spain, Wessex Water to France, Thames Water first to Germany then Australia, Smiths Electronics to the US, Associated British

Ports to Goldman Sachs based in New York, BT's offshoot O_2 to Spain, British Steel first to Anglo-Dutch Corus then to India, Liverpool Football Club to the US. By the time this book is published will Scottish Power be Spanish and will Sainsbury's, Boots, Rolls-Royce, Cable and Wireless, ICI, William Morris, HSBC and Barclays Bank also have gone? The loot taken by UK shareholders agreeing to these sales vastly exceeds that of the African kleptocrats whom we criticise for pocketing their countries' wealth.

Shareholders get rich. Wealth-creating companies leave the country. Government revenues plummet.

A large part of the global economy is centred on the London Stock Exchange. In 2006, its US rival Nasdaq tried to take it over but was prevented by the determination of Clara Furse, the Stock Exchange's Dutch-born chief executive. US hedge funds, however, own a quarter of Stock Exchange shares, so it may yet disappear into the dark pool of unregulated corporate finance. Britain may wake up one day to find that its last great asset, the lucrative financial services sector, has gone, that it has no industrial base left and that the Far East no longer needs its entrepreneurial or design skills.

Occasionally, governments react to the consequences of the global market. When Dubai Ports acquired P&O, imports and exports at Baltimore, Philadelphia, Miami, New Orleans, Houston and Newark would all have passed through Arab hands. This was a step too far even for dogmatic neoliberals in the US.

This free-for-all might just make some sense if nations were a thing of the past, if international commerce was the only economic discipline and if everyone played by the same set of rules. But this starry-eyed view of globalisation has little basis in reality.

France has 11 protected sectors. Spain snaps up foreign companies, then rapidly raises barriers when anyone tries to reciprocate. China takes advantage of everything that is up for sale. Its officials race around the world making deals with oil, natural gas, timber, phosphate and mining companies, often offering well over the market price. China's purpose, however, is not to become a major player in the international free-market casino but to secure access to dwindling global resources. India is catching up with the same policy.

When scarcity means that money can no longer buy essential resources, the casino will crash. Or, to use the analogy of 'pass the parcel', when the music stops he who holds the parcel will keep it.

Disney Corp. pays Haitian contract workers 28 cents an hour for sewing garments. Quadrupling this wage would add less than one per cent to the cost of a garment. No matter. Worker income is a company expense that must be kept to a minimum.

CSR

corporate social responsibility?

'OIKOS' (HOUSE), 'NOMIA' (manage). Economics, according to the Greek origin of the word, is about human housekeeping. It is about the welfare of people, their work, their future and the environment.

Modern corporate law, however, has other objectives for the economy. Profit takes precedence over concern for people's welfare, their work, their future or the environment. Some business directors have resisted this approach, but ultimately the individual has little strength against the mighty corporation.

- Henry Ford believed that his company should be more than a profit machine and should be run only "incidentally to make money". He paid his workers substantially over the going rate and rewarded customers with yearly price cuts on his model T cars. He was taken to court in 1916 on the grounds that profits belong to shareholders and he had no right to give their money to others. He lost. The judge said a "corporation is organised and carried out primarily for the benefit of stockholders." This precedent has been enshrined in corporate law.

- Anita Roddick refused to separate her personal values from her business. "I just want an extension of my home," she said, "I want to be able to bring my heart to the workplace." The Body Shop became one of the world's most successful businesses. When it became a public company she wanted to continue with this ethic, but things came to a head after the anti-WTO protests in Seattle in 1999. She called on The Body Shop to take a stance against the WTO but it refused. She now looks back on the stock flotation as a "pact with the devil. Because it has to maximise profits, everything is legitimate … using child labour or sweatshop labour, or despoiling the environment."

- CEO John Browne took BP out of the Global Climate Coalition (of oil companies) that had spent millions on lobbying against the Kyoto protocol. He said BP "had left the church of the oil industry" to become the world's first green oil titan. Environmentalists praised him for his ethical responsibility. Members of the Gwich'in Nation, Alaska, thought they could persuade him not to "come to the Arctic to destroy us." But they failed.

Browne then explained his green agenda. "This is not a sudden discovery of moral virtue, it is about long-term self-interest, enlightened, I hope, but self-interest none the less." So, there is no inconsistency with his refusal to reconsider Arctic drilling. "The fundamental test of our company," he said, "is performance." And the new logo, 'Beyond Petroleum'? "The days when our business had a captive market for oil are ending. There are new sources. Fuel cells will give us cars with different engines. We have to compete to ensure that oil remains a fuel of choice." Will long-term self-interest one day persuade even oil companies to choose survival over runaway global warming?

- Warren Anderson vowed to spend the rest of his life making amends when he first heard that 3,500 people – a number matched later by the destruction of the World Trade Center in New York – had been killed by gas escaping from his Union Carbide factory in Bhopal, India. One year later he said he had overreacted and would lead the company in its fight against paying any damages. What had changed? Nothing. His first reaction was human, his second, corporate.

The psychologist Dr Robert Hare says that many of the attitudes people adopt as corporate operatives can be characterised as psychopathic. "They try to destroy their competitors, and they are not particularly concerned with what happens to the general public so long as it's buying their product. Then they go home, they have a warm and loving relationship with their families; and their friends are friends rather than things to be used." They themselves are not psychopathic, just schizophrenic.

"A corporation is the property of its stockholders," said Milton Friedman, Nobel laureate and one of the world's most eminent flat-earth economists. "Should it spend the stockholders' money for purposes which it regards as socially responsible but which it cannot connect to its bottom line? The answer, I would say, is no." He added that this would be insincere when the real aim is profit. The corporation is duty-bound to perpetrate damage to communities and the environment, if this makes more money for its shareholders than the fines it would have to pay if prosecuted. In corporate law neither the shareholders – the owners – nor the directors can be held personally liable for the crimes of corporations. No 'real' person can get away with murder,

but it is acceptable for an 'artificial person' like a corporation to murder if it increases profits. Corporate murder by oil and logging firms is frequently reported in the media but no corporation has had its licence to trade revoked.

Corporations are given the right to be treated as 'persons'. But they are not mortal, they do not have feelings, they do not have a conscience and we choose not to punish them like real people. This gives them a huge advantage over individuals or small businesses that have to take responsibility for their actions. A person who kills, even by accident, usually has his activities stopped. Not so with some UK corporations. For example:

- Balfour Beatty, 1994. Collapsed tunnel. Fined £1.2 million. Continued in business.
- Great Western Trains, 1997. Killed 7, injured 139. Fined £1.5 million. Continued in business.
- Thames Trains, 1999. Killed 31. Fined £2 million. Continued in business.
- Transco, 1999. Killed 4. Fined £15 million. Continued in business.
- Balfour Beatty and Network Rail, 2000. Killed 4, injured 102. Fined £10 million. Continued in business.
- BP, 2005. Killed 15. Fine awaited. Continued in business.

In no cases were any directors held personally liable for manslaughter.

Every corporation these days has a department that consults citizens and publishes CSR (corporate social responsibility) reports. This is a necessary public relations exercise, but it does not get in the way of its main business. The only way to influence a corporation against

malpractice is either to demonstrate that it could benefit financially from better practice, or to persuade enough consumers not to buy its products or shares. Even these are blunt instruments, though, when each corporation is involved in a wide variety of activities, some good and some bad.

Corporations cannot operate in the absence of regulations. Governments grant them rights, such as the ability to limit liability. Governments created the World Trade Organization to protect their interests and introduced the notorious General Agreement on Trade in Service (GATS) allowing them to take over public services in poor countries. Corporations therefore spend millions to ensure that governments continue to regulate in their favour.

The ethical campaigners' only real chance of success is to persuade governments to regulate in favour of the people: corporations could then be a force for good. But corporate lobbies have infinitely greater funds than campaigners.

Western society has chosen to make corporate activity an ethics-free zone. It need not be so. The American Founders struggled against corporate tyranny and won – for a while.

Corporate law should protect people from the power of corporations.

Ending tyranny
the struggle of the Founders

"I believe in this beautiful country. I have studied its roots and gloried in the wisdom of its magnificent Constitution. I have marvelled at the wisdom of its founders and framers. Generation after generation of Americans has understood the lofty ideals that underlie our great republic. I have been inspired by the story of their sacrifice and their strength. But today, I weep for my country." Senator Robert Byrd, 2005

BOSTON'S CITIZENS THREW $15,000 worth of tea into the harbour in 1773. That was a lot of money then, and a lot of tea. The tea belonged to the East India Company, the world's first multinational corporation (MNC). The British government then decreed that the harbour would be closed until the people of Boston reimbursed the Company. This led to war and rejection of the tyrannical regulations imposed by a remote government on behalf of a corporation. Poor countries today have similar feelings about the privileges given to corporations by governments far away.

The American Founders were determined to prevent tyranny enslaving the New World, whether the tyranny of an aristocracy or of standing armies. But it was trade that aroused their greatest passions. At the time, virtually all members of the British parliament were stockholders with the East India Company: a tenth had made their fortunes through the Company, and the Company funded parliamentary elections generously. British traders and politicians prospered through the activities of this first MNC as it sucked wealth from around the world. The parallel with today's corporate and political life, particularly in the US, is remarkable.

The Founders introduced many measures in the New World to prevent corporate tyranny. Corporations received charters from individual states and had them for a limited period, not in perpetuity. They were only allowed to deal in one commodity, they could not hold stock in other corporations, their property holdings were limited to the needs of the business, their headquarters had to be located in the state of their principal business, monopolies had their charges regulated by the state, and all corporate documents were open to the legislature. Any direct or indirect political contribution was treated as a criminal offence. Corporations had their charters removed if the state considered their activities harmful to its people.

Railroad companies were traditionally referred to as 'artificial persons'. When the Fourteenth Amendment (ratified in 1868) gave all 'persons' equality before the law these companies desperately tried to claim that equal rights applied not just to slaves but to them as well. For 18 years the Supreme Court consistently ruled that corporations did not have the rights of human persons. Then the Santa Clara County vs. Southern Pacific Railroad case reversed this. Corporate tyranny in the US and beyond can be traced back to this one legal ruling.

Textbooks do not provide details of the case but only quote the head-note, which said that corporations now had the right to be treated as persons. It was the writer Thom Hartmann who eventually unearthed the original records in Vermont, only to find that the judge had specifically stated that the case did not relate to corporate personhood. The head-note had been written a year after the hearing by the Recorder, whose life had been devoted to the railroads. By then the judge was too ill to check it. American corporate law is therefore based on a fraud.

It is not surprising that Hartmann received death threats after publishing his book *Unequal Protection*, in which he reveals the real purpose of the Founders and the American Constitution.

The second step to corporate tyranny occurred when the US signed up to the North American Free Trade Agreement (NAFTA) in 1994 and to the WTO in 1995. It is commonly thought that these are both beneficial to the US. Wrong. The agreements prevent US citizens and authorities from making decisions about their local environment and trade, giving power instead to foreign bureaucrats. NAFTA's effect on Mexico, where eight million fell from the middle class into poverty, has been well documented. But in the US, 2.6 million jobs vanished (many replaced by low-paid service sector jobs), workers lost $28 billion in bonuses, wages fell 28%, working hours increased, environmental laws were

overruled and the trade deficit soared. Only corporations benefited, through overturning local laws and forcing down the cost of labour.

All the protections against corporate power sought by the American Founders have been lost. Corporations, with the right to 'personhood', now have the right to meet and influence 'their' elected representatives. Chemical corporations, quoting the Santa Clara case, claim the right to privacy to prevent uninvited inspections of their toxic sites by the Environmental Protection Agency. Corporations have the right to sue an objector at a public meeting for slander, and frequently exercise it, not to win so much as to intimidate protestors with the threat of legal fees. Corporations, asserting the right to free speech, used a perverse advertising campaign to kill off Clinton's proposal for health-care protection for the 40 million Americans who are uninsured.

Can the US return to the values of its Founders? Reversal of the Santa Clara case would be the first step to subjecting corporations to the control of the people. The federal government, each state, each township, could then regulate corporations to the benefit of its citizens and help local economies flourish once again. Indeed, in California, local governments have already passed laws that deny corporations the status of persons, while in Pennsylvania some townships have forbidden corporations from owning or controlling farms in their communities.

Huge questions remain. Deprived of personhood the corporations would still have financial bully-power. But, because of its unique constitution, the US could lead the world once again towards government of the people by the people for the people – not by and for corporations.

Hell in Nigeria
a corporate imperative

"How necessary it is that the English plantations in America should have a [sufficient] and constant supply of Negro-servants for their use."

Founding Charter, The Royal African Company, 1672

BETWEEN 1672 AND 1807, 12 million people were deported from West Africa and sold into slavery in the Caribbean and the Americas. The Royal African Company (RAC) was responsible for starting this forced displacement – unparalleled in scale – and for developing the triangular trade between Britain, Africa and the Americas, of which slavery was a major part.

In their book *The Next Gulf*, Andy Rowell, James Marriott and Lorne Stockman say that up to 38 million people died in this process of enslavement and transport. They describe how men, women and children were stripped naked and branded with red-hot pokers to identify ownership. Up to 400,000 guns each year were shipped from Britain to Africa in payment for the slaves, while tobacco and sugar, grown on plantations with slave labour, brought prosperity back to Britain. Such wealth enabled Christopher Wren to build some of London's most glorious churches.

This RAC's trade was succeeded in the 19th century by the Royal Niger Company's palm-oil business, which lubricated Europe's industrial machine. Any African trying to cash in on the trade was imprisoned or deported. The interior of the country was invaded and occupied, towns and cities were looted and razed to the ground, and whole populations were massacred.

In 2006, Shell delighted its shareholders by announcing an annual profit of $23 billion – a new record. Shareholders received proceeds from these oil sales without having to endure Shell as a neighbour. Oronto Douglas, however, did have to live with Shell next door. "Wherever oil reigns," he said, "life is hell."

The situation is described by Rowell, Marriott and Stockman in *The Next Gulf*. The Niger Delta, once a breadbasket, is now a wasteland. The people live in poverty and insecurity; many villages lack clean water, electricity or basic health care. Shell has been working there in a joint venture with the government since 1956, keeping its partner happy while ignoring the local community.

The vast sums involved have made corruption inevitable. More than 4,000 oil spills have poisoned farmland. Natural gas associated with the oilfields could have been captured and used, but this would have hindered the more lucrative exploitation of oil. A volume comparable to the UK's North Sea gas supply has simply been flared, contributing to climate change and throwing away a valuable resource. The flares roar like jet engines day and night, and pollute the air with benzene and sooty particles. Communities near these flares have never experienced darkness. Fish die in the rivers

An Ijaw child points out an oil spill by his village in the Niger Delta

and mangroves are destroyed. The toxic cocktail causes childhood respiratory illness, asthma and cancer. Shell calls in the army to deal with protests even if deaths are likely to follow.

Ken Saro-Wiwa, the writer and leading activist of the Ogoni community, saw the parallels between Shell's activities and previous centuries of foreign exploitation of his country: first for slaves, then palm-oil and now oil. He said that the Delta was "faced by a company whose management policies are racist and cruelly stupid," and he demanded that Shell take responsibility for its devastation. In 1995 he and eight others were tried in secret, tortured and hanged. Shell claimed that it had no moral obligation to intervene with its business partner in this process in spite of having an observer at the show trial. Meanwhile, it made payments to Lt. Col. Okuntimo, who was personally responsible for the 1994–1995 campaign of terror in support of oil extraction.

Shell's reputation was blackened. In 1996, it launched a public relations campaign costing £20 million to clean up its image. It succeeded in swaying western opinion, though it then lied to its shareholders about the size of its oil reserves.

Ten years on there has been little change. Pipes that should have been replaced 25 years ago continue to rust and cause spills in the villages and fields. Flares, banned since 1984, still burn. The army is still called in to suppress protest. In 2005, the Nigerian government ordered the company to pay $1,500 billion for its environmental damage. Shell, of course, refused.

Back in 1990, Ken Saro-Wiwa, a non-violent activist following in the tradition of Gandhi and Martin Luther King, wrote an article entitled,

'The Coming War in the Niger Delta'. The area would erupt into violence, he warned, if western companies and the state failed to meet local people's demands. By the 11th anniversary of his death in 2006, his prediction had come true. With repressive state tactics continuing, oil prices rising and three quarters of the Ogoni population living on under $1 a day, a bombing campaign began. Youth militias attacked the Delta's creeks, blowing up oil installations, abducting workers, taking on the military in bloody shoot-outs, occupying rigs and stealing a sizeable proportion of the production.

A new colonial chapter is under way. Having caused chaos in the Middle East the US now aims to diversify its oil supplies. The Gulf of Guinea, with Nigeria as the principal player, is the new Gulf from which the US hopes to acquire a third of its oil. It may also provide a new source of terrorism. A US military presence is increasing and the tiny independent islands of São Tomé and Príncipe are set to become the regional US base. But China is also desperate for oil supplies and is quietly developing contracts in the region too: Angola has taken over from Saudi Arabia as its largest supplier.

Colonialism has not changed. The west will 'apologise' for the slave trade but will continue to enslave the Nigerian population as long as it needs to exploit their resources. More than 300 years after the Royal African Company's charter was written, the present, unwritten, charter seems to read : "How necessary it is that western society should have a sufficient and constant supply of oil for its use."

Ken Wiwa, son of Ken Saro-Wiwa, has pointed to the link between the oil industry and the changing climate in the Niger Delta, warning

that a one-metre rise of sea levels will inundate three quarters of their land. "For God's sake, and for your own sake," he said in 2005, "if you wish to survive global warming, leave our oil in the ground and allow us to farm in peace."

It is ironic that Nigeria, after generating such wealth for the west, should have a national debt. World leaders have promised to cancel this debt on a number of conditions: one is that production of on-shore oil intensifies. More flares, more degradation, more protests, more brutal military intervention and more fossil fuel for changing the world's climate. Debt 'forgiveness' is a political tool being used in the service of Britain's largest corporation.

Lobbycracy
and the gang of eight

"Fascism should more properly be called corporatism, since it is the merger of state and corporate power."

Benito Mussolini, Italian dictator (1925–1943)

IN THE 1998 US elections, Republicans and Democrats received $660 million from the top 500 corporations in the country. The donors were richly rewarded by policies that favoured business over society, health or the environment. In the 2004 elections the donations doubled: US business gave $1,200 million directly to the parties, a figure that did not include the funding of conventions and advocacy groups.

The vast majority of American citizens – 99.75% – made no significant donations to either political party in these elections.

The rewarding of corporate donors reached new heights in the US after 2004. Corporate backers acquired access to decision making, and industry lobbyists were appointed to lead government agencies, task forces and advisory committees. Dick Cheney, former CEO of Halliburton, the oil industry construction company, was elevated to vice president. That was only the tip of the iceberg. In the twelve months from May 2004 President Bush installed more than a hundred top officials who had once been lobbyists or spokespeople for the very same industries they would now be regulating. As a result, profound changes favourable to business and industry are affecting carbon emissions, drug laws, health care, food policies, land use, logging, pollution standards, clean-air

regulations, social security, storing of nuclear waste and drilling for oil in nature reserves.

In Brussels there are an estimated 15,000 professional lobbyists working in 1,000 lobby groups, hundreds of public relations firms, corporate think-tanks and UN affairs offices run by corporations. Brussels has become the world's second biggest lobby centre after Washington. It is routine for MEPs to submit parliamentary amendments drafted not by themselves but by industry lobbyists. A significant number of

MEPs go through the 'revolving door' to receive large salaries in big business – provided they have behaved as requested while in parliament. Regulatory and transparency requirements are absurdly weak, far worse even than in the US.

EU officials actively seek corporate guidance to shape policies. This is a result of the collective obsession among European politicians with becoming the world's most competitive economic bloc. The president of the European Commission since 2004, José Manuel Barroso, said that these competitive goals would receive absolute priority during his presidency.

The G8, the group of eight states whose leaders meet annually, are more responsible than anyone for the present state of the world. They have set the agenda for the global economy for 30 years. All G8 leaders support the corporate agenda. Paul Martin, former prime minister of Canada, summed up their approach: "Our prosperity and security, the quality of life of our communities and the strength of our families, depend on our ability to access markets and to compete with determination and resourcefulness."

The G8 has no democratic legitimacy, being self-appointed from countries that comprise only a seventh of the world population. Individually, their morality makes their suitability for public office questionable: allegations have been made about initiating illegal wars (Bush, Blair, Putin), lying to parliament (Blair), introducing laws to avoid prosecution for corruption (Berlusconi, Chirac) and condoning torture (Bush). They may shed crocodile tears for Africa, but their primary aim is to exploit its resources to the full.

This gang has presided over the establishment of a lobbycracy in which money rules the rat race of competition, corruption, lawlessness and violence. The G8 used to meet openly in capital cities. Now it can only meet in obscure locations that are easy to seal off from a public that is desperately calling for economic justice and environmental sustainability.

Since 2002, numerous US companies – including Enron and World Com – many of them with special relationships to the president, have been found guilty of outrageous financial fraud. This led to a presidential directive in 2005 that exempts businesses from reporting transactions that might affect national security – a notion open to wide interpretation that would let most companies off the hook for similar offences. "The basic conditions of markets are now gone," said the former assistant US housing secretary, Catherine Fitts. "The black budget can now be the official budget for both government and private banks and corporations. Organised crime is now officially legal and combined with the stock and capital markets. This is the economic infrastructure for fascism."

For 40 years it has been known that many modern chemicals are responsible for birth defects and cancer. The new set of European regulations, REACH, however, was subject to the most concerted lobby campaign by industry ever. Toxic chemicals continue in use.

The first MNC
leading to empire

THE EAST INDIA COMPANY was the first major shareholder-owned multinational company (MNC). It found India rich in the 17th century and left it poor 350 years later.

When the company was established in 1600 there was not much Europe could export that the Far East wanted to buy. Spices, textiles and luxury goods sailed west. Only silver – and violence – sailed east. It was the ability to acquire land and control government services that made the fortunes of the Company, and destroyed those of India. Nick Robins' account of its social effects in his book, *The Corporation That Changed the World*, paints a rather different picture from the numerous corporate histories of 'John Company'.

As the mighty and opulent Mughal Empire declined, the Company acquired land beyond its vulnerable trading ports, extorted taxes from the people, manipulated terms of trade in its favour, and built up a private army. In 1757, Robert Clive fought and defeated the Nawab of Bengal. Later, Lord Cornwallis defeated Tipu Sultan in the south. In both cases, and in many lesser incidents, the Company's executive officers succeeded in extracting huge ransoms and accumulating vast wealth – not through their fashionable society customers back in England so much as from their suppliers in India, from defeated rulers and from taxes. India thus effectively financed its own impoverishment.

Under the Mughals, taxes had been collected through an intricate pattern of mutual

obligation. This was too complex for the Company. At a stroke, the 'zamindars' (tax farmers under the Mughals) were transformed into landlords and Bengal's 20 million smallholders were deprived of all hereditary rights. Just five years after the Company secured control of Bengal in 1765, tax revenues had tripled. These conditions turned one of Bengal's periodic droughts into a full-blown famine, in which an estimated ten million people died. Rather than organise relief efforts, however, the Company actually increased tax collection during the famine. Granaries were locked and grain was seized by force from the peasants to be sold at inflated prices in the cities. The devastating effects last to this day.

The Company became feared for the brutal enforcements of its monopoly interests. It cut off the thumbs of weavers found selling cloth to other traders, thus preventing them ever working again. In rural areas two thirds of a peasant's income was taken in tax, nearly double the rate under the Mughals. The Company's performance, through pursuing profit for its shareholders and its chiefs, contrasted starkly with its claim that it ruled for the moral and material betterment of India.

The British government followed the Company's approach. To maintain a monopoly in salt, for example, the colonial administration made it illegal for Indians to produce their own. The consumption of salt was forced down below even the minimum amount prescribed in English jails. This disgraceful control of an essential

commodity was only withdrawn after Gandhi's famous Salt March in 1930.

In Britain, the Company was so influential that attempts to control its affairs could bring down governments. An attempt led by Edmund Burke in 1783 to place the Company's Indian possessions under parliamentary rule led to the dismissal of those in power. The general election that followed was so generously funded by the Company that it secured a highly compliant parliament: a tenth of the seats were held by 'nabobs', a term derived from the Hindi word 'nawab', meaning an important rich man.

Booty from India created this new nabob class, the chief executive officers of Georgian England. The nabobs themselves had no conscience about their wealth. Robert Clive, having extorted a fortune after the Battle of Plassey in 1757, defended himself at a corruption enquiry by saying that he was "astounded" at his own restraint at not having taken more. Only a few dissenting voices, such as that of the Quaker William Tuke, pointed to the humanitarian disaster that the Company had wrought in India. But the case for reform was overwhelming and in 1784 the India Act transferred executive management of the Company to a Board of Control answerable to parliament.

The Company made out that its mission was to make Indians 'useful and happy subjects', but the underlying ethics of this public–private partnership remained the same. By the 1850s, just £15,000 was being spent on non-English schools in India, while the military budget stood at £5 million. Railways were built to speed up the access of British goods to Indian markets. Mill-made cloth brought from Britain shattered the local village economies, which were based

on the integration of agriculture and spinning. The great textile cities of Bengal collapsed. The governor general reported: "The misery hardly finds parallel in the history of commerce. The bones of the cotton weavers are bleaching the plains of India."

Indians were worn down by British rule, by the unfair trading regulations, the crippling taxes, the draining of India's wealth and the contempt with which they were treated. The final insult was forcing sepoys to use a rifle cartridge greased with cow and/or pig fat – an outrage to both Hindus and Muslims.

History seems to repeat itself over and over.

Retaliation was inevitable and catastrophe struck in 1857 when the Indians' fury exploded. The British could not fathom the hatred their policies had caused, so they called the violence a 'mutiny'. The killing of Europeans by the Indians generated, in turn, a ferocious bloodlust in English society that led to brutal reprisals. The government used the event to bring to fruition long-standing plans to take control of all aspects of Indian life and economy – full spectrum dominance. In 1858, the East India Company was abolished and direct rule by Queen and parliament was introduced.

So corporate exploitation induced a catalysing event (the mutiny) that in turn led to Empire.

The US empire
full spectrum absurdity

"All this talk about first we do Afghanistan, then we do Iraq; this is entirely the wrong way to go about it. If we just let our vision of the world go forth, and we embrace it entirely and we don't try to piece together clever diplomacy, but just wage total war, our children will sing great songs about us years from now."

Richard Perle, *The Guardian*, March 2003

THE ABOVE QUOTATION read like the ranting of a deranged psychopath back in 2003, but its ideas were soon adopted as official US policy. The Pentagon's 2006 Quadrennial Defense Review was presented to Congress as 'The Long War', to replace the War on Terror, which had replaced the Cold War. The Review envisaged a war unlimited in time and space: "The struggle may well be fought in dozens of countries simultaneously and for many years to come."

The 'Project for the New American Century' set out the blueprint for the US empire in June

1997. Later, in September 2000, it said that, "The process of transformation, even if it brings revolutionary change, is likely to be a long one, absent some catastrophic and catalysing event – like a new Pearl Harbor." One year later 9/11 was the catalysing event.

Following 9/11 George Bush proclaimed, "I am a war president." He referred to himself as commander-in-chief, with the right to override the Constitution. He secured unlimited war powers free from Congressional accountability to target countries at will, on the mere suspicion of harbouring terrorists. This was accompanied at home by curbs on civil liberties, the crushing of domestic dissent, the legitimisation of illegally obtained evidence even under torture, the legitimisation of torture itself, a new era of indefinite secrecy for presidential records and the criminalisation of legitimate protest. Anyone who has "purposefully and materially supported hostilities against the US" can be thrown into prison without the right to trial or the right to be represented. The president has adopted the arbitrary powers that Saddam Hussein enjoyed.

The dominant position of the US could have provided global peace and stability through co-operating with other nations in a world of weak governments, ethics-free corporations and anti-elite insurgency groups. But it has chosen to act outside international law by refusing to sign the Kyoto Protocol, violating the Montreal Protocol on ozone, rejecting the Clean Energy Plan, breaking the Nuclear Non-Proliferation Treaty, rejecting the Comprehensive Test Ban Treaty, withdrawing from the ABM Treaty with Russia, violating the Biological and Toxic Weapons Convention, refusing inspection of its weapons of mass destruction, refusing to sign a treaty on the rights of the child, 'un-signing'

the treaty for an International Criminal Court, ignoring the Geneva Conventions. The list goes on: land mines, small arms, weaponisation of space, business corruption, law of the sea, economic espionage, harmful tax competition, racism. And it continues. In October 2006, the US dropped the policy requiring space operations to be "consistent with treaty obligations." It now also rejects international agreements that would limit US testing or use of military equipment in space.

"There is no United Nations," said John Bolton before being appointed as ambassador to the UN. "There is an international community that occasionally can be led by the only real power left in the world – and that's the United States – when it suits our interests and when we can get others to go along."

In 2004 the 'Interim Global Strike Alert Order' introduced the concept of pre-emptive war ('kick the door down,' to use US military language) by presidential order without recourse to Congress. These attacks could include the use of nuclear weapons. "We are now on alert," said General Bruce Carlson, commander of the 8th Air Force. "We have the capacity to plan and execute global strikes," which could take place "in half a day or less." The order brought about a new era of international lawlessness in which countries opposed to US hegemony need to obtain nuclear deterrents of their own. And it prompted former president Jimmy Carter to say recently, "We have now become a prime culprit in global nuclear proliferation."

The weird alliance of a Labour party in Britain with the most extreme right-wing lawless administration in US history makes the UK complicit and a prime target for retaliation.

'Intelligence' has become the creation of facts to support policy. The world now knows that deliberate manipulation of intelligence was used by the White House and the UK Cabinet to justify the invasion of Iraq. After the Second World War the United Nations established unanimously that "to initiate a war of aggression [unsanctioned by international treaty] is not only an international crime, it is the supreme international crime differing only from other war crimes in that it contains within itself the accumulated evil of the whole." Nazi leaders were held responsible and hanged for this crime.

No international treaty or United Nations resolution sanctioned the invasion and occupation of Iraq.

By October 2006, 650,000 Iraqis had died. Many more had been mutilated. Others had been dissolved by phosphorus. Children had had arms or legs blown off from playing among unexploded cluster bomblets. Treasures dating from the rise of civilisation had been destroyed or plundered. The economy had been destroyed. Widespread radioactive contamination from the use of depleted uranium will continue to cause cancer and horrific birth defects forever. The country has descended into a vortex of violence. These horrors testify to the insight of the UN judgement that to initiate a war of aggression unsanctioned by international treaty is the supreme international war crime.

The American 'neo-cons' assumed that the overthrow of Saddam Hussein would open Iraq to democracy and allow its oil to be freely traded. Instead, the failure to establish security under the occupation opened a can of worms. Shia against Sunni violence is accompanied by Arab against Persian, Islam against coalition, Saudi against Iran, US against Iran, US against Russia and a global spread of terrorism. However, the US and Britain have forced the puppet government to sign away its oil to corporations. If they can make this stick they will regard the occupation as a success regardless of the carnage. This theft will be a continuing casus belli.

The US has a military presence in Kazakhstan, Afghanistan, Pakistan, Iraq, Egypt, Algeria, Yemen, Qatar, Bahrain, Kuwait, Saudi Arabia, Oman and Lebanon, and supports dictatorships in many of them. It is not difficult to see this as coordinated aggression against the Muslim world rather than simply a grab for oil.

And now Somalia. For 15 years the US supported warlords who were generally viewed, in the words of a Somalia specialist, as "absolute bastards; illiterate, syphilitic, irrational killers." Then, in early 2007, the US backed the invasion of Muslim Somalia by Christian Ethiopia. *The Economist* commented: "Although the Islamists were austere, they delivered security, orderliness and even a sense of pride to many in Mogadishu. Where the warlords had road-blocks, the Islamists had street cleaners … It might be that Mogadishu's few months under 'terrorist' Islamic rule will come to be viewed as a golden moment."

The US seeks universal hegemony through military power. The mission statement of all its armed forces is 'full spectrum dominance': dominance on land, the oceans, the airwaves and intelligence, and in space. In the last Iraq war, 83% of communications were sent via satellites. Space is the new lawless frontier. The US aims to revolutionise warfare with space-based laser weapons – invulnerable satellites that circle the earth and can target any stationary or moving object on the ground, in the air or in space, at the speed of light. It also aims to drop missiles from space (the 'rods from the gods' programme). "The globalisation of the world economy," says the US space command's 'Vision for 2020' report, "will continue with a widening between haves and have-nots. From space the US would keep those have-nots in line." And the commander-in-chief of space command said, "We're going to fight *in* space. We're going to fight *from* space and we're going to fight *into* space" (his emphasis).

In 1985, as part of its Star Wars programme, the US demonstrated its ability to destroy satellites (though most of its attempts failed). Recently, it said that it would "deny adversaries the use of space capabilities hostile to US national interests" and "oppose the development of new legal regimes that seek to limit US access to or use of space. Proposed arms control agreements or restrictions must not impair activities in space for US national interests." China and Russia repeatedly pressed the US to sign agreements outlawing arms in space, but Washington rebuffed their overtures. As with its nuclear posturing, its threats were bound to provoke a reaction: in January 2007, China shattered one of its own redundant satellites as a demonstration of its capabilities. But junk in space gradually builds up. When one piece crashes into a satellite, more pieces are created that will crash into more satellites. A chain reaction will develop as junk multiplies, making space unavailable even for peaceful purposes.

The US is renewing the Cold War by extending its Star Wars bases into Europe. Friendly states provide moral support and allow intelligence facilities, but their interests will be ignored when they are no longer useful. France discovered this when it questioned the legality of the Iraq invasion, and Britain will be similarly sidelined when it no longer has a leader totally committed to the Project for the New American Century. Less friendly states suffer economic or military aggression. Poor countries, like the 35 that refused to guarantee the immunity of US citizens from prosecution, have had aid terminated.

"In Russia's opinion, the [US] militarisation of outer space could have unprecedented consequences for the international community, and provoke nothing less than the beginning of another nuclear [arms race] era." Vladimir Putin, 2007

Reliance on overwhelming power and technical wizardry does not make peace; on the contrary, the chaos of Iraq and destruction of Lebanon showed that heightened hatred and insurgency are the outcomes. Could this be intentional? Some evangelical Christian groups, following a fundamentalist interpretation of their holy texts, see the war on terror in terms of the apocalyptic prophesies of Armageddon. They twist their scriptures so that peacemaking becomes contrary to God's will, while they ignore the more apposite Biblical proverb: "pride comes before disaster, arrogance before a fall."

The economic decline of the US empire may be the only hope that its arsenal will not spread further destruction and that the civilised values of many Americans, which used to be so admired, will once again guide its policies.

The new century

look east

"Bush's America is a hollowed-out debt-ridden economy engaged in using its last card, its vast military power, to prop up the dollar and its role as a sole world superpower." William Engdahl, *Financial Times*, February 2007

FOR WASHINGTON THE Cold War has never ended. Its leaders define their current agenda as the 'Project for the New American Century' with the military objective of 'full spectrum dominance'. Russia is the only country with the remotest capability of responding to a nuclear strike: now the US is surrounding it with bases and is moving the Stars Wars 'defence' system up to its borders. With nuclear primacy the US hopes to be able to dictate to the entire world.

Not surprisingly, Russia, China and East Asian countries are co-operating with each other to resist this threat.

Washington's investment in military hardware is effective at extermination, but counterproductive in the conflicts of today. The first application of the Project – the invasion and occupation of Iraq – demonstrated the limits of military power for subduing and governing a society. The catastrophe in Iraq may mark the beginning of the geopolitical decline of the US, and the focus of the global economy moving east.

In East Asia, Japan stood out as an economic member of the western world in the days when modernisation meant westernisation. That has changed. South Korea developed a strong economy without westernising; Malaysia prospered by rejecting the IMF's neoliberal

model; China's GDP, in terms of purchasing power, is likely to overtake that of the US in just over a decade. If India collaborates, an East Asian economic bloc would contain half the world's population.

The Association of Southeast Asian Nations (ASEAN) is the main institution linking countries in the region. It has half the population of China, roughly the same as Europe, twice that of the US, and has been a focus for trade, security and cultural collaboration. It boasts that no tension has escalated into armed confrontation between its ten member countries since it was set up in 1967. The members of ASEAN+3 (including China, Japan and South Korea) are now negotiating to become a free trade bloc. China's trade within the group is increasing by 40% a year.

The US imposed nuclear sanctions on India following its 1998 nuclear tests. But there has been a dramatic change over the past two years. In early 2005, Ashley Tellis, an analyst in Washington, wrote, "There is a real fear that China might some day turn its rising economic and military power against America. In this context the US needs to look at a re-ordering of its relationship with India, which today is not only a key ally in the war against terror but a counterbalance in Asia against China's

Victoria Harbour, Hong Kong – a centre of the rising East Asian economy

dominance." Manmohan Singh, the Indian prime minister, was invited to Washington in July 2005 and accorded the maximum honour of a 19-gun salute, state banquet and a deal to supply nuclear material that went far beyond New Delhi's expectations. In March 2006, President Bush paid a return visit and made it clear that India was now accepted as the 'sixth' member of the nuclear club, by the US at least. The two nations regularly conduct joint military exercises and hardly a week goes by without a senator, admiral or diplomat visiting New Delhi.

There is little chance, however, that India will become a US poodle. Its present policy is to remain equidistant between the US and China. It is signing agreements with Iran in spite of US pressure. Imports from the US, being virtually nonexistent, have been described as 'flat as a chapatti' and US requests for liberalisation of the retail, insurance and banking sectors have not been met. The future may be co-operation between India with its IT skills and fluency in English and China with its industrial might.

But middle-class India is currently wallowing in a trough of consumerism, while the majority of its population remains desperately poor. Class, caste and religious violence, linked with increasing inequality, could easily undermine economic development.

China is content within its borders (if one accepts its occupation of Tibet) except for the dispute over Taiwan, which is based largely on its claim for the whole of the oil-rich East China Sea. This is an area of potential conflict with Japan and the US. Meanwhile, China has used its role in talks with North Korea to forge a close relationship with South Korea, resulting in a slow but steady marginalisation of US

hegemony in northeast Asia. So far, China has taken care not to step into the Soviet Union's shoes with military confrontation, though it is now increasing its military budget faster than the growth of its GDP.

While the US has been preoccupied with its problems in the Middle East, China's global influence has been growing. It does not require the political strings that the US has consistently imposed on its trading and diplomatic partners and it is relaxed about human rights. Its primary purpose is to secure key resources such as oil, natural gas and phosphorus.

China has borders with oil-rich Russia and Kazakhstan, which means it can install pipelines directly without crossing other countries. US hostility to Iran means that Iran's oil and gas will flow east to both India and China. The US hoped that, through its support of the military regime in Pakistan and with the Taliban supposedly gone, the pipeline across Afghanistan would deliver oil to the west. But China has built a terminal port, and the Taliban may yet control the security of the pipeline. China has also been making deals for oil with African countries, such as Sudan and Angola, and is welcomed in Central and South America as a counterbalance to the US history of intervention.

Predictions about the global future are mostly based on continuity with the past: "Britain had the 19th century, America the 20th. Who will have the 21st?" Or: "The ability to create wealth has grown steadily, therefore it will continue to grow with China in the driving seat."

But the 19th and 20th centuries had a seemingly inexhaustible supply of cheap energy and resources. This will no longer be available.

Coal could destroy the climate. Conflict over oil could become more intense as extraction no longer meets demand. Over-fishing and acidification could threaten the supply of food from the oceans. Loss of nutrition from the soil and depletion of aquifers could seriously reduce food from the land. Deserts are spreading. Some Chinese rivers no longer reach the sea. These are the first devastating effects of climate change. All these factors could limit the future for China – and for all countries.

China has immense environmental problems. But so did Britain at the beginning of the Industrial Revolution, and prospered. It is addressing these problems seriously. Logging has been stopped, trees are being planted on a massive scale and research into renewable energy technology is overtaking that of other countries. In 1950, 13% of Chinese lived in cities. This figure is now up to 40% and expected to reach 60% by 2030. Dongtan, on an island off Shanghai, will be the world's first eco-city, as close to carbon neutrality as is possible today. All housing will be within seven minutes' walk of public transport; most citizens will work in the city; electricity and heating will be provided entirely from renewable sources; there will be no emissions from vehicles; food will be produced on the island; buildings will be constructed with local materials using new technology; and vegetation will be moved from the ground to roof level.

Present forecasts suggest that the future might well be in the Far East. But can we be so sure? Our world is beset by unknowns and any attempts to define the future are based on just a few current trends. One thing we do know: it will be different from what we expect.

"Dreams and predictions ought to serve but for winter tales by the fireside."

Francis Bacon (1561–1626), *Essays Civil and Moral: Of Prophesies*

Collapse
and complex civilisations

EASTER ISLAND, 2,500 miles from mainland South America, has always captured the imagination of dreamers and travellers. How could such a small, isolated community construct and move such gigantic stone statues? With their stylised, long-eared and legless forms, the haunting images of the moai feature in every picture book of the Pacific. Why did the islanders bother?

The answer lies with the intensely hierarchical society that discovered this fertile wooded island in about 900 CE. Trees were cut down to clear the land for agriculture and they were used to make canoes and build slides for dragging the statues from the quarry to platforms. Eventually no trees were left, the land lost its fertility and the population crashed.

There were up to ten clans of Easter Islanders, and each chief wanted to outdo the others in erecting bigger and better moai. The clan leaders were so preoccupied with competition and conflict that they ignored the effect they were having on the island's resources. As conditions deteriorated, the populace turned on its rulers in a wave of anger and toppled the statues.

Not all societies harmed their environment. The tiny Pacific island of Tikopia, with an area of 4.7 square kilometres and a population of just over a thousand, was much more vulnerable to degradation than Easter Island, but it has been occupied continuously for 3,000 years. Politicians love to talk about making 'tough' decisions but seldom have they had to face

such difficult ones as the Tikopian leaders. To address the most obvious threat of over-population, chiefs would perform an annual ritual in which they preached celibacy, coitus interruptus, abortion, infanticide and 'virtual suicide' – encouraging dangerous exploits, particularly those of young bachelors. Today, the only control is by emigration. Tikopia remains the least stratified of societies: the chief shares the same work, kinship values and rituals as everyone else; and the land is micro-managed for maximum nutrition.

Moai statues on Easter Island

Some see human survival to be dependent on grass-root activism as practised on Tikopia. Others say that government action is essential. Both have precedents in history. Whereas Tikopia's society was non-hierarchical and bottom-up, Japan's was the reverse. It survived a major crisis through government intervention.

In the 1600s, with the advent of peace and prosperity, the shogun Ieyasu and many 'daimios' (nobles) indulged their egos by constructing huge timber castles and temples. Urban construction used yet more timber, particularly for reconstruction after fires. By 1700, most old-growth timber, other than on steep slopes, had been felled. Disputes developed over wood for fuel and between boat and house builders, wildfires increased because second-growth timber was more flammable, soil erosion set in due to a shortage of the fertiliser that had been collected from forests, and lowlands were flooded from quick rainwater runoff. All these factors decreased crop yields, just as the population was growing. Major famines resulted. An outside visitor might have concluded that Japan was on the brink of societal collapse triggered by catastrophic deforestation. However, from that point on, successive shoguns invoked Confucian principles to limit consumption and accumulate reserves. An elaborate system of woodland management was introduced, and trees were treated as a slow-growing crop. By 1800, Japan's long decline in forests had been reversed.

Japanese deforestation was then exported, first to Korea and now to Australia.

When settlers first arrived in Australia they were deceived into thinking that the land was highly productive because of the magnificent woodlands and lush vegetation. But after the loggers had removed trees and sheep had grazed the standing crop of grass, they found that trees and grass grew back very slowly. The soil was to blame. In northern Europe we have fertile soil because glaciers in the Ice Age scraped minerals from the rock base; countries like Indonesia and New Zealand have received regular coatings of mineral-rich ash from volcanic activity. Australia, however, has had neither of these benefits and its soil lacks fertility.

Economic theory has blinded Australian leaders to the effect they are having on the country's resources. Cars and electronics are bought from Japan in exchange for timber, coal and minerals, and no difference is recognised between constructive economic activity and income from the depletion of resources. It is ironic that Australia, with the least forest cover of any industrialised country – three quarters of its original forests having been destroyed or degraded – is exporting timber to Japan, the most forested industrialised country with three quarters of its land covered by trees. The Styx valley forest in Tasmania has wonderful biodiversity and the tallest hardwood trees in the world, but it is being cut down for low-grade woodchips to feed the Japanese paper market.

By deforesting, on top of its history of overgrazing, Australia can be described as mining whatever fertility its land possesses – to match the income it receives from mining minerals. Mining is a one-way process.

Jared Diamond, an evolutionary biologist and author of the book *Collapse*, has identified five factors for the collapse of past societies:

- human environmental impacts, especially deforestation;
- political, social and religious reasons, as demonstrated by the competitive mindset found on Easter Island;
- climate change, as when the Little Ice Age (1400 CE and 1800 CE) destroyed the Norse civilisation in Greenland;
- attacks from the outside;
- loss of support from trading partners.

In most cases of a society collapsing, several of these factors were combined. The collapse of the Norse in Greenland is of particular interest since all five factors were involved.

Diamond found that societies seldom follow a pattern of gradual rise then gradual decline. The collapse has almost always happened at the height of their achievements, from causes that were not high on the list of their priorities. On Easter Island, for example, the size of statues gradually increased and the last ones were the most ambitious – they failed even to make it out of the quarry.

The modern world has chillingly obvious parallels with Easter Island. We have no threat from outside neighbours, whether friendly of not, because we are now one global society. But, like the Easter Islanders, we have been so preoccupied with competition and conflict that we have failed to notice the effect we are having on global resources and the climate.

The decline and fall of Rome, which has long fascinated historians, is another example of

societal collapse. The nations the Roman Empire conquered footed the bill for further conquests and expansion: the treasury of the king of Macedonia in 167 BCE enabled Marcus Aurelius to eliminate taxes; Pompey raised even greater sums from the accumulated wealth of Syria in 63 BCE; Julius Caesar's conquest of Gaul brought in so much gold that the metal lost a third of its value. Following his conquest of Egypt, Octavian distributed money to the people of Rome and relieved shortages in the state budget out of his personal fortune. He assumed the title Emperor Augustus and then terminated the policy of expansion.

The empire was becoming so extensive that little more could be administered. The one-off injections of wealth from conquests were used up and the taxes needed to administer an overblown dominion laid an increasing burden on its subjects. Some communities preferred to forgo the benefits of empire for a freer life with the barbarians. In the period of its expansion, Rome could survive the trauma of Hannibal's army overrunning its countryside from 218 to 203 BCE. But when administrative complexity and declining returns were sapping its strength, it collapsed with a relatively weak incursion in 410 CE.

The anthropologist Joseph Tainter, in his classic thesis *The Collapse of Complex Societies*, studied 18 civilisations and argued that societies collapse when their investments in increasing social complexity reach a point of diminishing returns. Easy-to-acquire resources are extracted in the initial period of expansion, but these become scarcer and more costly to acquire as they deplete. As problems arise with administration and social organisation they require increasingly elaborate solutions

that cost more and deliver less. Research and development moves from generalised knowledge that is widely applicable and obtained at a low price, to specialised topics that require great investment and are only narrowly useful. As the cost of maintaining complexity increases, fewer resources are available to meet crises of the kinds outlined by Diamond.

Collapse is an emotive word. It brings to mind invasions, revolution or meteorites. But if collapse is usually the result of diminishing returns from increasing investment, it can be studied as a mundane economic matter and avoided, or at least delayed, with appropriate changes of policy.

What about today's increasing complexities and diminishing returns?

Global medicine invests massively in hugely expensive but marginally useful research while neglecting the most common diseases affecting the world. The complexity of Britain's centralised National Health Service, or the even greater sums spent in the US on a system that fails many of its citizens, contrast starkly with the effective community-based health care of Cuba, which is run on a shoestring. Food distribution, particularly in the west, is a sophisticated and complex network that is vulnerable to catastrophic disruption. Britain's trains use energy bought on the international market at the same price as that used by Indian trains, but passenger tickets cost 50 to 100 times more per kilometre travelled.

The global financial system has become so complex that no one seems to understand what is going on. Jean-Claude Trichet, president of the European Central Bank, said at Davos in

2007, "There is now such creativity of new and very sophisticated financial instruments that we don't know fully where the risks are located. We are trying to understand what is going on but it is a big, big challenge."

These and many other examples suggest that we are at a stage of precarious complexity that absorbs all our resources while leaving no reserves to meet unanticipated shocks.

The UK's New Economics Foundation says that, in spite of ever-increasing GDP in Britain, the measure of domestic progress – in terms of the quality of life – started to fall in 1976. Many people in the west are reacting against the stress of being a full member of our complex pressurised society. Some are 'downshifting' from city executive to manual worker, others are going part time, and a small number are even trying to live self-sufficiently, disconnecting altogether from public services.

The US, matching Rome's period of expansion, has relied on wealth brought in by the dollar's use as an international currency, but it has used this one-off source for global adventures rather than for establishing a sustainable economy of its own. The period during which it receives tribute is now coming to an end.

Europe, in spite of horrific traumas, has avoided collapse over the past 1,500 years. The mutual interaction of its neighbouring administrations has included both exchange and conflict. Any collapse to a lower level of complexity by one country has been an invitation to neighbours to dominate or take over.

Civilisation is universally seen as the ultimate accomplishment of human society, having produced, on the one hand, the sheer beauty of Islamic architecture and Bach's cantatas, and on the other, the doubtful benefits of nuclear power. Collapse, by contrast, is seen as a catastrophe. In the overall history of our species, though, it is only recently that complex forms of human organisation have emerged. They are an anomaly and take constant creative energy to perpetuate. So collapse can instead be seen not as a catastrophic end of humanity but as a return to the normal, earlier, human condition of lower complexity.

Might a simpler life not be more satisfactory in the end?

Past civilisations, that had limited agrarian economies and used only natural materials, have left ruins that are valued as part of our heritage. But the relics of a collapsed global society like the one we have today will not be so benign. We will leave behind towering steel and glass structures that will never meld into the environment, persistent synthetic chemicals that will poison any life that comes into contact with them, genes that have not been subject to the process of evolution, radioactive waste and, above all, a changed climate. The future lot of Homo sapiens is never considered in our relentless pursuit of progress.

Life
nature, food and science

"No man is an island entire of itself; every man is a piece of the continent, a part of the main. If a clod be washed away by the sea, Europe is the less ... Any man's death diminishes me, because I am involved in mankind. And therefore never send to know for whom the bell tolls: it tolls for thee."

John Donne, *Meditation 17* in *Devotion Upon Emergent Occasions* (1624)

EVOLUTION IS A MIRACLE of complexity and inventiveness. From the billions of bacteria in our ecosystem to the few top predators, nature is a finely balanced wonder. And yet we wreak havoc upon it.

Mankind is only one small part of the planet's biodiversity. If we adopt sufficient humility and care, we might, just, avoid our residence on earth being abruptly terminated.

Don't predict
just be systematic

"HEAVIER-THAN-AIR flying machines are impossible," declared the eminent physicist Lord Kelvin in 1895. Fifty years later, the chairman of IBM said: "I think there is a world market for maybe five computers." Years after this, scientists believed that nuclear electricity would be too cheap to meter.

Predictions are often wrong, so how can we know if the latest technofix will, in time, provide benefits? Perhaps we can't. We do know, however, that society is systematically altering some properties of nature on which human life depends. Rather than focussing on each crisis as it arises, are there principles that society should follow to prevent further damage?

In a remarkable consensus-building process with other scientists in the 1980s, Professor Karl-Henrik Robèrt, one of Sweden's foremost cancer scientists, came up with the fundamental conditions that society must accept if our life on earth is to be sustained. Further discussion refined these conditions to their bare essentials:

- Nature must not be subject to increasing concentrations of substances extracted from the earth's crust.
- Nature must not be subject to increasing concentrations of substances produced by society.
- Nature must not be subject to increasing degradation by physical means.

If we systematically infringe any one of these conditions the future of our species will be endangered. At present we are systematically infringing all three.

The first system-condition. We mine and dispose of materials at a faster rate than they are absorbed back into the earth's crust. An obvious example is the carbon from fossil fuels that harms the atmosphere. But there are many other examples. Lead has caused problems since the Romans. Mercury gets into fish and from there into the food chain. Excessive extraction from aquifers brings arsenic into the water supply. We must understand how these substances are absorbed or neutralised and then limit what we take from the earth accordingly.

The second system-condition. We live in a balanced ecology that has evolved over a period of four billion years. When we introduce novel molecules, bacteria, viruses, plants, creatures and radioactivity that have not been subject to the processes of evolution, they will disturb the balance and cause problems somehow, somewhere, sometime. Typical examples are dioxins and PCBs that concentrate in fatty tissue and disrupt the endocrine gland, endangering reproduction of humans and other animals. The effect of these chemicals was first appreciated in the 1960s and has become more evident with the increase in allergies and degenerative disorders.

The third system-condition. Damage to the natural world is constantly reported in the media. Deforestation prevents carbon being absorbed from the atmosphere; over-fishing may lead to the collapse of ocean fisheries; the mass extinction of animal species is well under way; crop species are being lost through monoculture and cloning may do the same to animals.

And there is a fourth condition. People must not be subject to conditions that systematically undermine their capacity to meet their needs.

We must test each human activity systematically and reject it if it offends any of these four system-conditions. There is nothing woolly about sustainability: it is uncompromising, hard-edged, quantifiable and scientifically rigorous. **The rules are set by nature, not by man.**

It took four billion years for living cells to transform the virgin soup of the atmosphere – a toxic mix of methane, sulphurous compounds, carbon dioxide and other substances – into the beautiful and bountiful world that we inherited. We are now digging up what was laid to rest, spreading new chemicals and life forms, and degrading nature. The earth is running backwards into the chaos from which it started.

We would also love to predict the economy, but it is similarly uncertain. Financial advisers like to tell you that it always rises, forgetting that they were saying this just before the crash of the 1930s.

Like our natural environment, the economy will not survive if we continue to ignore the four system conditions. Alan Greenspan, as chairman of the US Federal Reserve, made certain that he could not be held to predictions. "If I seem unduly clear to you," he once told a congressman, "you must have misunderstood what I said."

Cod
a symbol of our times

THE BEST FISHING grounds in the world were once off the coast of New England. The prize fish were cod. After Cabot's voyage there in 1497 he reported that, "The sea is swarming with fish which can be taken not only with the net but in baskets let down with a stone." Within a hundred years the fishing grounds were serving the whole of Europe with salted cod, and fish the size of men were said to be caught there.

Cod swim in large shoals just above the seabed. They have a long life cycle, spawning only after four years. When factory trawl nets were introduced in the mid-20th century they scooped up all the fish, big and small, and few lasted long enough to spawn.

It was not until the 1980s that the fishermen of New England realised that, thanks to big offshore trawlers, the cod were disappearing, but the US government took no action. By 1992 the cod were gone. With the fish went the fishermen, another unique species hard to replace. Their skills in navigation, gutting, net mending and fish marketing couldn't save them. The tourists who go to enjoy the picturesque sailing ships in Gloucester harbour are now served filleted cod from Russia. Former fishermen cut the hotel lawns.

The cod may never return. Young cod are no longer migrating to warmer waters to spawn, perhaps because there are no older cod to lead them. Arctic cod, which have no market value, are moving in and eating Atlantic cod eggs and larvae. Other species and other predators are upsetting the natural balance and may also prevent rejuvenation of the cod stocks. Harvesting of shrimp and crab is still allowed but it prevents the return of biodiversity. So the most prolific fishing grounds in the world may now be dead forever.

Norway also had a crisis in the 1980s, but with a different outcome. Fish stocks were seriously depleted and catches were falling. The government took drastic action that put many fishermen and boat builders out of work. But within three years the stocks were improving and the fishing trade was saved.

The First and Second Great Fishing Experiments took place from 1914 to 1918, and 1939 to 1945. During these periods of fighting no fishing could take place in the North Sea. By the time each war had ended, the ocean had once again filled with an abundant supply of fish. The lesson was not learned, however, and over-fishing soon resumed. For eight years scientists have been saying that fishing should stop, and for eight years politicians have ignored them and handed out quotas. But the North Sea is fortunate in having more biodiversity than Newfoundland: although catches are small, cod have not totally disappeared.

The story of cod demonstrates that fundamentalist market economics – in which free trade determines what can be done with natural resources – is a remarkably silly idea. Cod were once a symbol of hope; they are now a warning to the world.

There are four areas in the world where winds push the surface water away from the coast and draw up cold, nutrient-rich waters from below to make abundant fishing grounds. Two are found off Africa's west coast.

In Senegal, fishing is the main source of employment – for 600,000 people – and provides the country's staple food. This will soon end. The government has given concessions to international companies without consulting the fishermen; but the companies fail to keep to their designated areas, taking fish from coastal waters. As the catch decreases and livelihoods are lost, the fishermen are starting to smuggle migrants to Spain for an alternative income. "Fishery laws are worthless if they cannot be enforced," says Nelson Dias, head of the local office of the International Conservation Union. "We need a satellite system to ensure that we can comprehensively monitor all our waters, but we do not have the financial means."

Coral reefs are the rainforests of the sea, being the treasure store of ocean biodiversity. Only ten per cent of Caribbean coral reefs are still intact. Regulation can work, however. St Lucia, realising its coral reefs were over-fished and damaged, designated half of them out of bounds. The fish are now back in large numbers with somewhere to breed once more.

The world's fishing industry produces $70 billion worth of fish – so long as stocks last. It receives $54 billion in subsidies.

New Internationalist, February 2007

Bees
an indispensable service

"If bees disappeared from the earth, man would have only four years of life left. No more bees, no more pollination, no more plants, no more animals, no more man."

Albert Einstein, quoted by Professor Haefeker in *Der Kritischer Agrabericht* (2005)

YOU CAN THANK the pollinators for producing a third of your food: from apples, oranges and almonds to onions, broccoli and potatoes. Only a few staple crops such as wheat and rice don't need this service – a service that is mostly provided, free of charge, by bees.

Bee colonies are extremely complex organisms that have adapted to changing conditions over millennia. During the past ten years, however, wild varieties have declined – in the US to half their previous number. Honeybees are also under threat as they become increasingly vulnerable to fungal, viral, bacterial and mite infections.

At the end of 2006, the situation in the US suddenly became catastrophically worse. No one knows the cause for certain except that it must be something to do with human activity. Bees are simply leaving hives and failing to return. The phenomenon is known as Colony Collapse Disorder (CCD). At the time of writing nearly three quarters of the remaining US honeybees in 24 states have disappeared.

Various culprits have been suggested for both the general decline and for CCD. A major suspect is genetically modified (GM) crops that are grown all over the US and release genetically modified pollen that is carried by bees along with their nectar. Research in the US has shown no pollination deficit in organic fields, a slight deficit in conventional fields and high pollination deficit in GM fields. Likewise bees were most abundant in organic fields and least abundant in GM fields, indicating that GM technology seriously reduces the bee population. If bees are attempting to avoid GM crops, being forced to fly longer distances, they may be dying while trying to find acceptable pollen.

The bees' ability to distinguish between GM and normal plants is a dramatic indication that the biotech industry's claim of there being no fundamental difference between the two kinds of crop is totally false. Watch out for those bright gold acres of oilseed rape that are being grown for biofuel: because they won't be entering the food chain, the GM versions may be considered safe. A study in Germany by Professor Hans-Hinrich Kaatz found that an alien gene in GM oilseed rape had moved to the guts of honeybees. GM rape producing GM bees – not a happy thought.

The general use of pesticides is obviously a contributing factor, supported by the fact that no reports of CCD have been received

A varroa mite feeding on bee larvae

from organic farmers. In 1997 professional beekeepers in France lost 70% of their honey harvest. The reason was clear. Sunflower seeds had been treated with an insecticide that had travelled from the seed into the sunflower and its nectar. After collecting the nectar the bees lost their orientation and failed to return to the hive. Also in France, Monsanto was challenged by beekeepers in 2004 for using an insecticide called Fipronil that was found to be killing bees. It withdrew the chemical, though it was allowed to use up stocks and introduce a replacement that was not yet adequately tested. Other pesticides have also been found to affect the ability of bees not only to navigate but also to smell and communicate.

Then there are antibiotics: bees are very vulnerable to bacterial infection and beekeepers regularly give them antibiotics to control it. If bugs develop resistance to a particular antibiotic, its continued use will kill competitors and leave the field open to resistant bugs.

Stress is another possible reason for the decline of bees. California produces more almonds than anywhere else in the world and 1.4 million – yes, million – hives of honeybees are moved from all over the country between mid-February and mid-March to pollinate orchards. Many of the hives are moved three or four times a year to different locations. As colonies around the US collapse, hives full of bees are being brought from elsewhere, even all the way from Australia. The constant need to adjust to new environments may be severely weakening the bees' immune systems.

The practice of breeding queen bees from the larvae of worker bees has been used for 95 years. Rudolf Steiner wrote in 1923 that this process would have long-term detrimental effects so grave that, "within a century all breeding of bees will cease if only artificially produced bees are used." The practice is now supplemented with artificial insemination to increase honey production, but this further reduces genetic diversity. Following the general practice of industrial farming, bees are bred to be larger and this makes them more susceptible to the blood-sucking 'vampire' mites than normal sized ones. This gradual move away from their natural origins may be the reason why modern honeybees are so vulnerable.

The dramatic increase in high voltage cables – long known to affect bee behaviour – could well be another factor undermining the populations of both wild bees and honeybees. Research projects have shown that if mobile phones are placed near hives the bees fail to return. Bees have fascinatingly complex means of navigation, so it may be that the rash of cell phone, radio and TV towers – the electronic smog of modern living – is disrupting their GPS systems.

Each theory has adherents that claim it to be the main cause. However none of the theories satisfies all the contexts in which problems occur. Perhaps the general decline of bee populations is a combination of several damaging practices that are inherent to our current way of living and farming.

But why such a catastrophic collapse in the US, and only in the US, at the end of 2006? There is one, most likely suspect. The winter of 2006 in North America was unusually mild but it was followed by a period of extremely cold weather. Researchers have found that extreme temperature shifts have a detrimental effect on bees' immune systems. This suggests that the bees, weakened by many of the other stresses resulting from industrial farming and modern technologies, were finally pushed over the brink by extreme weather conditions. Europe may have escaped Colony Collapse Disorder so far, but a changing global climate could wreak havoc on the weakened bee populations here too in the not so distant future.

There are thousands of wild bee species in the world that have special niches in the biodiversity of nature. Their interaction with honeybees can lead to a five-fold increase in pollination efficiency. But in areas of monoculture farming there are no wild bees at all. Dr Claire Kremen, at Princeton University, says that farmers have been relying too heavily on honeybees. "I think of wild bees as being our insurance policy," she says. "If we don't protect the wild pollinators we don't have a backup plan."

Over the past 25 years the diversity of wild bees in Britain, the Netherlands and Germany has declined. Common species have slightly increased but those bees that were always relatively rare in the past have become rarer still, while some species have died out.

Scientists researching this phenomenon turned their attention, almost as an afterthought, to plants pollinated by certain bees and found a close correlation between their decline and that of the bees. Common plant species have increased and rare ones have decreased. This parallel between wildflowers and their pollinators seems too strong to be a coincidence. But which is the cause and which the effect?

Scabious bees and field scabious plants are both declining. The early cutting of meadows means that the scabious often fails to reach the flowering stage. So, in this instance, cultivation may be responsible for the decline of bee species. But sometimes it is the other way round. Researchers refer to a vicious circle of decline caused by intensive farming and the loss of wild habitats. "We were shocked by the decline in plants as well as bees," said Dr Koos Biesmeijer of Leeds University. "If this pattern is replicated elsewhere, the pollinator service we take for granted could be at risk."

Another research project, this time in Costa Rica, showed the value of natural environments for maintaining healthy bee populations. It found that in coffee farms situated near untouched tropical forests, greater pollination by wild bees produced a 20% higher yield.

The steady decline of wild bees and the increasing fragility of honeybees are warnings that our methods of food production are destroying the equilibrium of the environment. We have consistently ignored these warnings. CCD may indicate that the end of industrial farming is nigh. In the future, instead of fighting for oil and water, industrialised nations may go to war over food produced by countries that have succeeded in protecting their pollinators.

Mammals
revenge of the elephants

BRAHMAN IS, FOR HINDUS, the one god: the god without shape and form, neither male nor female, transcending time and space, the highest intelligence. Brahman commands reverence but does not exactly encourage intimacy.

Ganesha, the cuddly son of Shiva and Parvati, with an elephant's head and plump child's body, led a charmed life and is a much more approachable deity. What's more, he removes obstacles from your life and work. He is the favourite among the gods and his image is found all over India – like the Virgin Mary's image in Catholic countries – at the roadside, in temples and hanging in car windscreens. The temple elephant leads processions on festive occasions and symbolises our relationship with all other species. Humans and elephants, when living near each other, seem to develop a special bond.

And yet, in one Indian state elephants have recently killed 600 people. Why? Possibly because so much of the forest has been taken away from them. In retaliation, angry villagers have killed 270 elephants.

This is part of a phenomenon that has developed since the mid-1990s and is being studied by Gay Bradshaw at Oregon University. "Everybody pretty much agrees that the relationship between elephants and people has changed dramatically," she says. "What we are seeing today is extraordinary. Where for centuries humans and elephants lived in relative peaceful coexistence, there is now hostility and violence."

Elephants live in communities and bury their dead. They use many forms of communication – visual, auditory, vibrating – for long distance

and close interaction. Their intense burial and mourning rituals include week-long vigils over the body, carefully covering it with earth and brush. They revisit the site for years afterwards, caressing the bones and rubbing their trunks along the teeth of the skull's lower jaw, the way elephants greet each other when alive. We can easily empathise with many aspects of their lives.

Elephants are among the most sociable animals on the planet. The elders – the matriarchs and bulls – protect and guide the herd and initiate younger elephants into the group's customs. But it is precisely these elders that are targeted by poachers for their tusks and even by park rangers in culling programmes. Without elders to bring them up, the juveniles are at a loss to know how to behave.

Elephants have voracious appetites, so they cannot coexist with agriculture. In parts of Uganda high elephant populations fought off the spread of agriculture well into the 20th century.

But Uganda provides an uncomfortable parallel between the plight of elephants and the plight of people on a continent riven with poverty and strife. Idi Amin introduced a reign of terror throughout the 1970s, killing over 300,000 of his political opponents. Later, full-fledged war developed in the north of the country between the government and The Lord's Resistance Army (LRA), which routinely 'recruited' children from villages, sometimes forcing them to kill their parents before pressing them into service as soldiers. To escape the LRA, most of the population in the north have moved from their villages into more than 200 camps set up for displaced people. There are few elders in these camps, most having been systematically eliminated during Amin's time. The children

therefore grow up without parents, schools, hospitals or any kind of infrastructure. They form roaming, violent gangs that have been described as completely wild.

In the mayhem caused by the LRA, not only individual elephants were killed for their ivory but whole elephant families were slaughtered with automatic rifles and hand grenades. Their numbers crashed from nearly 4,000 to fewer than 150. The last elephants of Queen Elizabeth National Park never left one another's side. One matriarch remained and gathered them together from their various hideouts and led them as one group into the open savannah. She held the group together, moving as one until her death.

Africa's elephant population now seems to be poised on the brink of madness, showing all the signs of chronic stress and venting their rage not just on humans but on other species as well. In one area they have been reported as killing villagers, attacking safari vehicles, raping and killing rhinos, and killing each other. All these attacks seem to have been by adolescent males that are orphans and have witnessed their families being exterminated.

Only where human densities are low do people have a deep acceptance of their wild surroundings. As densities increase, more conflict develops. Forty per cent of the earth's land surface is now dedicated to human agriculture, leaving less and less virgin land for large animals, which need the conditions of freedom under which they evolved.

Elephants, like many other large mammals, may have no future. The sixth mass extinction in the history of the world is under way. It is the first to be caused by one of the earth's species.

Soil
storehouse of nutrition

"Maintenance of the fertility of the soil is the first condition of any system of permanent agriculture." Sir Albert Howard, *An Agricultural Testament* (1940)

IN A SPOONFUL of healthy soil there can be a billion organisms from over 10,000 species. Soil is alive. It is a mineral, animal and vegetable kingdom all in one. It is the storehouse from which plants extract resources and in which they lay down reserves for the future. The science of how plants use the soil is so complex that we are only just beginning to understand it.

A single worm can shift 30 tonnes of earth in its lifetime. Together with insects, the worms aerate the ground, drag rotting material down, digest and excrete it, and begin the process of transforming plant matter into humus. Bacteria, fungi, protozoa and algae then work on the rotting matter and release the nutrients from it in the form of minerals, proteins, carbohydrates and sugars. Plants extract up to 10,000 of these naturally occurring compounds from the soil. Known as phytonutrients, they are essential for nourishing and protecting plants from pests and disease.

Then there are mycorrhizae, the white fuzz around the plant roots. Mycorrhizae create a living bridge of organic acids between the plant, the minerals and the microbial community. The plants grow and feed insects and other animals. Falling plant matter and manure is then deposited onto the soil, returning the nutrients that the plants extracted. The cycle of life continues and the topsoil becomes richer.

For thousands of years farmers have worked with nature, noticing when things go wrong, sometimes badly wrong. In the Fertile Crescent of the Middle East, rising salts destroyed both the crops and the empires that depended on them. In the Roman Empire, returning generals invested wealth from conquests in farms and ran them with managers and slaves, while the farmers became soldiers and their agricultural knowledge went with them. Rome declined and fell, and the fertility of Italy has never recovered.

Fifty years ago agribusiness entered the field. Through growing hybrid crops that require artificial fertilisers and a lot of water it increased yields. Industrial farming concentrated control into a few hands, machines assumed the role that labourers had had and traditional knowledge was lost. The soil is now largely used as a sponge to hold chemicals while the crops grow. It has lost the rich life that held it together and much of it has simply blown away. Future generations will have to struggle with land that has been robbed of its goodness.

Plants extract their nutrients from the soil and animals get theirs from plants. These mineral trace elements keep plants healthy and, in turn, are essential constituents of human bones, teeth, muscle, soft tissue, blood and nerve cells; they are involved in almost all the body's metabolic processes. British government records from 1940 to 2002 showed a disastrous drop of minerals in the food we eat:

- The iron content of 15 different meat items had fallen by 47% and their magnesium content was down 7%. Turkey had lost 71% calcium and 79% iron. Streaky bacon had lost 87% calcium and 78% iron.

- The iron content of milk had dropped by 62%, magnesium 21%, and its calcium content was also down.

- Cheddar cheese provided 9% less calcium, 38% less magnesium and 47% less iron. Parmesan had lost 70% of its magnesium and all its iron had gone.

Selenium, potassium, phosphorus, iodine, molybdenum, chromium, manganese – over 20 trace minerals have been analysed and the quantity of all of them has been diminishing in a wide variety of fruit and vegetables. The loss of these elements in our food has contributed to an increase in allergies. "Minerals have been easy to detect and measure since the 19th century," said Dr Tim Lobstein, the Food Commission's co-director. "Today's agriculture does not allow the soil to enrich itself but depends on chemical fertilisers that don't replace the wide variety of nutrients that plants and humans need."

With increasing knowledge, one would expect agricultural science to have found ways to correct this trend and ensure that the food we eat contains the trace nutrients that our bodies need. The reverse is happening. The primary objective of agricultural science has been to increase profits for the food industry. Soil throughout the world is losing its fertility.

Organic farming
respecting nature's way

"If mankind cannot devise and enforce ways of dealing with the earth that will preserve the source of life, we must look forward to a time – remote it may be but clearly discernible – when our kind, having wasted its great inheritance, will fade from the earth because of the ruin it has accomplished." Professor N.S. Shaler, *Outlines of the Earth's History* (1898)

EVE BALFOUR, ONE of the founders of the environmental organisation the Soil Association, saw land as a fountain of energy flowing through a circuit of soils, plants and animals. She defined food as living channels that conduct energy upwards, while death and decay return it to the soil. In 1946 she warned that chemicals such as DDT would enter, and work their way up, the food chain. This hazard took 40 years to enter the consciousness of administrators.

Twenty years later the scientist Rachel Carson wrote *Silent Spring*, a book that helped to start the ecology movement. It warned of a countryside depopulated, devoid of wildlife and devastated by chemicals. And yet, since then, our attack on nature has intensified to all-out warfare, with tractors compacting the soil, herbicides destroying the humus, and pesticides killing micro-organisms, insects and natural predators. During the 20th century the US lost half its topsoil. It can take at least 500 years to develop an inch of topsoil, so the damage is immense. If agricultural scientists claim credit for improving the yield of specialised crops, then they must also admit responsibility for the tragic results of their myopic interventions. At last, at the opening of a new century, the general public is beginning to realise that our inheritance hangs in the balance and it is starting to demand organically produced food.

When a farmer changes from chemical to organic farming, the productivity of his farm immediately drops. This is because chemicals have degraded the soil and killed off predators. It takes several years to restore the land to full productivity. However, comparative studies for corn, wheat, soybeans and tomatoes have found that fully restored organic fields average between 94% and 100% of the yields of nearby

Sixty per cent of UK aquifers could fail EU quality standards for water quality due to nitrates from industrial farming.

conventional crops. But these comparisons ignore scale. The smaller the farm, the greater the yield. A small organic farm with mixed crops, intercropping and animals can have a considerably higher yield per hectare than large conventional mono-crop farms. This is the farming that can do most to feed the world and can prevent farmers in poor countries being

Small plots of farmland in Cuba

forced off the land into city slums where they cannot grow food for their own needs and have little chance of employment.

Eve Balfour linked the land with our mental, social and spiritual experience. She insisted that contact between town and country should be encouraged, and that farming should be an integral aspect of education. It will be many years before this vision of truly organic sustenance can become a reality. It bears very little resemblance to 'supermarket organics' that use aeroplanes and lorries to move produce around the world.

In the past decade, sales of organic produce have grown faster than any other sector in British and US agriculture. Organic farming is already 95% as productive as conventional farming in spite of the research and subsidies doled out to agro-industry. So why is organic produce more expensive? Because the market is distorted.

The market, which should reward producers according to the value of their product, does not apply in cases where massively funded agribusiness lobbies target the government and its agencies. Society, not the farming industry, carries the costs of pesticide contamination, polluted water and other health and environmental impacts associated with industrial farming. The industrial food system, moving its products all over the country, is dependent on our roads, ports and airports but does not pay anything towards their cost. Oil-based farming is depleting the world's fuel supplies and damaging the atmosphere, but it is not penalised. Organic food represents the true cost of food in an undistorted economy. If these hidden costs were apportioned, food from industrial farms would be considerably more expensive than organic food.

In Britain, feeding chopped-up bits of cows to cows – an example of sloppy industrial farming practice – resulted in mad cow disease and the horrors of CJD, the human equivalent. Cows were culled, imports increased and no one would buy our beef. This need not have happened. Organic farmers had not been allowed to feed animal protein to ruminants since 1983 (three years before the first case) and there have been no recorded cases of BSE in any animal born and reared organically. Industrial farming was also responsible for outbreaks of swine fever and the spread of bird flu.

Organic farming bans irradiation and oestrogen-mimicking, gender-bender pesticides (POPs and EDCs). In contrast, non-organic food can contain more than 500 chemicals.

Cuba, through necessity, provides some interesting lessons for the rest of us. The trade embargo and the collapse of the Soviet Union meant that, since the 1990s, it has not been able to import fertilisers, pesticides or fuel for tractors. Most of the food in Cuba is grown in huertas – private urban plots of less than an eighth of a hectare – and sold from stalls outside the growers' homes, at street corners and under the covered walkways of Havana's elegant, crumbling colonial buildings. Inside the city, chemical fertilisers and pesticides are forbidden and compost is made from household waste.

The government took up the challenge of a local, science-based, low input, sustainable agriculture. Unused city land was given to anyone who wanted to cultivate it. Forty per cent of state farms became co-operatives while the rest were divided into small units. Thousands of jobs were created – 200,000 in 2001 alone. "The secret is in the high productivity of small urban units," said Nelso Compagnioni of the Institute for Tropical Agriculture. "Every dollar of produce on a small plot costs 25 cents to produce; as soon as you increase the area you get higher costs. And we have no need for transport; customers collect their food on the way home from work."

What will happen when sanctions are lifted? "There will be tough negotiations," said Mavis Alvares, director of the Association of Small Farmers. "It simply isn't the policy of the government to have cheap imported food. We have put an immense educational effort into sustainability."

Does Cuba suffer from being unable to benefit from the productivity that comes with scale? To answer this we have to consider the two ways of measuring productivity. First: the amount one person can produce. Second: the amount one hectare can produce. Big business, using the first measure, requires people to be replaced

by chemicals and machines regardless of the amount of land used or food wasted. Flat-earth economists call this high productivity.

But what matters more is the second measure: productivity per hectare. The most productive land is the vegetable plot of an enthusiast who feeds her family and gives or sells produce to neighbours. In countries where the local market is functioning properly, small farmers take care over all aspects of their mixed production. By contrast, the large-scale cultivation of cash crops is very unproductive, as mixed cultivation is not possible and anything that is not absolutely uniform must be discarded. Productivity per hectare therefore reduces as size increases.

In 2006, the UK government rejected advice from the Royal Commission on Environmental Pollution for protecting the public against the dangers of pesticide spray. It did not even introduce a buffer zone alongside residential property, schools, hospitals and retirement homes. "If the government won't look after people's health by acting on the best scientific advice," said Lord Melchett, "the answer has to be a large-scale move to organic farming and the end of all pesticide sprays in the British countryside."
BBC Science News, February 2006

Biomimicry
science's new frontier

THERE IS A SPIDER, the Nephila clavipes, that makes six different kinds of silk. Its web can stretch by 40% when hit by a fast-flying moth and then return to its original size unaffected. The US army is researching spiders because their web is stronger and has better energy-absorbing elasticity than Kevlar, a fibre so tough that it can stop bullets. Kevlar is made by pouring petroleum-derived molecules into a pressurised vat of concentrated sulphuric acid to be boiled at many hundred degrees Celsius and then subjected to high pressures. **To make its silk, a spider just needs to eat a fly or two.**

A hummingbird can fly forwards, backwards, up, down or sideways with equal ease. It can fly across the Gulf of Mexico on a fraction of a gram of fuel and, when picking up its fuel, fertilise the flower to provide more fuel in future. Compare the resources consumed and the damage done in building and flying a Chinook. We have a lot to learn.

Architects have long been fascinated by the ability of termites to build structures that maintain a constant temperature in their interior chambers. Computer scientists think that studying ant behaviour might help them create parallel, rather than linear, computers. And if we want a lot of hydrogen, nature produces it all the time with the help of a particular enzyme. **Can we mimic nature?**

Material scientists boast about achieving incredibly high pressure to make very hard ceramics and producing high temperatures to forge special steels and elaborate chemical processes. But they can't beat an oyster for sheer strength, nor can they match a mollusc for effective underwater glue. Scientists use outmoded Stone Age technology – heat, beat and treat. Some agricultural researchers are noticing that nature does not use the plough. Plants grow naturally as mixed communities, with seldom fewer than four species together. Nature favours perennials. Even organic farming still has much to learn from nature.

And then there's energy. Almost all our energy comes from the sun – via plants. Coal, oil and gas are embodied energy from the sun, captured millions of years ago. Duckweed captures solar energy with 95% efficiency, many times better than manufactured photovoltaic cells. A leaf takes in water and carbon dioxide; the carbon forms sugars, which store the sun's energy, and gives off oxygen. But how? Scientists say it is 'membrane potential', where a positive electron is moved to one side of a membrane and a negative electron to the other. If we could mimic that, and if the process needed simply water and daylight and produced as little waste as duckweed, we would have a truly sustainable energy source. **The scientific race is on.**

Genetic knowledge is the biggest recent leap forward, but experience suggests that immensely powerful new technologies should be approached with caution. We should be warned by fossil fuels, which are so incredibly versatile that they are largely responsible for our present lifestyle. They are also largely responsible for overpopulation, land degradation, changing climate, rising sea levels and resource wars.

We are on a unique planet on which life has evolved in a unique way and we must live within the planet's unique patterns. In three billion years, all sorts of diverse properties have been combined, like crystals and membranes in a spider's web. But not everything. Boundaries have been erected, and it is these boundaries that we excitedly destroy when we take genetic inheritance into our own hands. Novel genes could well cause havoc as they move vertically and horizontally through future generations of bacteria, plants, animals and us. **Tampering with evolution requires extreme caution.**

Biomimicry introduces an era that is based not on what we can extract from nature, but on what we can learn from her. "Doing it nature's way," says Janine Benyus, author of *Biomimicry*, "has the potential to change the way we educate our children, grow food, make materials, harness energy, heal ourselves, store information and conduct business."

NPK

the agrichemical revolution

"Only by faithfully returning to the soil everything that has come from it, can fertility be made permanent and the earth be made to yield a genuine increase."

Lord Northbourne, *Look to The Land* (1930)

BEFORE NPK (nitrogen, phosphate, potassium) world agriculture supported one and a half billion people. After NPK, when its full impact is felt, the world may be able to feed even fewer.

N. Nitrogen

Over three quarters of the earth's atmosphere is nitrogen. It is contained in all plant and animal tissue. The route that it takes through the ecosystem is fascinating: bacteria on leguminous plants extract it from the air and make nodules on their roots; these transfer it to the soil from where it is taken up by other plants. Some of the plants rot back into the ground, leaving the nitrogen for others to use. Animals eat the plants and return the nitrogen to the soil in their dung. By eating plants and herbivorous animals, humans absorb nitrogen into the body and release it in urine. This cycle has formed the basis of agriculture for millennia.

1909 was the turning point. It was the year in which ammonia (NH_3) was first made from natural gas using the Haber–Bosch process. This provided vast quantities of nitrogen fertiliser, which made modern agriculture possible. The plentiful new supply of fertiliser allowed the development of hybrid plants (which also require a lot of water). The resulting Green (Agrichemical) Revolution confounded Malthus's prediction that the population would increase faster than the supply of food. The reverse happened: the expectation of plentiful food encouraged people to have more babies.

But various problems arose. Less than half the applied nitrogen is taken up by plants; the rest seeps into groundwater. Excess nitrates in drinking water can interfere with the oxygen-carrying capacity of a child's blood, causing shortness of breath, blueish skin and even death. Fifty-five per cent of Britain is now designated as 'nitrate vulnerable zones'. The nitrogen takes a long time to move through the ground into aquifers, so we are not certain where or when the extraction of groundwater for drinking purposes may have to be abandoned.

"Diffuse nitrate pollution puts a big question mark over the future compatibility of UK food production and public water supplies," said Professor Bradley of the environmental agency ADAS in 2006. "What's more, this problem isn't limited to the UK but applies across much of Europe. The only way to safeguard the future of our water resource is to convert much of our existing arable land into unfertilised, restorative grassland or forest." We can have industrially farmed food or drinking water. Not both.

Cropland without humus and manure relies on imported nitrogen. It deteriorates over time and, deprived of the roots of weeds that bind it together, blows away easily in the wind.

Most nitrogen fertiliser is made using natural gas. Already the extraction of natural gas is past its peak in the US, resulting in less fertiliser being manufactured. There is still a lot of natural gas in the rest of the world but it is difficult to transport, it is in high demand as oil supplies deplete, and its price is rising.

Nitrogen fertilisers will have to be abandoned in due course and farming will have to return to crop rotation in order to 'fix' nitrogen from the air. The benefits of the Green Revolution will be lost, and it will take a long time for the soil to regain its natural fertility.

P. Phosphorus

Photosynthesis, by which food is created, requires phosphorus. Plants cannot grow without it. Adenosine triphosphate is a nucleotide phosphorus molecule found in every single cell in your body and it drives the thousands of biological processes needed to sustain life, growth, muscle-contraction, movement and reproduction. Phosphorus is not just another nutrient. It is an essential element of the food that we eat. It has no gaseous phase so it cannot be captured from the air, and there is a limited amount of it present in the soil. If soil loses its phosphorus content it loses its fertility.

Farmers have always known that dung from their cattle needs to be returned to the soil in a cycle of nutrients. Before artificial fertilisers were introduced, human excrement was returned to the earth too.

Phosphorus travels from the ground into crops, from crops into people and from people into pipes that convey it to sewage works. Only a small proportion of the phosphorus is captured to return to the land. The modern sanitation

Eighty-five per cent of the
€32.5 billion European
agricultural grants go to
giant agribusinesses that are
totally dependent on NPK.

Jack Thurston, www.Farmsubsidy.org,
March 2007

system is a one-way conveyor belt for transporting the fertility of the soil out to sea, where it is lost forever.

Bird droppings are rich in phosphorus. In France, one of the reasons for building pigeonniers all over the country was to produce natural fertiliser. As farming intensified and cities grew, the pigeons failed to provide enough, so the hunt for such fertiliser extended abroad. Pacific islands were found covered in up to seven-metre deep layers of guano – droppings of fish-eating sea birds – that are even richer in phosphorus than pigeon faeces. Competition for mining the guano became so intense that Peru went to war over it, first with Chile in 1852 and then with Spain in 1865. Later, the US granted its citizens the right to claim ownership of islands that could supply the stuff. Some of these islands, like Narau, became fabulously wealthy in the 20th century until the guano ran out. Most are now a wreck of spoil heaps.

Rock phosphate from Florida, Brazil and Morocco then became the main source of phosphorus. But rock phosphate, like all historic deposits, is a limited resource. The mining industry likes to say there is so much in the

ground that it will last for 300 years and there is nothing to worry about. But its availability follows the same bell-shaped curve as oil and uranium: the easy bits are taken first, followed by lower grade ores that require more energy to extract. If the amount of energy required rises at 5% a year and if the cost of energy also rises at 5% a year, rock phosphate will double in price every seven years and phosphate fertiliser will soon become too expensive. Agriculture will, once again, depend on the nutrient cycle by which phosphorus is returned to the soil, though the soil will take many years to become as fertile as it once was.

Is water-based sewerage the answer for world health? Our present practice of flushing away urine, faeces and rainwater and losing most of their nutrients out to sea will have to stop.

The Swedish scientist Folke Günther says that the retention of phosphorus is not just an agricultural issue: it will have profound effects on the planning of settlements, perhaps limiting their size. It will require the integration of farming land into cities. And it will require the re-thinking and re-engineering of all our sewage systems, not just replacing crumbling Victorian sewers with modern concrete ones. Some communities in Sweden already have toilets that separate faeces from urine at source, since urine carries most of the nutrients. They also keep rainwater separate so that fresh water is retained and not lost out to sea as well.

A research institute at Wardha, near Gandhi's ashram in central India, is working on sewage systems for rural villages. The director, Dr Samer Kurvey, described a pilot project where a village was provided with a complete water-flushed system leading to a septic tank. When he returned a year after the installation, he found that it was not used. The villagers resented the amount of water it needed when they had hardly enough for their crops. He also came to the conclusion that the porcelain fittings cost far too much for general application in villages.

The institute today has an intriguing display park, which might be mistaken for a fairground from a distance. The fittings on show can be made using clay and other local materials at almost no cost. The faeces are guided into two dry pits, alternately, where they rest for a year before being distributed onto fields. The urine, from a separate aperture, flows into another pit where the smell is removed organically. It is then diluted and bottled for sale as fertiliser. Dr Kurvey claims that if this system were introduced universally India could do without chemical fertilisers altogether.

Both excess nitrogen and phosphorus from industrial farming are washed into watercourses, rivers and estuaries where they cause algae blooms that use up all the oxygen in the water, suffocating the fish. Dead zones are found at the mouths of almost every major river.

K. Potassium
Potassium is the third element essential for animals and plants. There is no shortage, but it is not much use without the other two.

Pelicans on guano-covered rocks on the Ballestas Islands, Peru

Food security

the high cost of cheap food

"Modern agriculture is intrinsically destructive of the environment ... The widespread application of conventional agricultural technologies such as herbicides, pesticides, fertilisers and tillage has resulted in severe environmental damage in many parts of the world."

The Royal Society and the US National Academy of Sciences, *Transgenic Plants and World Agriculture* (2000)

ONE DAY THE prime minister will wake up to news that the supermarket shelves are empty. When hungry crowds besiege the House of Commons who should take the blame?

'Stark raving mad' is the best way to describe how food travels from field to plate in the UK. Count the lorries you pass on the motorway and you will find that two out of five are part of the food distribution system. A cabbage from Cornwall is taken to a processing plant in the Midlands then transported back to Cornwall for sale. Even organic milk from a cow in mid-Wales may well travel to Cardiff, then to London, then back to Cardiff, then to a supermarket in Bristol. Even more ludicrous are the apples and onions flown from New Zealand when both are in season in Britain. The government spends £6 billion a year on roads as a part of its subsidy for this insane merry-go-round.

Supermarkets, some keeping 40,000 or more products on their shelves, no longer have any storage space. Just-in-time deliveries are made twice a day from vast regional or national distribution centres. These work through the night with endless production lines responding to hi-tech information systems that connect checkout tills, sorters, growers, accountants, gang-masters, transporters and many others who are essential to the system. Some of the distribution centres feed 700 lorries a day, each tracked on GPS systems, from all over Europe as well as the UK. As an exercise in precision and complexity it is unrivalled.

All sections of this vast operation – the computers, information transfer, the labelling systems, the work gangs, the machinery – are dependent on each other, and a breakdown of any part could bring the whole to a grinding halt. In 2000, lorry drivers objected to the government's fuel escalator tax, which aimed to increase slowly the cost of petrol and diesel. As reports came in of supermarket shelves stripped bare the government panicked and abandoned the tax. The Federation of Bakers commented, "We came within hours of the country not having a loaf to eat." With a fuel crisis or a carefully targeted terrorist incident the whole country could be without food within a day.

Finding or growing food has been the primary occupation of communities throughout history. More than half the population in many poor countries still feed themselves off the land; they have only a tenuous connection to the market economy through selling their surplus.

Agriculture is of little importance to economists because it contributes only 2% to the national economy. However, a third of the UK population is involved in getting food from the ground to the dining table. Few of them see the food growing or even know where the food comes from because they are working in packing sheds, or driving lorries, managing spreadsheets, processing accounts, tying up contracts, arguing in court, moving tins around or sitting at checkout tills. The food industry, as opposed to agriculture, is one of the most profitable sectors of our economy.

The purpose of the food industry is not to provide a secure source of food for people – or a steady income for small farmers – but to make money for shareholders. At the beginning of the last century, most food was grown and distributed locally. By the year 2000, just 20 multinational corporations controlled a food trade that had become international.

Transporting food from country to country fills the air with greenhouse gases. The power of food corporations is putting farmers in crisis throughout the world and small farmers are committing suicide in China, India, the US and Europe. Food corporations are not concerned about nutrition. They have been prepared to let children suffer a plague of obesity until the public become so outraged that the corporations' profits are endangered. Their only concern is to obtain food at the lowest possible price, handle it, and sell it at the highest possible price. Flat-earth economists refer to this as 'value added', being unable to distinguish between price and value.

Supermarkets, with their unchallenged buying power, have been able to drive down farm-gate prices and dictate policy to farmers. You can blame them for what happens, or you can blame the government's insistence that competition on price should regulate all aspects of our society.

Industrial farming requires animals to be treated as machines for manufacturing food. The systematic cruelty that this involves – in a supposedly civilised country – is hard to believe.

Fifty years ago farmers in Britain received over half the money that shoppers spent on food. Now they receive less than a tenth.

Chickens are kept in cages the size of an A4 sheet of paper. Their legs are too weak to support their overweight bodies, they are defecated on by the chickens above, they never see daylight, and then they are shackled upside down to a conveyor belt to be slaughtered. Scientists could hardly design better factories for incubating viruses like salmonella, E. coli, Newcastle disease, bird flu and MRSA bacteria.

Animals kept in these unnatural conditions are unhealthy – to put it mildly. Most so-called free-range chickens are treated little better; only organically-raised poultry are systematically kept in conditions humane enough for them to develop resistance to disease. Read Felicity Lawrence's *Not on the Label* for the full horror. People would never buy non-organic chickens from supermarkets if they knew the facts about poultry factories.

Bird flu hit Britain in 2007. A year earlier, Genetic Research Action International had

studied the origin of the virus and concluded that: "The deadly H5N1 strain of bird flu is essentially a problem of industrial poultry practices. Its epicentre is the factory farms of China and southeast Asia and its main vector is the transnational poultry industry, which sends the products and wastes of its farms around the world." Poultry factories around Quinghai Lake discharge waste into the water and feed

chicken faeces to fish farms. Factory farms in Turkey import new birds from the Far East and truck old chickens to local markets. *The Lancet*, the world's leading independent peer-reviewed medical journal, said, "The geographical spread of the disease does not correlate with migratory routes and seasons. The pattern of outbreaks follows major road and rail routes, not flyways." In other words, live poultry, chicks, fertilised eggs, bird feed and other poultry products spread the virus.

In the light of the previous BSE crisis, it is scarcely believable that chicken feed is still permitted to include poultry litter (bird faeces), feathers and waste meat. Russian scientists said that such feeds were the prime suspect for an outbreak of H5N1 at a factory farm in Kurgan where 450,000 birds had to be killed.

When global warming threatened the vastly profitable oil industry it mounted a well-funded campaign to deny that carbon emissions were involved. Expect the same from the multi-billion dollar poultry industry.

Its first tactic was to say that migrating wild birds carried the virus, and therefore small farms with free-range birds were the most likely to pick it up. Their media promotions showed markets in poor countries teeming with people handling chickens from their back yards. The message was clear: ignore the scientists, chickens are best kept indoors and sealed from any contact with other birds or people.

Strange that the first poultry to pick up the virus in Britain were on a well-managed farm with 160,000 birds kept in sheds sealed from the outside and with the highest bio-safety standards in the country. It was obvious from the outset, to anyone not subject to the industry lobby, that the trade in factory-reared poultry between East Asia, Russia, Turkey, Europe and Latin America could spread viruses around the globe in a matter of days. Poultry factories are incubators for pandemics.

MRSA, the 'superbug' with resistance to antibiotics, has become endemic in UK hospitals. Affecting fewer than 20 people in 1993, it killed over 1,600 in 2005; the number of deaths is still rising. Bacteria resistant to Staphylococcus aureus (SA) are now being found in people outside hospitals and even in their pets. When the bugs reach farm animals they will find ideal conditions to multiply. An antibiotic drug kills susceptible bacteria but removes competition from any bug resistant to it, so the continued use of certain antibiotics for animals that are kept in unhealthy, crowded conditions will be the best way to spread MRSA. Will there then be a mass slaughter of infected animals? And will they pass the superbug back to humans?

Factory farming of animals has given us warnings with mad cow disease, swine fever and bird flu. Those were serious, but only warnings. Our pursuit of cheap food at any cost may eventually deprive us of meat altogether.

In May 1974, Ulster had its fuel supply cut off. Richard St George, from the Schumacher Society, recalled how this event produced a near-collapse of basic food supplies. "The Ulster Workers Council objected to the Sunningdale Agreement for power sharing between the Catholics and Protestants so they declared a strike. It represented a small fraction of the population and had little public support."

However, on the first day it managed to close the Belfast oil refinery. The oil-fired power station had some reserves but shut down on the fourth day. The authorities immediately ordered all frozen food to be destroyed as it was now a health hazard. The sale of milk was then banned because, by law, it has to be pasteurised. Farmers milked their cows by hand and poured the milk into the river. There was fuel in the filling stations but no hand pumps had power. Pressure in the gas mains dropped dangerously, so the gas supply was shut down. Without gas, the bread ovens could not be heated, so there was no bread. About 50,000 battery hens a day died from hypothermia when the heating went off: they had lost too many feathers from being kept in cages to keep themselves warm.

Part of Belfast is below sea level and as the sewage could not be pumped out, it flooded and contaminated the water supply. The distribution of emergency water supplies was hampered by lack of fuel. The rural telephone service had one week's battery backup, so it started to collapse in the second week. Towards the end of that week there were reports of raiding parties slaughtering livestock, dragging them into town and cooking them on fires of broken furniture.

The government capitulated. Our society is a miracle of electronically controlled efficiency – until it goes wrong.

The absurd UK food swap

• pork:	exports	195,000 tonnes
	imports	240,000 tonnes
• lamb:	exports	102,000 tonnes
	imports	125,000 tonnes
• butter:	exports	49,000 tonnes
	imports	47,000 tonnes
• fresh milk:	exports	119,000 tonnes
	imports	114,000 tonnes
• poultry:	exports	170,000 tonnes
	imports	363,000 tonnes
• live pigs:	exports	110,000 pigs
	imports	200,000 pigs

The absurd food swap apparently makes sense to flat-earth economists but it spreads disease, provides a route for pandemics, wastes money and contributes to global warming through all the fuel used for transport.

Caroline Lucas MEP, *Relocalising Europe's Food Supply* (2001)

Making new plants
either GM or organic, not both

"Current gene-containment strategies cannot work reliably in the field."

Editorial, *Nature Biotechnology*, vol.20 no.6 (2002)

THE BIOTECH INDUSTRY would like us to believe that genetic engineering (GE, GM, GMO) is just a development of plant-breeding techniques practised since the dawn of civilisation. No honest scientist would be prepared to make this claim.

Conventional breeding transfers genetic information between related organisms – members of the same species or, more rarely, of closely related genera. Genetic engineering, however, overcomes barriers that have existed for three billion years of evolution and transfers genes between unrelated species, genera and plant or animal kingdoms. Excited biotechnologists have produced a green rabbit, a pig that glows in the dark, a ready-to-roast chicken with no feathers, a mouse with a human ear, and a potato with the gene that stops a fish freezing. These scientists are lords of creation.

Genes are units of heredity – they reproduce themselves from one generation to the next. They are fragments of the DNA sequence that have cohesive ends, enabling them to be extracted and re-combined. Hence, genetic experimentation is often referred to as recombinant DNA technology.

Forty years ago, molecular scientists dreamed up the simplistic 'central dogma' that genes fully account for inherited traits. This gave rise

to a multi-billion dollar industry that has made a massive assault on US agriculture. Following this, the Human Genome Project, which found the DNA sequences of genes in all 23 pairs of chromosomes that exist in every human cell, was heralded as 'the ultimate description of life.'

In fact, however, the Human Genome Project destroyed the scientific basis of genetic engineering. It found that there were far too few genes to account for the complexity of our inherited traits: humans possess even fewer than a blade of grass. An industry that claims to lift agriculture and medicine onto new levels of scientific precision is actually based on a science and a technology in their infancy.

Hype reached the highest political level, and the height of absurdity, when US President Clinton described the genome as "the language in which God created life." Few noticed the sacrilege of suggesting that God could only speak one language.

Genetic engineering is an inexact process. The gene engineer aims at certain results but the outcome relies on trial and error. Very occasionally the transferred gene has the desired effect, though its position in the genome of the new plant may change during the plant's life or in future generations. Several processes are involved in the transfer:

Soybean crop ready for harvest in the Mississippi Delta

- A powerful vector must be used, usually Agrobacterium tumefaciens, a bacterium that causes tumours in plants by inserting DNA from its own genetic code. Its cancerous action is the reason for its effectiveness.

- A promoter is necessary for overcoming the plant's natural resistance to infection. Usually the Cauliflower Mosaic Virus (CaMV 35S) is used, a virus that affects bacteria, algae, plants, human cells, and is known to cause damage to the pancreas, liver and brain of an animal. The promoter 'turns on' the transferred gene (the technical term is hyperexpression) but often 'turns on' other genes as well. CaMV's dangers have at last been admitted by the biotech industry and it has been quietly withdrawn. But will the replacement be any safer?

- A marker gene is added because genetic modification is a haphazard process and the scientist needs to know where the gene has arrived in the host genome. Until recently antibiotic-resistant marker genes were usually used. It has now been found that these genes can be taken up by bacteria in the human gut and reduce the effectiveness of antibiotic medication. The British Medical Association says that the use of such genes is "completely unacceptable".

- Random extra genes get transferred. These are not planned, but strands of unexpected DNA have been found, for example, in Monsanto soybeans. This DNA may be unstable and move around the genome.

These are some of the ways in which genetic engineering alters plants. Can it really be described as similar to conventional breeding techniques? The biotech industry, with strange logic, claims that genetic engineering is no different from normal plant breeding, while also claiming that it is a radically new science.

Biotech companies insert toxins into every cell of certain food plants as insecticides. The toxins are also released into the ground where they kill susceptible insect larvae and degrade the soil. Low-level toxins in the cellular make-up of crops provide ideal conditions for developing resistance in weeds, insects and bacteria. As a result, dangerous compounds such as paraquat and atrazine have to be re-introduced to outsmart the pests, though they in turn will become ineffective.

The industry claims that GM crops reduce the use of chemicals. This is true for a time. But after three or four years, because bacteria develop resistance, the use of herbicides and pesticides on most GM crops increases. Since they kill weeds but not the crop, the chemicals can be applied just before harvest, increasing the residue left on food. Meanwhile, the top US scientific body, the National Academy of Sciences, warned in April 2002 that genetically engineered plants introduce allergens into pollen, which then spread around the environment. Allergies have increased dramatically in recent decades among the US population.

The regulation of genetically modified food for human consumption can fail: StarLink maize was approved only for cattle because it contained an allergenic protein, but it contaminated half the US maize supply and entered the food chain in seven countries.

GM foods have been consumed in the US for seven years, supposedly without harm. The industry claims this proves that they are safe. But during this period food-derived illnesses have doubled. In California, the number of children with autism has doubled in the last four years. Allergies have greatly increased. But no one knows if these effects are consequence or coincidence because no monitoring of the long-term clinical or biochemical effects of GM has been carried out, either in the US or in Britain.

Now for the really scary stuff: horizontal gene transfer. Genes are part of the magic that shapes future generations. They go vertically from plant to seed, parent to baby. But genetically modified genes also move horizontally from plants to bacteria. They can also move from food to the bacteria in our gut, get into the bloodstream and breach the lining of the womb.

We are officially warned that baby food should not contain GM organisms. Expectant mothers should therefore avoid any GM elements in their food. Might they not be dangerous for us all?

Because of the concern over GM crops, the UK government did the right thing and held a public consultation in 2003. It said that it would respect the public's view. The result was absolutely clear. Only 2% said they would be happy to eat GM food. Since then, the desire for organic produce has escalated at 30% a year while there remains zero demand for genetically modified food.

Since the consultation, however, Britain has objected to all the European Parliament's GM bans, the prime minister has consistently promoted GM, and the government has provided grants for GM research (worth more than £12 billion under New Labour). A previous environment minister, Eliott Morley, led a

campaign in Europe to allow the commercial growing of GM crops, and the EU trade commissioner, Peter Mandelson, is allowing GM varieties to be nodded through the European Commission without reference to members of the European Parliament.

Our government, in pursuit of global competition, appears to have contempt for the views of its citizens.

In 2006, the UK government admitted that there can be no safe buffer distance between GM and non-GM crops. Once GM crops are introduced, genetic contamination can spread from one area to another until all crops are in danger of contamination with novel genes. The government also said that food can be called organic even if one in a hundred mouthfuls contains genetically modified organisms. If this continues, true organic food will be a thing of the past and pregnant women will be unable to protect their foetuses.

A study by Cornell University of 480 Chinese farms found that gains from (GM) Bt cotton peaked after three years. Later the farmers were spraying their crops 20 times each growing season.

Having failed to convince the British public through argument, the biotech industry is now trying moral blackmail. Would you deny the benefits of GM crops, they ask, to poor countries? Golden Rice is the example quoted most often: it is genetically modified to provide vitamin-A and will supposedly save millions of people from blindness.

In south India much of the population, particularly children, suffer from night blindness caused by vitamin-A deficiency. SCAD, a non-governmental organisation in Tirunelveli, found that vitamin-A pills helped the sufferers, but they were expensive and impractical to administer. So, instead, SCAD incorporated cowpea, a weed rich in vitamin-A, into biscuits. Two biscuits a day, costing virtually nothing, totally eliminated night blindness in all their 400 villages.

Farmers in SCAD's villages had been asked to consider growing Golden Rice to increase their vitamin-A intake, but they rejected it because it would have reduced the wide variety of seed that they used. This would have increased the risk of famine in the context of changing climate conditions and of plant diseases, which spread rapidly in a monoculture. A commercial seed would also have put villagers into debt. At present, most of their crop is grown from seed saved from the previous harvest.

Hormones

Growth promoters are widely used for beef in Brazil and Argentina, and two thirds of cattle raised in the US are treated with these hormones. They are of great value to farmers as the effect is to speed the animals' development and maturity.

Unfortunately they have the same effect on people. The onset of puberty in young girls in the US, where hormone-treated beef is regularly eaten, has been lowered significantly. Tiny levels of hormones in food, previously believed safe, can in fact increase the incidence of genital abnormalities in baby boys as well as heighten the risk of breast, testicular, prostate and other cancers in later life.

The rate of breast cancer in the US is 97 per 100,000 against 67 in Europe, which, again, is likely to be due to the high consumption of hormone-treated beef in that country. Similarly, figures for prostate cancer in men are 96 per 100,000 in the US compared with 37 in Europe.

The EU currently bans the use of growth or sex hormones and bans the import of treated beef. The UK government is trying to have the ban lifted. No beef imported to the UK in the 18 months up to July 2006 was properly tested, and we have never tested beef for 17b oestradiol, the hormone-derived drug on which the greatest concern now centres.

> *A French researcher placed a single weed called 'fat hen', which had picked up atrazine-resistance, into a genetically modified maize field where atrazine was being sprayed for weed-control. It wasn't killed by the atrazine and after four years it had multiplied to over 100,000 plants.*
>
> *Crop Protection Monthly, issue 188, July 2005*

An honest scientist
and his fate

"The morphology and biochemical structures of rats are very similar to those of humans, and this makes the results we obtained very disturbing." Doctor Irina Ermakova, Russian Academy of Sciences, 2007

IN OCTOBER 2006 Russian scientists reported that over half the offspring of rats fed on genetically modified soya died within three weeks of birth. The rest had half the normal bodyweight. An Italian researcher then found changes in the liver and pancreas of mice fed on GM soya. In Australia, GM peas caused such serious inflammation of lung tissue in mice that the research had to be stopped. Further results from Russia in April 2007 showed abnormalities in baby mice. Evidence mounts.

In his book, *Don't Worry, It's Safe to Eat*, Andrew Rowell claims that, eight years ago, similar findings were suppressed when the UK government thought they would harm the biotech industry. Since then, no research institute has dared repeat the tests for fear of losing government grants. The story could be out of a James Bond film. According to four witnesses at the Rowett Institute in Aberdeen, telephone calls from Monsanto to Bill Clinton, from Clinton to Tony Blair, then from Blair to the Institute, stopped a key project. Is this just a conspiracy theory? Maybe, but then, what else would explain subsequent events outlined below?

Dr Arpad Pusztai is one of the world's leading experts on plant lectins with 35 years of laboratory experience. In a project for studying the effects of GM food (won in competition

against 28 other teams) he found that the small intestine, pancreas and brain of rats fed on a genetically modified diet developed differently from those of the control group. Their immune system was also affected. "I believe that this technology [genetic modification] can be made to work for us," he said in a short interview on television, but "it is unfair to use our fellow citizens as guinea pigs. We have to find guinea

pigs in the laboratory." The head of the Rowett Institute commented on how well Arpad had answered the interviewer's questions. He added, "A range of carefully controlled studies underlie the basis of Dr Pusztai's concerns."

The next day Pusztai was told to hand over his data from the project. All GM research was stopped, the team was dispersed and he was threatened with legal action if he spoke to the press. He was banned from his laboratory and his phone calls and emails were diverted. Later, his collaborator and his biochemist wife were given early retirement.

The promise of lucrative returns can even influence a scientist's advice.

The Royal Society, Britain's leading scientific body, was consulted by the government over Pusztai's findings and rushed out a condemnation of his work without obtaining his final report. The government's chief scientific officer said that Pusztai had caused undue public alarm and damaged the biotech industry. Then his private files were stolen from both his home and the Institute (what burglar would be interested in these?). His work was peer-reviewed six times before being published in *The Lancet* (whose editor was then threatened with loss of pension), despite being well received at a scientific conference and backed by 30 international scientists.

When research is contested, the scientific method is to reproduce it to see where the fault lies. This was not done – except, it is thought, by Monsanto, who refused to release

its findings. Eventually, in 2003, the European Union asked Monsanto to do research into GM maize (MON-863). The results were kept secret for two years, and then only a summary was released, which stated that the rats had developed abnormalities to internal organs and blood, affecting the immune system. Assessments of this research by European scientists known to be critical were kept quiet. In the end, Professor Serlin and Dr Pusztai were allowed to see the report but they had to sign a declaration of confidentiality. It was leaked that they criticised the methodology and were alarmed at the dangers to health should this maize enter the food chain.

A vote was held and 14 of the EU environment ministers were against releasing the maize and only seven (including the UK) in favour. Disregarding democratic processes, the European Commission allowed the maize to be grown for animal feed in Europe. Dr Brian John of GM Free Cymru said, "Our attempts to open the MON-863 secret dossier to public scrutiny show that there is corruption right at the heart of the GM approvals process."

A brief and balanced comment by a scientist like Pusztai destroys his career. Similar findings by Monsanto have the whole apparatus of government defending the corporation. What is the message? First, that government places the interests of big business above the interests of its citizens – but this is well known. Second, that biotech members of the most highly respected scientific body in the UK, the Royal Society, were prepared to dispense with scientific integrity in the interests of a commercial agenda. Scientists are very motivated individuals and the general public depends on them, so the second message is the saddest.

POPs and EDCs
synthetic time bombs

"Man talks of a battle with nature, forgetting that if he won the battle he would be on the losing side." E.F. Schumacher, *Small is Beautiful* (1973)

IN JANUARY 1999, nine litres of transformer oil in Belgium were accidentally mixed with fats destined for animal feed. The oil contained two synthetic compounds: PCBs and furans. Ten animal feed manufacturers sold products containing this oil to 1,700 farmers, who gave the feed to countless pigs, chickens and cows.

Although the exposure in each mouthful of feed was minuscule, the contaminants concentrated in the animals' fat. By the end of May, retailers throughout Belgium had dumped all poultry and egg products, farms had slaughtered any

animals suspected of carrying the poisons and governments throughout the world had banned imports of all Belgian animal products.

PCBs and furans are POPs (persistent organic pollutants) and POPs are a legacy of the agrichemical revolution. They revolutionised farming because they killed pests and increased yields. The benefits were so widespread that anyone questioning their use was accused of being anti-science, obstructing agricultural and industrial progress, and depriving the poor of protection against disease.

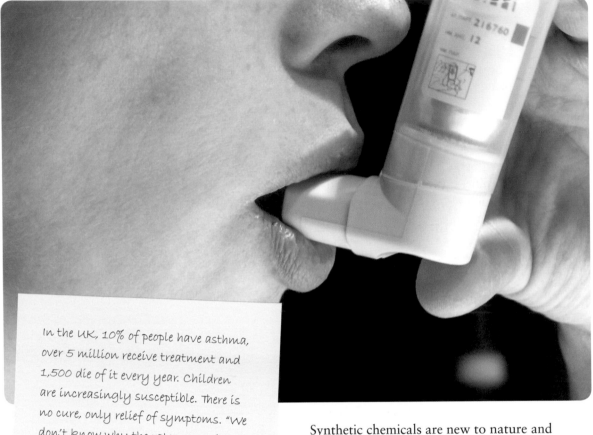

In the UK, 10% of people have asthma, over 5 million receive treatment and 1,500 die of it every year. Children are increasingly susceptible. There is no cure, only relief of symptoms. "We don't know why the rates are going up," says Sarah Boseley, health editor of The Guardian. "Only one thing is clear: the causes of this worldwide epidemic lie in our western lifestyle."

The Guardian, November 2007, and Tiscali Lifestyle, 'Asthma Statistics,' 2007

These chemicals were developed for explosives and nerve gases during the Second World War; Monsanto later produced Agent Orange, which was used for defoliation in Vietnam. At the end of both wars there were huge stocks of chemicals and equipment left over, so the manufacturers converted weapons against people into weapons against the land.

Synthetic chemicals are new to nature and have not been subjected to life's evolutionary processes. It is not possible to dispose of POPs. Bacteria won't degrade them. They can't be neutralised by incineration. Having killed someone they are free to roam again. POPs are in the environment and they will stay in the environment – forever. They are now found everywhere. And they are working their way up the food chain from fish and gulls to seals and eagles. Mothers have many POPs, including dioxin and PCBs, in their breast milk.

Five of the twelve most common POPs are endocrine-disrupting chemicals (EDCs). The endocrine gland controls hormones, the central nervous system and other key functions of the body. Products can be tested at a few parts per billion for carcinogenic properties, but a few parts per trillion are capable of affecting hormones. Strangely, large doses of EDCs might have no effect, but when tiny doses are administered to rats at a key stage of pregnancy, such as when their hormones trigger limbs to develop, they have a devastating effect.

This may explain some strange findings. In the St Lawrence River, the population of Beluga whales was in decline despite a ban on hunting. It was eventually discovered that their testes and ovaries were horribly deformed, preventing reproduction. Similar problems have been found with alligators, polar bears, monkeys, gulls, otters and shellfish – all animals that, like us, are at or near the top of the food chain.

The chemical industry denies that POPs or EDCs can harm humans – "where are the corpses?" – and pressurises politicians to allow it to continue selling hugely profitable products. But there is a steady increase in autism, attention deficit hyperactivity disorder (ADHD), dyslexia and uncontrollable aggression, which now affect one in five children in the US. Thousands of babies in Puerto Rico are experiencing premature breast development. The sperm count of men, globally, has halved in the last 50 years. These symptoms, and many more, are directly related to disruption of the endocrine gland.

Contraceptives and many other synthetic drugs have already found their way into plants, mammals, birds, fish and drinking water via the sewage system, indicating that we may all be ingesting drugs prescribed for others. A third of male fish in English rivers have changed sex. Genetically modified crops are not tested for endocrine disruption. There is more reason, however, to suspect that the endocrine gland will be affected by changed genes (which are integral

to living organisms) than by novel chemicals, which can be seen as inert influences.

There are more than 100,000 synthetic chemicals on the market today. Only 140 have been tested in the last decade – no one knows whether the other 99,860 might be harmful. By any reasonable logic, the industry should be required to prove that its chemicals are safe before releasing them on the public. But it is the consumer who has to prove that they are harmful before any action is taken.

Synthetic time bombs are ticking. The United Nations wishes to phase out the use of POPs, against strong opposition from Britain, the US and the industry itself. Chemical corporations, with sales of $600 billion a year, are conducting a vast uncontrolled experiment on humankind.

Chemicals act slowly but surely. Viruses are faster. In the 1350s, the plague killed half the European population. A flu virus in 1918 killed more people than died during the First World War. But antibiotics have prevented similar occurrences since the Second World War. However, the over-use of antibiotics for humans and animals has enabled bacteria to evolve that are resistant to almost all antibiotic drugs. Pandemics are, once again, not only possible but increasingly likely.

They don't seem to realise how dangerous these chemicals are.

Two Japanese farmers
back to basics

WEEDING PADDY FIELDS is very labour intensive. Japanese farmers therefore eagerly adopted chemical weedkillers when they became available, even though they did not help to improve yields. Only a few farmers held back from the Agrichemical Revolution and sought alternative methods.

The Furunos are a Japanese farming couple who do not use chemicals. Instead, their system uses ducks to fertilise the fields and eat the weeds. As a result, their rice has a very high yield and they have four different products to harvest on their farm: rice, fish (roach), eggs and ducks. In spite of a life spent perfecting the system they are happy for it to be adopted by anyone. "Financial success is not important," they say. "We did not patent the method, we just want it to be widely adopted." Ten thousand farmers now follow their example in Japan and it is spreading throughout southeast Asia.

It is the norm among farmers all over the world to share their methods and experiences. Only agribusiness aims to prevent others using their agricultural knowledge unless they pay for it.

Masanobu Fukuoka inherited a farm from his father. He claims to have a lazy approach to running it. "If things grow in the wild on their own, why does one have to do so much hard work?" he asks. In a short time his inactivity destroyed his father's orange orchard and was having similar success with the rice. But he persisted with his unusual convictions and over the years developed a system of 'do nothing'

farming. He does not flood his rice fields, he does not weed them, he does not dig or plough and, above all, he does not use any chemicals. Yet his crops are resistant to pests, yield as much as traditional or industrial paddy fields, and require much less work.

But the system does require careful management and knowledge of the particular location; the farmer needs to be observant and to know the

microclimate. In the autumn, Fukuoka sows rice, clover and winter barley and covers the soil with straw. The barley grows immediately and is harvested in May. The spring monsoon weakens the weeds and allows the rice to grow through the ground cover. Nothing more needs to be done until the rice is harvested in October. Over the years, with no ploughing, no removal of the straw and no addition of manure or fertilisers, the soil has become noticeably richer. "This is a balanced rice field ecosystem," he says. "Insect and plant communities maintain a stable relationship here. It is not uncommon for a plant disease to sweep through the area leaving the crops in these fields unaffected."

Fukuoka has a similar approach to his restored orange orchard, where a variety of vegetables now grow under the trees. His method of care rather than intervention in farming leaves him time to be a philosopher too.

Both the Furunos and Fukuoka achieve yields that could make Japan self-sufficient in food, but the government persists in supporting chemical methods using alien seed. "Because the world is moving with such furious energy in the opposite direction," Fukuoka says, "it may appear that I have fallen behind the times, but I firmly believe that the path I have been following is the most sensible one."

Patenting life
wait a minute!

"Every rose that is sweet-scented is telling the secrets of the Universal."

Rumi, *Masnavi* 1:2022

MANY PEOPLE AROUND the world know trees by their medicinal properties, and the idea that anyone should pay a fee for using them is inconceivable. Throughout history it has been accepted that anyone can use the properties of nature – until 20 years ago.

A genetically engineered micro-organism, designed to consume oil spills, started the attempt by corporations to privatise and profit from the fundamental biological components of life. The US Patents and Trademark Office (PTO) rightly rejected this first application, arguing that living things could not be patented under US law. But, at appeal, the patent was allowed by a narrow majority on the basis that the micro-organism was "more akin to inanimate chemical compositions than to horses and honeybees." The PTO, still believing that patenting life forms was wrong, appealed in

turn. The Supreme Court still upheld the patent, even though four of the nine judges strongly opposed it.

Then, in 1987, the PTO did an astonishing about-turn. It issued a ruling that all 'genetically-engineered' living organisms could be patented – including human genes, cell-lines, tissues, organs, and even genetically altered human embryos and foetuses. This unprecedented ruling opened the floodgates.

Under intellectual property law, things have to be 'novel, non-obvious and useful' to be patented. No one has ever argued that oxygen or helium, for example, can be patented just because a chemist has isolated, classified, and described their properties. These elements are not novel; they exist in nature. However, the PTO now holds that anyone can claim a human invention simply by isolating and classifying a gene's properties and purposes even though these also pre-exist in nature.

The first mammal to be patented was a mouse with human genes. The team that created Dolly the Sheep applied for a broad patent to cover all cloned animals. The Briocyte Corporation was given a patent on all umbilical cords of new-born babies for pharmaceutical purposes, simply because they needed to isolate the cells of one of them – for which no inventive step was required.

They'll patent me over my dead body!

A businessman, John Moore, received hospital treatment for a rare form of cancer and found that the University of California-Los Angeles had patented his body parts and licensed them to a pharmaceutical company at a value of $3 billion; the California Supreme Court ruled that Moore had no rights over his own body tissues.

Broad patents that give protection for future, as yet unknown, uses have caused a furore. Patents for the properties of the Neem tree and of Basmati rice by US companies have provoked violent anger throughout India. A US professor failed in his attempt to patent turmeric for medicinal purposes but it cost India $500,000 to fight the case. India can't afford to fight every ludicrous suit – financial might, not right, wins – but don't be surprised when yet more corporate property is trashed by angry farmers in India.

The arrogance of this new colonialism is breathtaking. Papua New Guinea was furious when the US government patented cell lines from its citizens. Patents take no account of the transformation of wild grasses and tubers into crops by indigenous people over millennia. They literally allow western companies to hijack information that has been common knowledge to everyone in a society and charge others for using it. But poor nations fear sanctions if they do not adopt western practice.

The world took a wrong turning in the US 20 years ago. Might China and India, asserting their new strength in world affairs, declare that the fundamental elements of life are global commons and should never be up for sale to private interests at any price? All life knowledge, at present in private hands, would then be freely available in these countries and they would be able to lead the world in the life sciences.

Dolly the Sheep

Microbes
tougher than humans

HUMAN BEINGS MAY be clever, but the humble microbe will outlive us.

Let's start with the big picture. It took four billion years for living cells to transform the toxic soup of the atmosphere into conditions that could support life. We have microbes to thank for this re-ordering. But modern civilisation is reversing it. We are stirring up everything the microbes 'fixed,' we are creating novel materials, plants and gases and disgorging them onto the earth's crust and into the sky.

But the microbes are still at work. Bacteria, viruses, protozoa, yeasts and algae live in the soil, in water, in the air, on our skin and in our bodies, and are key players in maintaining suitable conditions for life. They recycle nutrients for plants, and in our gut they provide vitamins and aid digestion.

These microbes have awesome power. A single bacterium can, given the right conditions, take less than a day to multiply to a thousand billion cells. So a policy of understanding and co-operation, as practised in organic farming and in much eastern medicine, would be more enlightened than zapping them whenever they harm our crops or cause us pain.

In the 1960s many doctors believed that infectious diseases would soon be conquered.

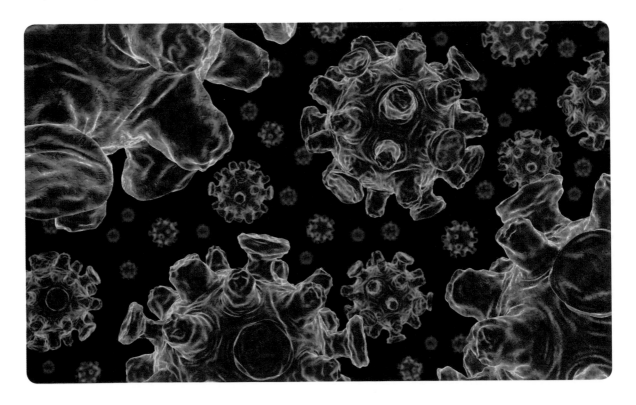

This hope is now fading and medicine is increasingly seen as a race to keep ahead of pathogenic microbes. As soon as cures or new drugs are found, resistant bacteria seem to develop. Many hospitals have had to close wards due to untreatable bacteria or viruses. Malaria is spreading north from the tropics. Tuberculosis is coming back and some strains are already untreatable. New infections such as the West Nile virus can cause panic; but, when everything in sight is sprayed, the spray may cause more damage than the infection it is supposed to control.

Our close contact with domestic animals at the dawn of civilisation allowed microbes to jump from them to us, producing many of our 'crowd' diseases: smallpox and tuberculosis came from cattle, the common cold from horses. We developed partial immunity through long contact, but Polynesians and indigenous Americans had virtually no defence when they first came into contact with Europeans carrying these diseases. Pigs have a bad record for passing on viruses and this suggests that we should be cautious over xenotransplantation, where pigs are used for growing human spare parts.

Other viruses may spread from forest regions. Aids, for example, came out of Zaire in the 1960s. The west has liked to blame Aids on Africans eating bushmeat, but as they have always done this why should the syndrome emerge when it did? One theory is considered closely in Edward Hooper's book, *The River*, in which he describes how, from 1957 to 1960, the Wistar Institute injected nearly a million Africans in the Congo (now Zaire) to test a new polio vaccine called Chat, derived from chimpanzee kidneys. The 'volunteers' did not have polio at the time: a polio epidemic occurred soon after, probably caused by the vaccine. No cases of Aids had been found before this experiment took place, but the syndrome clearly spread from this part of Zaire.

Matt Ridley, the science writer, reviewed the situation in the June 2000 issue of *Prospect* magazine. The Wistar Research Institute had kept phials of the vaccine but refused to allow independent testing for 40 years, after which it released just a few samples to biotech scientists at the Royal Society. Unsurprisingly, they were found to be free of infection. The biotech industry, of course, would not like its practices to be held responsible for such a terrible pandemic, and the US would always defend one of its companies. Africans have little chance, then, of denying responsibility or blaming reckless western scientific experiments in turn for the origin of Aids.

The 1918 flu virus infected most of the planet within a year of its appearance. It made a third of humanity sick and, of these, it killed three per cent – one per cent of the world's population. The virus then died out. The US Armed Forces Institute of Pathology in Rockville, Maryland, resurrected it in 2005 by isolating and sequencing the virus from a frozen corpse. The experiments were carried out at only the second highest level of containment, samples have been sent to other laboratories and the people handling the virus do not wear full protective suits. If someone catches the infection it could prove impossible to contain.

Human presence is the flicker of an eyelid in the timescale of microbes. We cannot assume that humans are somehow above the evolutionary battle and are bound to survive, however much we dominate the planet.

Nanotechnology
good or bad – who knows?

DECONSTRUCT A POTATO atom by atom, store the information on a computer, broadcast it to the other side of the world where they can feed dust into a few trillion nano-assemblers and, hey presto, they reconstruct the potato. That is an extreme, but not improbable, description of what could be the defining technology of the coming century.

Nanotechnology aims to manipulate atoms. At this level of physics, air and rock, life and non-life, mind and matter are all assemblies of atoms arranged in different ways. It is the ultimate 'convergence' science that spans all academic disciplines, from physics to biology to health to cognitive neuroscience. A layperson can't hope to understand the science, but it sounds exciting: it will solve humanity's material needs – we can have a better quality of life while working less – electricity will be too cheap to meter (we've heard that before) – neurons could be re-engineered so that our minds talk directly to computers or artificial limbs – fine tuning our metabolism could stop ageing – computer networks could be merged with biological networks to develop surveillance systems – viruses could be re-engineered as weapons. These are some of the longer-term claims.

A shorter-term prediction recorded by *The Economist* may be a more realistic reason for the hype: "It will be a trillion-dollar business in ten years' time."

For 200 years new sciences have transformed human life and capabilities. We are always optimistic that the next science will solve the problems left by previous ones. But the fruits of the tree of knowledge seem to suffer from a curse. The Industrial Revolution has given developed countries undreamed of riches but it also started the process of global warming. Nuclear science threatens global holocaust. Antibiotics have been only a temporary miracle. Persistent synthetic chemicals have been put to a multitude of uses but they have worked their way up the food chain and now affect reproduction and the central nervous system of humans and other animals.

With genetic science we are now reaching out for the fruits of the tree of life. But corporations control the science for profit and the downside is concealed. New sciences have both good and bad aspects and the stronger the science the more extreme the consequences.

Nanotechnology may be the most powerful technology that has ever existed, and consequently it has highly dangerous potential. Ultra fine particles (UFPs), for example, of a size that is extremely rare in nature, can penetrate skin and alveolar membranes, leaving the body wide open to toxic effects. UFPs are already being used in a wide range of applications from drug delivery to sun creams. A particularly jolly warning by Bill Joy, chief scientist of Sun Microsystems, was that out-of-control self-replicating nanobots might be able to reduce global ecosystems to grey goo in a matter of days. Imaginative science fiction? Let's hope so, but keep your fingers crossed.

Commercial eugenics
a new Golden Age?

"If society passes through the Singularity, the world will be different on the other side. It is likely that those people ready for change will benefit the most; those resisting will be swept aside."

William Sims Bainbridge and Mihail Roco, *Managing NBIC Innovations* (2006)

ECONOMIC INEQUALITY HAS become extreme. But the redistribution of wealth is unpopular among the rich who wield power. Instead of trying to overcome it, they may take inequality into a whole new sphere: genetic modification. This would also be one way to solve humanity's biggest problem – the growing population.

Our mental capacity evolved to meet the needs of hunter-gatherers. It is built into our genetic makeup, so all the new gadgets we make today have to be capable of manipulation by these limited mental abilities. Even the most isolated indigenous people, for example, given the right training, can use the internet easily.

Evolutionary psychology provides a cause and effect theory that is used in many different ways to explain our human oddities. An art historian, for example, might suggest that the numerous landscape paintings with an edge-of-forest feel to them reflect the sense of excitement our ancestors had when hunting in the forest, and their feeling of safety when gathering food in open countryside. The fact that men are more promiscuous than women can be put down to genetic determination: he has plenty of opportunities for his seed to produce offspring whereas she has only an annual chance.

Scientists have latched onto this cause and effect concept; it captures the imagination and helps them acquire funds. Almost daily, they claim to find genes for some condition or other: for alcoholism, for aggression, for depression, for dyslexia, for obesity, for cancer …

Finding and neutralising the gene for Down's syndrome would certainly be one of the great achievements of modern medicine. If we could find the correlation between a gene and aggressive behaviour perhaps we could also reduce violence and crime: in California genetic scans are already used in the sentencing process to determine whether a convicted criminal is likely to re-offend.

Increasingly, insurance companies will ask us to declare any tests that show genetic pre-dispositions. Employers will want to check that their investment in trainees is not likely to be wasted. Billionaires will want to ensure that their progeny are tall, beautiful, intelligent and sociable – traits that, it is claimed, can be enhanced by genetic modification.

Our genetic make-up was developed for hunter-gatherers and is ill adapted to modern society. But we can supposedly now change our genes to suit our present needs. In today's market-driven society those that can afford to do this will.

James Watson, co-discoverer of DNA and an advocate of genetic re-design, is quoted as saying, "If you are really stupid, I would call that a disease; so I'd like to get rid of that." Some scientists in the biotech community see these new technologies as just another step in our inexorable technological progress, leading towards the 'transhuman' state. It is more like a cult than science and has startling similarities to the evangelical Christian belief in the rapture, when the chosen few will ascend to heaven. "Transhumanists view human nature as work-in-progress, a half-baked beginning that we can learn to remould in various ways," says Nick Bostrom, a professor of philosophy and leading transhumanist thinker at Oxford University. "They look forward to the Singularity when a new superior species will emerge."

Molecular biologist Lee Silver, of Princeton University, is one of the scientists blazing a trail for a future of the 'Gene-Rich' and 'Natural' classes. The Gene-Rich, offspring of today's super-rich, will comprise about 10% of the population. Enhanced with synthetic genes and with the lifespan of Methuselah, the Gene-Rich will become the rulers of society – business people, musicians, artists, athletes and scientists. "With the passage of time," Lee Silver predicts, "the genetic distance will become greater and greater, and there will be little movement up from the Natural to the Gene-Rich class. Naturals will work as low-paid service providers or as labourers. Gene-Rich humans and Natural humans will be entirely separate species with no ability to cross-breed and with as much romantic interest in each other as a current human would have for a chimpanzee."

The higher human species may treat the lower one as we treat other species today. They may decide that a humane cull of the Naturals is necessary to tackle the adverse environmental effects of excessive population numbers.

The US Department of Commerce and the National Science Foundation commissioned the 2001 report 'Converging Technologies for Improving Human Performance', which endorsed many of the beliefs of the transhumanist movement. It deals with nanotechnology, biotechnology, information science, and cognitive science, shortened to nano-bio-info-cogno, or NBIC. The report said: "Payoffs will include improving work efficiency and learning, brain to brain interaction, perfecting human-machine interface including neuro-morphic engineering, enhanced human capabilities for defence purposes, ameliorating the cognitive decline that is common to the ageing mind ... If we take the correct decisions and investments today, many of these visions could be achieved within 20 years. Moving simultaneously along many of these paths could achieve a golden age that would be an epochal turning point in human history."

The NBIC project has received the biggest research grant in the US since the space programme. In a strategic bid to extend US commercial and military dominance it will develop brain implants, genetic modification, pharmaceuticals, nuclear weaponry and intelligent uniforms.

Some philosophers claim that technology is leading us ever onwards and upwards towards a glorious master race that will inhabit a golden age. Others are less impressed with this quasi-religious enthusiasm.

Understanding nature
and redesigning life

"Whence is this creation? Perhaps it formed itself, or perhaps it did not. The one who knows looks down on it, in the highest heaven. Only he knows. Or perhaps he does not know."

Rigveda 10.129 (circa 1500 BCE). Early manuscript of Hindu philosophy,

ST THOMAS AQUINAS saw the natural world as a Great Chain, a myriad of animals and plants in a descending hierarchy of importance. For him, nature meant dependent relationships and obligations among creatures that God had created. Diversity and inequality guaranteed the orderly working of the system. His portrayal of nature reflected the hierarchical structure of the medieval society in which he lived.

Later, Darwin's portrayal of nature also reflected the society in which he lived. The competitive capitalist market had parallels with his description of plants and animals. Evolution in nature produced better and better models just as each version of a machine was more sophisticated than the last. The intrinsic value of each living thing in the medieval paradigm was replaced by utility value. Individual, clan, village and town structures, in which people knew their place, gave way to types, categories and functional planning. Utility, rather than an established order, allowed dictators to act out theories in which people – as machines or competing economic units – could be manipulated to suit a particular social theory. It led to communism, to the eugenic experiments of the last century, and it culminated in neoliberal market fundamentalism.

Nature is now being cast in the image of the computer and information science. Creatures are no longer birds and bees, foxes and hens, but bundles of genetic information without sacred boundaries between species. In commerce, new groups of companies are emerging with shared relationships within complex embedded networks that can respond quickly to fast-changing flows of information.

Information, for a generation brought up in a computerised society, is the basis for understanding nature. It reassures us that the infinite and chaotic complexities and multi-faceted expansions of all our activities, our ever-shifting life-styles, and our experimentation with genes, are in harmony with the evolutionary processes of nature. Thus, we avoid feeling confused and threatened.

In the 1940s, Norbert Wiener pioneered the concept that "all living things are really patterns that perpetuate themselves. A pattern is a message and may be transmitted as a message." The fact that we cannot telegraph the pattern of a person from one place to another, he suggested, seems to be due only to technical difficulties. Star Trek fans will recognise this concept – "Beam me up, Scotty!"

The ability to handle information, rather than to develop knowledge or wisdom, is typical of modern life: today's fad gives way to tomorrow's, we must be continually open to new scenarios, we can reinvent ourselves through drugs and plastic surgery, life and work are games to be played.

Molecular biologists no longer talk of laws of nature or objective reality but of scenarios, models, creative possibilities; this is the language of architects or artists. Those at the cutting edge see their ability to handle almost unlimited information through computers as a natural extension of evolution. Evolution has now passed into their hands. Molecular biologists are the artists of new forms of life; they will modify and design future generations. They are the God of St Thomas Aquinas and the invisible hand of Darwin's natural selection.

However, we may also be seeing the emergence of a new consciousness in which people are becoming more aware that they share the world with other cultures, other creatures and a myriad of life forms, and with this consciousness they are increasingly filled with awe, humility and reverence.

"We need to make a fundamental shift, a paradigm shift, from ownership to relationship. We do not own nature – we have a relationship with nature. Nature does not belong to us – we belong to nature."

Satish Kumar, *Resurgence* magazine, March 2006

Intuition
imagination, common sense and morality

"Failing to understand the consequences of our inventions seems to be a common fault of scientists and technologists. We are being propelled into the new century with no plan, no control and no brake."

Bill Joy, Chief Scientist of Sun Microsystems, *Wired* magazine, April 2000

SCIENCE IS LARGELY responsible for our progress and prosperity, so it is natural to look to science for the answers to difficult questions.

But science, almost by definition, is reductionist: it looks at the simple constituents of complex things. Science can improve crop yields but not get the additional food to hungry mouths. Scientists are open about their ignorance of the political effects of nuclear energy, which have proved more significant than the science itself. Governments like to claim scientific support for their policies, partly because it allows them to make decisions within a cabal of experts, bureaucrats and corporate managers, hiding from the public behind obscure language. But recent events suggest that we should give more weight to intuition, imagination, common sense and morality than to scientific advances.

Citizens seem far more intelligent than governments.

Intuition might have prevented the British turning cows into cannibals. We would have avoided BSE, cattle would have suffered less, and we would have saved £6 billion.

Imagination would suggest that clear labelling of the content and origin of food products would enable epidemiologists to trace what is happening in a complex food system. It would also help consumers to make informed decisions about what they buy.

Common sense would tell us that a centralised food system is dangerous. Without such a system nine litres of transformer oil would not have destroyed Belgium's entire food economy in 1999. Common sense tells us that planting crops genetically new to nature, on the basis of "let's see what happens," could be like releasing rats to see if they spread bubonic plague. Common sense tells us that the cost of coal, oil, gas and water should reflect depletion and contribution to climate change, not just the cost of extraction.

Morality tells us not to keep chickens in such crowded conditions that they cannot walk, live only six weeks and are then shackled upside

down to a conveyor belt to be killed. Without this cruelty we would not have Salmonella and other food scares. Morality tells us to ban BST hormone treatment because it causes mastosis and acute suffering to cows, let alone the suffering it might cause humans. Morality once told us to stop slavery: now it tells us not to participate in inhuman trading practices. Morality tells us not to steal the earth's precious resources, like oil and phosphorus, from our children and grandchildren.

When intuition, imagination, common sense or morality – let alone science – suggest that a new policy, product or procedure is suspect, it should be the responsibility of the promoter to prove that the objections are unfounded. This is the precautionary principle. The British government and the World Trade Organization act on the basis that no restriction must be allowed until conclusive evidence shows that the policy or product is harmful. By then, though, the damage has been done.

Citizens' juries – chosen at random from people with no intellectual or financial links to the issues being presented – are sometimes used to decide whether a certain area of research is worth pursuing. The jury is presented with the technical background and can question experts. The jurors then come to a verdict as to whether the proposed research seems reasonable and fair, by criteria that they themselves develop. Both scientists and political theorists have been surprised and impressed by the results.

In the US, the Jefferson Center has conducted citizens' juries since 1974, covering a wide variety of issues such as property tax reform, assisted suicide, environmental risks, traffic congestion pricing, agriculture and water policy, and electricity futures.

We all believe in democracy but we all know that lobbyists and activists influence decision-makers. The citizens' jury provides an unparalleled opportunity for a group of citizens to assess a proposal using their intuition, imagination, common sense and morality, and for legislators to hear the people's authentic voice. It has worked well in countries as diverse as the US, Germany and India. Sceptics have been surprised and impressed by the positive and sensible outcome of these juries.

A test case

Anjamma is a farmer who works one and a half hectares of land with her children. They have two bullocks, eight buffalo and no machines. She was one of 12 people chosen to take part in a citizens' jury of small traders, small and marginal farmers, workers in the food industry and consumers to assess ambitious plans for farming reforms in their part of India.

The chief minister of Andhra Pradesh, Chandrababu Naidu, had been widely acclaimed for the state's modernising achievements in the field of Information Technology. If he could do it in IT, why not agriculture? US agricultural advisers were brought in and in 2001 the programme for Vision 2020 was drawn up. This aimed to bring millions of poor farmers straight into the 21st century with massive consolidation of farms, mechanisation of agriculture, irrigation projects, new roads and the introduction of genetically modified crops. The state government claimed that the programme would eradicate poverty in the region. Britain agreed and devoted its largest aid package for that year to the project.

The citizens' jury sat through days of evidence from politicians, seed companies, academics, aid donors and NGOs. Three scenarios were presented and advocates for each tried to persuade the jury that their particular approach would provide the best opportunity to enhance livelihoods and food security. An oversight panel checked that each proposal was presented in a fair and unprejudiced way.

The first proposal was the state's idea of Vision 2020. The second was for environmentally friendly farming to meet western demands for organic and fair trade produce. The third was based on increased self-reliance for rural communities, low input, local food production and local marketing. The jurors could either choose one of the pre-formed visions or suggest their own approach.

Their verdict was clear:

- They wanted encouragement for self-reliance and community control over resources.
- They gave priority to the maintenance of healthy soils (the farmers among them were conscious of the harmful legacy of pesticides and fertilisers).
- They wanted to maintain diverse crops, trees and livestock.
- They wanted to build on indigenous knowledge, skills and local institutions.
- They wanted to maintain control of medicinal plants and their export.

And their opposition was clearly expressed:

- They were horrified that Vision 2020's proposals would reduce those working the land from 70% to 40% in Andhra Pradesh. This would uproot 20 million people, leaving them with no livelihood.
- They did not want genetically modified crops, specifically not 'Vitamin-A' rice or 'Bt cotton'.
- They did not want consolidation of ownership into fewer and bigger farms for cash crops.
- They did not want an increase in contract farming.
- They did not want labour-displacing machinery.

Anjamma was asked what she would do if Vision 2020 went ahead. "There will be nothing for us to do," she replied, "other than to drink pesticides and die."

Mental equipment
reality beyond our grasp

"Brain: an apparatus with which we think we think."

Ambrose Bierce, *The Devil's Dictionary* (1906)

OUR BRAINS DID not appear suddenly from nowhere; they evolved in the same way as other parts of our bodies evolved. Gradually, over hundreds of thousands of years, individuals with greater mental abilities supplanted others. So our mental equipment today is appropriate for specific needs and is related to just five senses. It is not an abstract intelligence designed to comprehend all of existence, even if we use it to try to understand and manipulate the world around us. It has limitations.

To appreciate the implications you only have to consider the experiences and insights of people who lack one of the five senses. Think, for example, of a group of individuals who have been blind from birth, discussing what it means to see. They would have heard others talk about colour, about clouds, about mist, about distance and about beauty. How would they discuss these concepts among themselves? Some might say it is all a myth and deny that sight exists; some might be acutely frustrated that they cannot quite grasp the idea; some might develop a verbal description and try to convince the others to accept their definition; others might be more tentative and try to feel their way towards a more intuitive understanding.

If our cognitive equipment evolved to meet the needs of hunter-gatherers it is not surprising that some aspects of reality are simply beyond

our grasp. It's the same as dogs understanding only part of their owners' meaning: "blah blah blah Fido blah blah walk blah blah." But we do seem to sense further reality through a dark distorting glass. Our vague perceptions are the stuff of mystics, poets, musicians and painters. Religions have tried to tie these realities down into concepts and words.

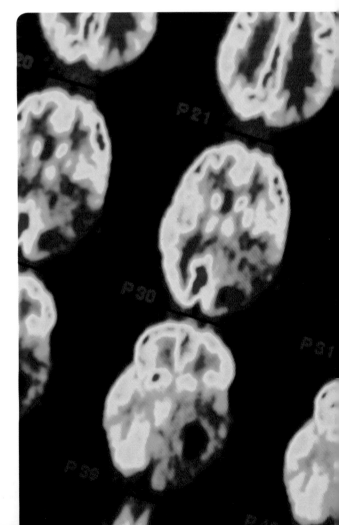

PET scan of a human brain

Physicists can now describe things that fall beyond our comprehension. Newtonian physics and Cartesian geometry once made sense to our five senses. This is no longer the case with modern science. The idea of matter as just chunks of stuff is being eroded. It is now described as a mass of energy or a web of interpenetrating vibrations. Particles of energy are connected to each other in mysterious ways, seemingly unlimited by space and time. Scientists now suggest that string, with ten dimensions and a whole world of magnitude below the size of molecules, could provide clues for understanding the infinite vastness of an expanding universe.

The theory of loop quantum gravity describes particles as tangles in space with no fundamental building blocks at all. There could be a parallel universe less than a millimetre away, but we are oblivious to it because that millimetre is in a fourth dimension. All these concepts point to connections at a level that we will never be able to comprehend.

If there were creatures whose cognitive equipment had evolved beyond ours, they might be amused at the way we describe concepts that are mysterious to us but clear and obvious to them. But they might also be alarmed that our technology allows us to play with things that have an interconnectedness that we cannot fully understand. They might be watching us wandering towards the precipice and they might just be shouting, **"STOP!"**

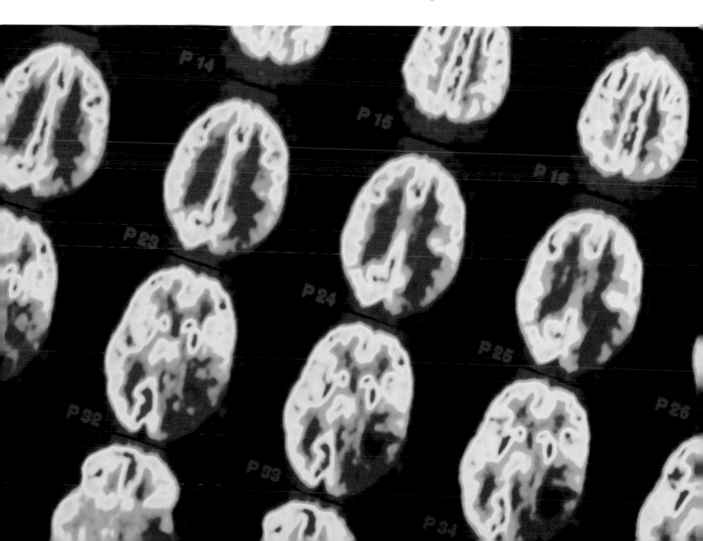

A message of hope

"It is no use saying, 'we are doing our best.' You have got to succeed in doing what is necessary." Winston Churchill, 1954

HUMANITY IS GALLOPING furiously in the wrong direction, as newspapers remind us almost daily.

There are, however, grounds for hope that we will find a new path. Optimism cannot be based on doing what we are currently doing a little better. We will only survive if changes are made to the foundations of our environmental, social, economic, trade and political structures. This book highlights changes that have been proposed by radical thinkers in these fields.

There are simple and obvious systemic conditions that must regulate all our interaction with the environment and its resources (see Don't predict, page 208).

Successful regulation of emissions that caused the ozone hole shows that global regulation can work (see Ozone layer, page 26).

Climate chaos can be averted with two measures: first, a cap must be put on the flow of fossil fuels into the economy; second, the benefits from the sky's ability to handle a limited amount of carbon emissions must be shared equally between all adults in the world (see Cap and Share, page 38).

There is no energy crisis – we waste most of the energy produced – and renewable energy sources will be adequate to replace fossil fuels provided we make some lifestyle changes (see Energy, page 42).

John Maynard Keynes proposed an international monetary system in 1944 that would have ensured fair trade and eliminated Third World debt. He was overruled. His proposals should be adopted and adapted to the current situation (see The first rule, page 130).

Our economy is not failing because of the greed of fat cats at the top but because it has faulty foundations. A different money system could reverse the constant increase of inequality (see Usury and greed, and Global eco-currency, pages 76 and 86).

Countries, including the US, rose out of poverty by protecting their infant industries. Poor countries must be allowed to follow this path (see Vibrant city regions, page 152).

Conflict arises from the desperate inequalities of global society and can be reduced by a just economic system and by replacing the UN Security Council with a Peace Council (see Tools of peace, page 159).

The American Founders were acutely aware of the dangers of corporate power, and American laws limited their powers – for a time. These laws should be reintroduced (see Ending tyranny, page 182).

The deepening harm and hazards associated with our food system can be replaced with healthier, more sustainable alternatives, such as local organic production and mimicking the way in which nature works (see Biomimicry and Food security, pages 224 and 230).

The direction of our research and investment may improve if guided by citizens' juries rather than by the vested interests of specialists (see Intuition, page 256).

These are just a few of the reasons outlined in this book that can make us optimistic about the future. We can choose to treat all humanity with respect and match our activities to the systems of this wonderful planet.

We, the rich, are living comfortably at present but our children may not be so lucky. A 13-year-old girl, Severn Suzuki, spoke up on behalf of future generations in front of world leaders at the Earth Summit in Rio – the 1992 UN Conference on Environment and Development:

"We've raised all the money to come here ourselves, to come 5,000 miles to tell you adults that you must change your ways ...

"I am here to speak for all generations to come. I am here to speak for the starving children around the world whose cries can't be heard. I am here to speak for the countless animals dying across this planet because they have nowhere left to go ...

"I am only a child and yet I know we are all in this together and should act as one single world towards one single goal ...

"What you do makes me cry at night. You grown-ups say you love us but I challenge you to please make your actions look like your words."

I, the fiery light of divine wisdom,

I ignite the beauty of the plains,

I sparkle the waters.

I burn the sun and the moon and the stars,

With wisdom I order all rightly.

I adorn all the earth.

I am the breeze that nurtures all things green.

I am the rain coming from the dew

That causes the grasses to laugh

With the joy of life.

I call forth tears, the aroma of holy work.

I am the yearning for good

Hildegard of Bingen (1098–1179)

Yeo Valley
good practice in action

THIS BOOK IS full of stories about big companies that do extreme harm to the earth and its people. Yeo Valley Organic is a rare thing: a family-owned dairy business that, in spite of considerable success, is determined to hold on to its independence and principles. This essay shows what a remarkable and very modern farming company can do.

The connection between Yeo Valley and Alastair Sawday Publishing is strong. We are only a few miles from each other; in fact, Tim Mead of Yeo Valley used to rear cows in what is now our office kitchen! We both won the Queen's Award for Sustainable Development in 2006 and both share a commitment to the organic philosophy.

Is Green always good?
The environment is at last at the top of the agenda – and not just for the usual eco-warriors. Governments, companies and individuals are finally, but swiftly, waking up to the 'new' reality of their fragile earth. This can only be a good thing; together we can effect real change.

Such notable changes in public opinion, however, spell one thing for many companies: a marketing opportunity. Look at the organic food market. Over the past decade it has passed through the various growth phases of 'niche', 'fad' and 'trendy' and is now worth over £1 billion in the UK. It is the fastest growing sector of the British food economy so it is no great surprise that multinationals are bringing new brands to the market, clothed in a gentle

greenwash. Is this a bad thing? Well, yes and no; new products provide new consumer choices and variety but there is the risk that the ideals and principles of organic food and farming are diminished by careless handling from international corporations and 'profit suckers'.

However, Yeo Valley Organic has become a major player in the organic market without compromising on quality or value. They make good organic food available to everyone.

A brief history
Yeo Valley's history is relatively short but it is eventful, with one overriding constant: the same, independent family ownership.

The story began on a small dairy farm in Blagdon, southwest of Bristol. Roger and Mary Mead bought the 60-hectare Holt Farm in 1961 and Roger, raised in a dairy farming family, set about developing his British Friesian herd. From the very beginning, his entrepreneurial spirit gave him a vision to find a way of selling his milk directly to his own customers.

This vision moved a significant step closer to reality in the early 1970s when the neighbouring, 24-hectare Lag Farm became available and the Meads started a Pick Your Own Fruit venture and opened a tearoom. Locally-baked scones and home-made jam were offered to the fruit-picking public and the tearoom menu soon featured Roger's clotted cream. Of course, taking the cream left the farm

with skimmed milk, so he used that to make his first trial batches of yogurt, then a fairly new product in Britain. So it was, that as a by-product of a farm teashop, Yeo Valley Farms was born 35 years ago.

Production at first was on a very small scale, using the clever idea of putting milk churns in pens of warm water to incubate the yogurt. The first manufacturing room was a converted barn, deliveries were made in an un-refrigerated Morris Minor van and the first customers were local shops and hotels.

The following years were testing, but by the early 1980s the dairy employed around 30 people and had attracted business from some of the emerging supermarkets. The Lag Farm yogurt dairy was expanded to meet the growing demand and Yeo Valley soon won a reputation for quality, flexibility and service that has resulted in constant sustainable growth.

This new dairy business required huge concentration, but Roger did not neglect his first love – dairy farming. He gradually extended his farm as neighbouring land became available for rent or purchase, and the prize-winning Lakemead British Friesian herd expanded.

Today, the farming enterprise covers 500 hectares containing two dairy herds whose milk is delivered daily to the Lag Farm dairy. The farm continues to invest in setting the highest environmental standards, with its own conservation team laying hedges, rebuilding traditional dry-stone walls, creating wide, permanent set-aside field margins and planting thousands of native broadleaf trees. The farm is now partly organic with the remainder currently undergoing organic conversion.

The successful completion of Roger's farming vision was, tragically, not something that he lived to see. He died in a tractor accident in 1990 at a crucial time for both the farm and the growing Yeo Valley dairy business. His widow, Mary, took over the reins of the farm and his son Tim, then aged 27 and recently returned to Somerset after qualifying as an accountant in the City, was faced with the huge task of running his father's yogurt enterprise.

Yeo Valley today – an authentic business?
Yeo Valley is now the biggest organic food brand in the UK, accounting for more than seven per cent of total yogurt sales. They buy all their organic milk from over 100 farmers in the southwest who are members of the Organic Milk Suppliers' Cooperative (OMSCo). The relationship with these farmers started with just half a dozen of them in 1994. This was (and remains) in stark contrast to the price-driven, often-aggressive policies that have been so damaging to British non-organic dairy farming. Fair and equitable relationships with the farmers who provide the milk are a cornerstone of Yeo Valley Organic's approach.

In 2005 author and green campaigner Neil Croft wrote the book *Authentic Business – How to Create and Run Your Perfect Business*. His criteria for an authentic enterprise were:

- a purpose beyond profit
- a purpose that is profoundly held
- a purpose that is socially and/or environmentally positive
- integrity between communication and action
- respect for others
- sensibility to exploitation of resources and customers
- a distinct and unique business personality.

According to Croft, businesses that understand these principles, such as Yeo Valley, are thriving.

As increasing globalisation sees more and more companies and brands becoming engulfed by multinational business, often with the loss of identity, ideals and jobs, Yeo Valley stands out as different. Their aim is not to be the perfect business – "we are only human, we have all sorts of flaws and hiccups," they say – but to be able to stand up to scrutiny. Scratch the surface and there is real substance behind their story.

For example, Yeo Valley don't pretend to be carbon neutral – simply not possible without questionable 'carbon offsetting' – but they have reduced their CO_2 footprint by over 50% in the past two years. They buy only 'green electricity', have special double-decker trailers and pursue an energy- and package-saving programme.

The ethics and the wider environmental impact of a switch to biofuels is described in this book as a 'dangerous distraction', with the potential to increase food prices at the expense of the poorer countries of the world. However, there are some opportunities for small-scale, local growing of energy crops that make sense. On their own farmland Yeo Valley have planted miscanthus (elephant grass) on land not normally cultivated or grazed. The annual crop will be harvested for burning in a new bio-boiler, which will replace an existing oil-fired heating system in their offices and farm buildings. This carbon-neutral energy from 20 hectares will replace about 50,000 litres of oil each year.

The Yeo Valley packaging is easy for consumers and retailers to recycle. Their unusual two-part pots, for example, have a thin inner plastic pot supported by an outer card-wrap. The card is made of unbleached, uncoated recycled paper, perfect for compost bins. This contrasts with some products that ask consumers to "Please recycle", when there are no commercial arrangements to do so. Yeo Valley continues to look for even more sustainable packaging; the technology for reliable GM-free biodegradable 'plastic' pots is still in its infancy, but will come.

The farmers behind Yeo Valley

Support for the region's organic farmers from a company like Yeo Valley can have a huge impact on rural economies and livelihoods.

Wills Barn – an educational facility for local schools and colleges

For some farmers, the constant slide in non-organic milk prices made the conversion to organic a desperate bid for financial safety. But it is encouraging to see how they have embraced organic principles and found a far greater sense of fulfillment.

OMSCo dairy farmers are one of the key constituents of Yeo Valley's success and the company plays a 'balancing' role in the fast-growing market. When UK supplies exceeded demand in the early 2000s, Yeo Valley rushed new products, such as milk and cheese, to market to help make use of the surplus. They were thus able to pay the contracted prices, flying in the face of conventional market practice. Yeo Valley's support for OMSCo helped it become the key organic farmer group in the UK and thereby calm a market that would otherwise fluctuate wildly and exploitatively.

Informing the new Green consumer

The growing interest in organic food and environmental issues brings an increasing demand for information. Yeo Valley is therefore developing several educational initiatives. A new BBC Learning Zone programme for teachers, due out in early 2008, follows the 'Journey of a UK Product' from one of OMSCo's farms, through Yeo Valley's Cannington dairy to a consumer in a supermarket.

In 2007 Yeo Valley opened a unique educational facility for local schools and colleges. Wills Barn is a 250-year-old sheep drover's barn that had fallen derelict. Keeping the character of the old Somerset stone farm building, it has been restored using the very latest environmental ideas. It is a showcase for energy efficiency and conservation – a sustainable structure with a new role for the next 250 years.

From the fields around it, you see a bank of photovoltaic solar panels using daylight to provide all the electricity the building needs. Careful design, high-efficiency insulation and ultra low-voltage lighting keep energy consumption to a minimum. Water is collected from the roof, filtered and stored beneath the barn for washing and toilets. A wood-pellet boiler provides the heating.

The aim is to give a greater understanding of the countryside and nature, raise awareness of the merits of both organic and conventional farming and improve knowledge about diet and good food. It is also a hands-on showcase for environmental studies, conservation and the growing need for a sustainable approach. See the website on www.willsbarn.co.uk.

Conclusion

Yeo Valley Organic has become recognised by most retailers as an 'anchor brand'. The team are acutely aware that, as the brand reaches a wider audience, it must not lose its real identity and distinctiveness. Many consumers, often with justification, suspect that successful businesses have sold-out, either physically or ideologically, in the quest to achieve commercial success.

Just as their first Queen's Award in 2001 helped reassure any doubters, the second Queen's Award for Enterprise for Sustainable Development in 2006 should do much to answer any critics. Yeo Valley's commitment to British farming and to a growing, profitable and sustainable organic dairy supply-chain is remarkable in this day and age. But the aim is also to produce affordable organic products of the highest quality – in an ethically sound and environmentally sensitive way. Unusually, Yeo Valley delivers first and talks later.

ORGANISATIONS AND INSTITUTIONS

The organisations and institutions listed here provided material for the book. Their websites are useful sources for further information. Their views and opinions are diverse and do not necessarily reflect those of the author.

ADAS. Agricultural Development and Advisory Service
www.adas.co.uk

ASPO. The Association for the Study of Peak Oil
www.peakoil.net

Bank of England
www.bankofengland.co.uk

Bradford Peace Studies
www.brad.ac.uk/acad/peace

CAAT. Campaign Against the Arms Trade
www.caat.org.uk

CAT. Centre for Alternative Technology
www.cat.org.uk

COC. Centre of Concern
www.coc.org

Christian Aid
www.christianaid.org.uk

CIA, The World Factbook
www.cia.gov/library/publications/the-world-factbook

Citizens Income Trust
www.citizensincome.org

Earth Policy Institute
www.earth-policy.org

Friends of the Earth
www.foe.co.uk

FEASTA. Foundation for the Economics of Sustainability
www.feasta.org

GCI. Global Commons Institute
www.gci.org.uk

Global Research
www.globalresearch.ca

Green Party, UK
www.greenparty.org.uk

Greenpeace International
www.greenpeace.org/international

INES. International Network of Engineers and Scientists for Global Responsibility
www.inesglobal.com

Jefferson Center, Citizens Jury Process
www.jefferson-center.org

Land Value Tax Campaign
www.landvaluetax.org

Met Office Hadley Centre
www.met-office.gov.uk

Mother Jones
www.motherjones.com

Move On, Democracy in Action
www.moveon.org

NAS. United States National Academy of Sciences
www.nas.edu

New Economics Foundation
www.neweconomics.org

NOAA. US National Oceanic and
Atmospheric Administration
www.noaa.gov

Oceana
www.oceana.org

ORG. Oxford Research Group
www.oxfordresearchgroup.org.uk

Pew Center on Global Climate Change
www.pewclimate.org

Post–Autistic Economics Network
www.paecon.net

Preparing for Peace
www.preparingforpeace.org

Rachel's Environment and Health News
www.rachel.org

Rio + 10
www.rio-plus-10.org

Royal Commission
on Environmental Pollution
www.rcep.org.uk

RSPB. Royal Society for the Protection
of Birds
www.rspb.org.uk

Soil Association
www.soilassociation.org

Survival, Movement for Tribal Peoples
www.survival-international.org

The Sky Trust
www.usskytrust.org

TJM. Trade Justice Movement
www.tjm.org.uk

TJN. Tax Justice Network
www.taxjustice.net/cms

TNS. The Natural Step
www.naturalstep.org

Traidcraft
www.traidcraft.co.uk

UCS. Union of Concerned Scientists
www.ucsusa.org

UNDP. United Nations Development
Programme
www.undp.org

UNEP. United Nations Environment
Programme, Global Environment
Outlook
www.unep.org/geo

UN WIDER. United Nations World Institute
for Development Economics Research
www.wider.unu.edu

Vostok ice core data
www.ncdc.noaa.gov/palco/icccore/
antarctica/vostok

WDM. World Development
Movement
www.wdm.org.uk

World Future Council
www.worldfuturecouncil.org

Worldwatch Institute. State of the World
Annual Report
www.worldwatch.org

WTO. World Trade Organization.
www.wto.org

REFERENCES

The *Big Earth Book* draws upon material from numerous books, magazines, journals and websites. Those mentioned here provide the key sources for each chapter and can be used for further reading. The opinions expressed in these publications do not necessarily reflect those of the author.

The Elements

Atmosphere

Ed Ayres, *God's Last Offer*, 1999.

Fred Pearce, 'The Ice Age that Never Was: Global cooling,' *New Scientist* 16/12/06.

Martin Rees, *Our Final Century*, 2003.

Runaway warming

Michael J. Benton, *When Life Nearly Died: The Greatest Mass Extinction of All Time*, 2003.

Maria Gilardin, 'Apocalypse Now,' *The Ecologist* 02/06.

Mark Lynas, *High Tide*, 2004.

NEF, *Up in Smoke*, 2004.

US NAS, *Abrupt Climate Change: Inevitable Surprises*, 2001.

Ozone layer

Maureen Christie, *The Ozone Layer*, 2001.

Public policy

CIA Military Advisory Board, *National Security and the Threat of Climate Change*, 2004.

William Nordhaus, *Stern Review: The Economics of Climate Change*, 2006.

Fred Pearce, 'State of Denial,' *New Scientist* 04/11/06.

Andrew Simms (NEF), *An Environmental War Economy*, 2001.

'The Heat Is On,' *The Economist* 09/09/06.

Rio and Kyoto

Christian Aid, *Coming Clean*, 2007.

Jeremy Leggett, *The Carbon War*, 1999.

Fred Pearce, 'Kyoto Promises are Nothing but Hot Air,' *New Scientist* 24/06/06.

'Sins of Emission,' *The Economist* 05/08/06.

Contraction and convergence

Mayer Hillman, *How We Can Save the Planet*, 2004.

Aubrey Meyer, 'Contraction and Convergence,' Schumacher briefing, 2000.

Cap and Share

Cap and Share, www.capandshare.org/howitworks.

Peter Singer, *One World*, 2002.

Energy

'Can Coal be Clean?' *The Economist* 02/12/06.

NEF, *Mirage and Oasis: Energy Choices*, 2005.

An energy policy

Alberto Di Fazio (Global Dynamics Institute), *The Fallacy of Pure Efficiency Gain Measures to Control the Future Climate Change*, 2000.

George Monbiot, *Heat*, 2006.

Trees

Larry Lohmann, *Carbon Trading*, 2006.

Gerald Traufetter, 'Planting Trees to Atone for Our

Environmental Sins,' *Der Spiegel* magazine 30/10/06.

SCAD, scad@yahoo.com.

Natural gas

Julian Darley, *High Noon for Natural Gas*, 2004

Biofuel

Economist Intelligence Unit, *Food Price Rise*, 09/02/07.

Fred Pearce, 'Fuels Gold,' *New Scientist* 23/09/06.

'Biofuel,' special issue, *The Ecologist* 03/07.

The future of oil

ASPO, monthly newsletters, www.peakoil.ie.

Kenneth S. Deffeyes, *Hubbert's Peak: The Impending World Oil Shortage*, 2001.

Feasta, *Before the Wells Run Dry*, 2003.

Thom Hartmann, *The Last Hours of Ancient Sunlight*, 1999.

Richard Heinberg, *The Party's Over*, 2003.

Rank, Report to the Pentagon, *Seizure of Saudi Oilfields and Saudi Investments in the US.*

Daniel Whitaker, 'Race for Riches is Africa's Torment,' *The Observer* 12/11/06.

Nuclear power

Frank Boulton, 'Civil Nuclear Power,' *The Friend* 16/02/07.

Paul Brown, 'Sellafield Staff Ignored 100 Warnings,' *The Guardian* 16/07/05.

'Bhopal's Search for Justice,' *The Ecologist* 11/06.

'Nuclear Meltdown Narrowly Averted,' *The Ecologist* 10/06.

Uranium

Uranium Information Centre, www.uic.com.au.

US Energy Information Admin., www.eia.doe.gov.

WISE Uranium Project, wise-uranium.org.

Oceans

Caspar Henderson, 'Paradise Lost,' *New Scientist* 05/08/06.

Oceana, *Oceans in Danger, European Trawlers are Destroying the Oceans* and other reports, www.oceana.org.

'State of the World's Oceans,' special issue, *New Internationalist* 01/07.

Fresh water

Andy Coghlan, 'Catch Every Drop to Fight World Hunger,' *New Scientist* 26/08/06.

Dilip D'Souza, *The Narmada Dammed*, 2002.

Jessica Marshall, 'Glaciers Heading for Point of No Return,' *New Scientist* 19/08/06.

Mark Reisner, *Cadillac Desert*, 1993.

Arundhati Roy, *The Cost of Living*, 1999.

The Amazon

Peter Bunyard, *Gaia, Climate and the Amazon*, 2005.

Nicola Graydon, 'Rainforest Action Network,' *The Ecologist* 02/06.

Derrick Jensen and George Draffan, *Strangely Like War*, 2003.

Alok Jha, 'Amazon Rainforest Vanishing at Twice Rate of Previous Estimates,' *The Guardian* 21/10/05.

'Welcome to the Rainforest – Pharmacy to the World,' www.rain-tree.com.

Money

Usury and greed

Douglas Dowd, *Understanding Capitalism*, 2002.

George Soros, *The Crisis of Global Capitalism*, 1998.

They make money

Derek French (NEF), *The Case for Community Banking*, 2001.

Michael Rowbotham, *The Grip of Death*, 1998.

The banking casino

Janet Bush, 'Sell Out: Why Hedge Funds Will Destroy the World,' *New Statesman* 31/07/06.

Tax Justice Network, *Closing the Floodgates*, 2007.

'The Dark Side of Debt,' *The Economist* 23/09/06.

'Private equity: Barbarians at the Door,' *The Economist* 03/03/07.

Monetary reform

David Boyle, *The Little Money Book*, 2003.

Bernard Lietaer, 'Beyond Greed and Scarcity,' *Sustainable Economics* 04/06.

James Robertson, 'The Need for Monetary Reform,' *Sustainable Economics* 08/06.

James Robertson and Joseph Huber, *Creating New Money*, 2000.

The bancor

Michael Rowbotham, *Goodbye America!*, 2000.

Robert Skidelsky, *John Maynard Keynes: Fighting For Britain, 1937–1946*, 2001.

Global eco-currency

Centre of Concern, *Rethinking Bretton Woods Project*, www.coc.org.

Richard Douthwaite, *The Ecology of Money*, 1999.

Hazel Henderson, *Beyond Globalisation*, 1999.

Land Value Tax

Charles Bazlinton, *The Free Lunch*, 2002.

Johnston Birchall (NEF), *A Mutual Trend: How to Run Rail and Water*, 2002.

Richard Bramhall, 'Land Value Taxation,' *Sustainable Economics* 02/05.

Kenneth Doyle, *The Social Meaning of Money and Property*, 1999.

David Roodman, *Natural Wealth of Nations*, 1999

Andrew Simms, Petra Kjell and Ruth Potts (NEF), *Clone Town Britain*, 2005.

Inequality

NEF and Friends of the Earth, *The (un)Happy Planet Index*, 2006.

UNDP, Human Development Reports.

World Institute for Development Economics Research, reports, www.wider.unu.edu.

'While There's a Market,' editorial, *New Scientist* 02/09/06.

Population

Virginia Abernethy, *Population Politics*, 1999.

Bill McKibben, *Maybe One*, 1999.

Economic growth

Herman Daly, *Beyond Growth*, 1996.

David Fleming, *The Lean Economy*, (forthcoming).

Donella Meadows, Dennis Meadows and Jorgen Randers, *The Limits to Growth*, 2004.

David Woodward and Andrew Simms (NEF), *Growth isn't Working*, 2006.

A paradox

Richard Douthwaite, *The Growth Illusion*, 1999

Wörgl

David Boyle, *Funny Money*, 1999.

Richard Douthwaite, *Short Circuit*, 1996.

Kenneth Doyle, *The Social Meanings of Money*, 1999.

George Huppert, *After the Black Death*, 1986.

Interest-free banking

Edgar S. Cahn, *No More Throw-Away People*, 2000.

Margaret Legum,
It Doesn't Have to be Like This, 2003.

Margaret Legum, 'New Complementary Currency,'
and 'The Talent,' *Sustainable Economics* 12/06.

Bernard Lietaer, *The Future of Money*, 2001.

Citizens' income

Peter Merry, *Why Work?*, 1997.

Götz W. Werner, *Einkommen für Alle*, 2007.

Bhutan

Jonathan Gregson,
Kingdom Beyond the Clouds, 2000.

'Happiness (and How to Measure It),'
The Economist 23/12/06.

Basic needs

Manfred Max-Neef,
From the Outside Looking In, 1992.

Helena Norberg-Hodge, *Ancient Futures*, 1992.

Them or us?

ASSEFA, www.actionvillageindia.org.uk/AVI/Assefa.

Peter Jones, *An Intelligent Person's Guide to the Classics*, 1999.

NEF, *Participation Works: 21 Techniques of Community Participation for the 21st Century*, 2001.

Wealth in poverty

Mari Marcel Thekaekara, 'Poor Relations,
The Guardian 27/02/99.

Daniel Quinn, *Ishmael*, 1992.

Daniel Quinn, *Beyond Civilisation*, 1999.

Just Change

Just Change, www.justchangeindia.com.

Stan Thekaekara, *Humanising Globalisation*, 2004.

Mosques and churches

Karen Armstrong, *The Battle for God*, 2001.

Power

The first rule

Daniel Abrahamson, 'Iranian Oil Bourse Opens for Business,' www.infowars.com, 2006.

Thomas Barnett (US Naval Institute),
Asia: The Military-Market Link, 2002.

William Engdhal (Global Research),
Crisis of the US Dollar System, 2006.

Loren Goldner, 'The "Dollar" Crisis and US,'
http://home.earthlink.net/~lrgoldner/, 2004.

George Monbiot, *The Age of Consent*, 2003.

The second rule

William Fisher and Thomas Ponniah,
Another World is Possible, 2003.

Joseph Stiglitz,
Globalisation and its Discontents, 2002.

'The Future of Globalisation,'
The Economist 29/07/00.

'The Great Unravelling,' *The Economist* 20/01/07.

Free trade in practice

Michel Chossudovsky,
The Globalisation of Poverty, 1997.

Benjamin Joffe-Walt and Oliver Burkeman,

'Coffee Trail,' *The Guardian* 16/09/05.

Claire Melamed (Christian Aid), *The Damage Done: Aid, Death and Dogma*, 2005.

NEF and The Open University, *The UK Interdependence Report*, 2006.

Joseph Stiglitz, *The Roaring Nineties*, 2003.

'Karnataka Poverty: Alarming Figures,' *New India Express* 16/01/04.

An oxymoron

John Gray, *Heresies: Against Progress and Other Illusions*, 2004.

James Lovelock, *The Revenge of Gaia*, 2006.

Jonathan Walter and Andrew Simms (NEF), *The End of Development?* 2002.

Odious debt

Joseph Hanlon, 'Take the Hit,' *New Internationalist*, 05/99.

David Korten, *The Post Corporate World*, 1999.

Third World debt

Susan George, *A Fate Worse Than Debt*, 1988.

Noreena Hertz, *The Silent Takeover*, 2002.

Damien Millet and Eric Toussaint, *Who Owes Who? 50 Questions about World Debt*, 2004.

John Ralston Saul, *The Collapse of Globalism*, 2005.

Vibrant city regions

Gita Dewan Verma, *Slumming India*, 2002.

Jane Jacobs, *Cities and the Wealth of Nations*, 1984.

The arms trade

Campaign Against the Arms Trade, www.caat.org.uk/publications.

Craig Unger, *House of Bush House of Saud*, 2004.

Weapons of war

Oxford Research Group, *Global Responses to Global Threats*, 2006.

Paul Rogers, *Losing Control: Global Security in the 21st Century*, 2001.

Gore Vidal, *Perpetual War for Perpetual Peace*, 2002.

Tools of peace

Dylan Matthews (Oxford Research Group), *War Prevention Works*, 2001.

Jakob von Uexkull and Herbert Girardet, *Shaping Our World*, 2004.

The terrorist

Michael Bond, 'The Ordinary Bombers,' *New Scientist* 23/07/05.

Clare Dyer, '"There is No War on Terror",' *The Guardian* 24/01/07.

John Gray, *Al Qaeda and What It Means to be Modern*, 2003.

Richard Norton-Taylor, 'Al-Qaida "planted information to encourage US invasion",' *The Guardian* 17/11/06.

Paul Rogers (Oxford Research Group), *The War on Terror: Winning or Losing?* 2003.

Nuclear war

Rob Edwards, '60 Years On,' *New Scientist* 16/07/05.

Rob Edwards, 'Hiroshima's Bomb May Have Carried a Hidden Agenda,' *New Scientist* 21/07/05.

Oxford Research Group, *Iran's Nuclear Programme, Beyond Terror*, and further reports, 2007.

Dan Plesch, 'Trident: We've Been Conned Again,' *New Statesman* 27/03/06.

'The Accidental War,' *The Economist* 22/07/06.

War

Robert S. McNamara and Brian Van de Mark,

In Retrospect – The Tragedy and Lessons of Vietnam, 1996.

Westmorland Meeting, *Preparing for Peace*, 2005.

Water distribution

Corporate Europe Observatory, *Reclaiming Public Water*, www.corporateeurope.org, 2005.

Ann-Christin Sjolander Holland, *The Water Business: Corporations Versus People*, 2005.

Vandana Shiva, *Water Wars*, 2002.

World Development Movement, *Dirty Aid, Dirty Water*, 2005.

Shareholders

Roger Cowe (NEF), *Stakes Not Shares*, 2001.

Marjorie Kelly, *The Divine Right of Capital*, 2003.

David Korten, *The Post-Corporate World*, 2000.

Shann Turnbull (NEF), *A New Way to Govern*, 2002.

'Buy, Buy, Buy,' *The Economist* 10/02/07.

CSR

Joel Bakan, *The Corporation: The Pathological Pursuit of Profit and Power*, 2004.

Sharon Beder, *Global Spin: The Corporate Assault on Environmentalism*, 1997.

Post-Autistic Economics Network, www.paecon.net.

Ending tyranny

Thom Hartmann, *Unequal Protection: The Rise of Corporate Dominance and Theft of Human Rights*, 2000.

Dan Plesch, *The Beauty Queen's Guide to World Peace*, 2004.

Hell in Nigeria

Lynda Polgreen, 'Nigeria: Oil and Misery,' *The New York Times* 10/12/05.

Andy Rowell, James Marriott and Lorne Stockman, *The Next Gulf*, 2005.

Nicholas Shaxson, *Poisoned Wells: The Dirty Politics of African Oil*, 2007.

Lobbycracy

Corporate Europe Observatory, *Brussels: The EU Quarter*, www.corporateeurope.org, 2005.

Paul Harris, 'Capitol Hill's Dirty Secrets,' *The Observer* 08/01/06.

Greg Palast, *The Best Democracy Money Can Buy*, 2003.

The first MNC

John Keay, *The Honourable Company*, 1993.

Nick Robbins, *The Corporation that Changed the World*, 2006.

Gordon Wood, *The American Revolution*, 2003.

The US empire

Elliott Abrams et al. (26 leading neocons), *Project for the New American Century*, 1997.

Noam Chomsky, *Power and Terror*, 2003.

Michael T. Klare, *Resource Wars*, 2002.

Ken Oates (ed) with Noam Chomsky (Bertrand Russell Peace Foundation), *Full Spectrum Absurdity: Will America Die of Defence?* 2001.

The Pentagon, *Quadrennial Defense Review*, 2006.

Richard Perle, 'Thank God For the Death of the UN,' *The Guardian* 21/03/03.

John Pilger, *Freedom Next Time*, 2006.

Ziaudinn Sardar and Merryl Wyn Davies, *American Dream, Global Nightmare*, 2004.

Peter Singer, *The President of Good and Evil*, 2004.

US Department of Defense, *Joint Vision 2020*, 2000.

'Somalia: By Dawn the Islamists Were Gone', *The Economist* 06/01/07.

The new century

William Engdahl, *Putin and the Politics of the New Cold War*, 2007.

Timothy Garton Ash, *Free World: America, Europe and the Surprising Future of the West*, 2004.

Herbert Girardet, *Cities, People, Planet*, 2004.

Global Witness, *A Choice for China*, 2005.

Martin Jacques, 'East is East – Get Used To It,' *The Guardian* 20/05/07.

Edward Luce, *In Spite of the Gods*, 2006.

James Martin, *Meaning of the 21st Century*, 2007.

Jonathon Porritt et al., 'Greening the Dragon,' *Green Futures* magazine 2006.

Amartya Sen, *The Argumentative Indian*, 2005.

Collapse

Jared Diamond, *Collapse: How Societies Choose to Fail or Succeed*, 2004.

Joseph Tainter, *Collapse of Complex Societies*, 1988.

Life

Don't predict

Jonathon Porritt, *Playing Safe,* 2000.

Karl-Hendrik Robèrt, *The Natural Step*, 2002.

Cod

Mark Kurlansky, *Cod*, 1999.

'For Cod's Sake Act Now,' editorial, *New Scientist* 11/11/06.

Bees

L'Abeille no. 936, 2007.

Michael Thiele (Bees for Development Trust), *The Need for Organic Beekeeping*, 2007.

Mammals

Shaoni Bhattacharya, 'Elephants Pay Homage to Dead Relatives,' *New Scientist* 26/10/05.

Caroline Williams, 'Elephants on the Edge of Fight Back,' *New Scientist* 18/02/06.

Soil

Gundula Azeez (Soil Association), 'From Black Gold to Brown Gold,' *Living Earth* magazine 2007.

Rachel Carson, *Silent Spring*, 1962.

Albert Howard, *An Agricultural Testament*, 1940.

Organic farming

Eve Balfour, *The Living Soil*, 1943.

Walter Schwarz, 'Cuba's Organic Revolution,' *Resurgence* magazine 05/02.

Soil Association, *Organic Works*, 2006.

Biomimicry

Janine M. Benyus, *Biomimicry: Innovation Inspired by Nature*, 1997.

NPK

Paul Brown, 'World Sewage Plans Should be Abandoned,' *The Guardian* 10/03/03.

Centre of Science for Villages, http://csvtech.org.

Folke Günther, *Making Western Agriculture More Sustainable*, www.hplpn.se/folke.

Jane Higdon (Linus Pauling Institute), *Micronutrient Information Centre: Phosphorus*, 2003.

Ingrid Steen (DARCOF), *Phosphorus Availability in the 21st Century*, 2005.

Food security

John Humphreys, *The Great Food Gamble*, 2001.

Felicity Lawrence, *Not on the Label*, 2004.

Helena Norberg-Hodge et al., *From the Ground Up: Rethinking Industrial Agriculture*, 2000.

Cóilín Nunan and Richard Young (Soil Association), *MRSA in Farm Animals and Meat*, 2007.

Craig Sams, *The Little Food Book*, 2003.

Peter Singer, *The Way We Eat*, 2006.

Colin Tudge, *So Shall We Reap*, 2003.

Making new plants

Greenpeace, *GM on Trial*, 2002.

Mae-Wan Ho, *Living With the Fluid Genome*, 2003

Soil Association, *Seeds of Doubt*, 2002.

'Biotech in Trouble,' article series, *Rachel's Environment and Health News* 2000.

'GM Giant Bids to Own the World's Food,' *The Ecologist* 10/05.

POPs and EDCs

Theo Colborn, Dianne Dumanoski and John Peterson Myers, *Our Stolen Future*, 1996.

'Modern Environmental Protection,' article series, *Rachel's Environment and Health News* 2000.

An honest scientist

Geoffrey Lean, 'When Fed to Rats it Affected their Kidneys,' *The Independent on Sunday* 22/05/05.

Andrew Rowell, *Don't Worry, It's Safe to Eat*, 2003.

Two Japanese farmers

Masanobu Fukuoka, *One Straw Revolution*, 1992.

Patenting life

Jeremy Rifkin, *The Biotech Century*, 1999.

Vandana Shiva, *Protect or Plunder: Understanding Intellectual Property Rights*, 2001.

Microbes

Julian Cribb, *The White Death*, 1996.

Edward Hooper, *The River: A Journey to the Source of HIV and AIDS*, 1999.

Matt Ridley, 'The Origin of Aids,' *Prospect* 06/00.

Nanotechnology

'Nanotechnology and the Precautionary Principle,' *Rachel's Environment and Health News* 2005.

Commercial eugenic

Richard Massey, 'Engineering Humans,' article series, *Rachel's Environment and Health News* 2001.

Bill McKibben, *Enough: GE and the End of Human Nature*, 2004.

Understanding nature

Jeremy Rifkin, *The Biotech Century*, 1998.

Edward O. Wilson, *The Diversity of Life*, 1992.

Intuition

The Jefferson Center, *Citizens Jury Handbook*, 2004.

Amartya Sen, *The Argumentative Indian*, 2005.

Mental equipment

Stephen Pinker, *How the Mind Works*, 1997.

Message of hope

Helen Burley and Chris Haslam, *Cool Life, Cool Planet*, 2008.

Friends of the Earth, *I Count – Step-by-Step Guide to Climate Bliss*, 2006.

Julia Hailes, *The New Green Consumer Guide*, 2007.

Tony Juniper, *How Many Light Bulbs Does it Take to Change a Planet?*, 2007.

GLOSSARY

aquifer an underground water-bearing layer of porous rock

ASEAN Association of South-East Asian Nations (ten nations with a total population of 560 million) (1967)

biodegradable substance that can be rendered harmless by natural processes

biodiversity the variety of species, floral and faunal within an ecosystem

biomass the total mass of biological material contained within a given area

biosphere the interlinked communities of animals, plants and micro-organisms that live on land and sea

biotechnology the manipulation of living organisms and their components, particularly genes, for specific tasks

Bretton Woods 1944 conference to establish post-war monetary and trade systems

BRICS Brazil, Russia, India, China, South Africa – a term for an association of nations that might challenge the Washington Consensus

carrying capacity the maximum population that an environment can sustain

CDM Clean Development Mechanism (in the Kyoto Protocol)

DNA substance that is the carrier of genetic information found in the chromosomes of the nucleus of a cell

ecology science of relations between living organisms and their environment

ecosystem a biological community in which organisms interact with their physical environment

EPA Environment Protection Agency (US)

eutrophication increased growth of an aquatic ecosystem due to excessive nutrient input, particularly nitrogen and phosphorus

FAO Food and Agricultural Organisation (UN)

FDI foreign direct investment

flat-earth economists Post-Autistic Economics Network term for colleagues who fail to relate their discipline to self-evident reality

GATS General Agreement on Trade in Services (WTO 1995)

GATT General Agreement on Tariffs and Trade (WTO 1948–1995)

GDP gross domestic product

GNP gross national product

GMO genetically modified organism

HDI Human Development Index (UNDP)

ICU International Clearing Union, the world organisation proposed by Keynes at Bretton Woods (alternative to IMF and WB)

IMF International Monetary Fund (Bretton Woods Agreement 1945)

IPCC Intergovernmental Panel on Climate Change (UN 1988)

IPR intellectual property rights

Kyoto Protocol addendum to the 1992 Rio Earth Summit agreement on climate change made in Kyoto in 1997

mangrove plant communities dominated by mangrove trees that colonise tidal mud flats in tropical areas

MNC multinational corporation

NAFTA North American Free Trade Agreement (1992)

NATO North Atlantic Treaty Organisation (military alliance of the US and mostly western European countries) (1949)

neoliberalism attempt to revert to classical economic policies of 18th and 19th centuries, including free trade, privatisation, market-determined exchange rates, maintenance of budget surplus and free reign for market prices

NGO non-governmental organisation

NOAA National Oceanic and Atmospheric Administration (United States)

OECD Organisation for Economic Co-operation and Development for rich countries (1961)

OPEC Organization of Petroleum Exporting Countries (1960)

organic class of chemicals formed from carbon; also relates to cultivation using fertiliser derived from animal or vegetable matter

POPs persistent organic pollutants: based on carbon chemicals that do not degrade

PPP purchasing power parity, discounting differences in official exchange rates between currencies

United Nations Security Council five permanent members with veto powers (China, France, Russia, UK, USA) plus ten others.

threshold point of transition from one state to another that may result in irreversible change

trace elements elements required in minute quantities for the health of plants or animals

TRIPS Trade Related Intellectual Property Rights Agreement (WTO 1994), to protect the patents of (largely western) corporations and to prevent countries using their own patenting laws

UNDP United Nations Development Programme, the largest multilateral source of development assistance in the world (1965)

UNEP United Nations Environment Programme, to encourage sound environmental policies, particularly in developing countries (1972)

UNFCC United Nations Framework Convention on Climate Change, made at the Rio Earth Summit in 1992

USAID United States Agency for International Development

USDA United States Department of Agriculture

Washington Consensus loosely used term for the group of neoliberal policies imposed by the US Treasury Department, IMF and WB on developing countries

WB World Bank: popular name for the International Bank for Reconstruction and Development (Bretton Woods Agreement 1945)

WHO World Health Organization (1948)

WTO World Trade Organization (1994)

INDEX

Author acknowledgements

I would like to thank everyone who has criticised and commented on the text. I am also grateful to those who I may or may not have met but whose ideas and phrases I have plundered. I would particularly like to thank Alastair Sawday who initiated the project and has inspired it from the start.

Publisher acknowledgements

Thank you, first and foremost, to Rachel Fielding who got the project off the ground and piloted it through its early development with immense dedication and skill. Thank you, too, to Rob Richardson for advice and support, Emily Walmsley for skilful and devoted editing, and Lyn Hemming for so competently taking the baton from Rachel and carrying the project through to the end. Also to Derek Edwards for his creative design, to Clare Edwards for allowing us to camp out in her front room for the duration of the design work, and to Company X for their initial concept work on the book design. Thank you to Julia Richardson for production support and management and to Tom Germain for tireless picture research.

Cover picture credits

Front (l to r): iStockphoto, iStockphoto, Neil Rees, T Dressler/Wildlife/Still Pictures, Francois Gilson/Still Pictures, Greenpeace/Roger Grace/Splashdown Direct
Spine: Sinopictures/Phototime/Still Pictures
Back (l to r): iStockphoto, iStockphoto, Michael Bader/Transit/Still Pictures, S Rocha -UNEP/Still Pictures, iStockphoto, iStockphoto

Picture credits

Aflo/Naturepl.com 2, 8; iStockphoto 4, 16,18, 21, 32/33, 35, 4, 46/47, 50, 53, 58/59, 62/63, 65, 66/67, 76, 78/79, 80, 81, 82, 86, 87, 95, 99, 102/103, 104, 111, 120, 128/129, 130, 132, 138, 139, 141, 142, 154, 156, 157, 158, 161, 170, 176, 181, 188, 192, 206/207, 216, 219,208, 224, 225, 226, 229, 232, 234, 237, 241, 242, 244/245, 248, 257, 258, 264; ardea.com 49 (Davud Nance), 203 (Jean-Paul Ferroro); Still Pictures 14 (Doug Perrine), 19 (Altitude) 22(Bruce Molnia), 28 (Sinopictures/Phototime), 37 (Belerra-UNEP), 57 (Julio Etchart), 68 (Joerg Boethling), 69 (Harrison). 70 (Jacques Jangoux) , 72 (S Rocha -UNEP), 116 (Michael Bader/Transit), 120 (T Dressler/Wildlife), 137 (Ullstein – Hartmann), 144/145 (Adrian Arbib), 151 (Hartmut Schwartzbach), 167 (Shezad Noorani), 169 (Sean Sprague), 185 (Adrian Arbib), 187 (Paul Glendell), 221 (Francois Gilson), 239 Markus Matzel/ Das Fotoarchiv), 251 (Mark Edwards); 24/25 Michael Hambrey (www.glaciers-online.net); 26 NASA (Goddard Space Flight Center Scientific Visualization Studio visibleearth.nasa.gov); 84 International Monetary Fund; Getty Images 60 (Scott Peterson/Contributor), 74/75 (Greg Schuster), 118 (Time&Life Pictures), 163 (Abid Katib), 199 (AFP), 222 (Panoramic Images), 247 (Handout), 260/261 (Jonathan Selig); 10, 13, 96, 122, 263 Misha Ostromecki (www.mishaphoto.co.uk); University of Pennsylvania Library 100 (Edgar Fahs Smith Collection); Alamy 89 (Simon Rawles), 108 (Marion Kaplan); Majority World 112 (Suchit Nanda/Drik), 146 (Shehab Uddin/Drik), 172 (Shezad Noorani/ Drik); New Economics Foundation 114/115 (www. neweconomics.org/ www.happyplanetindex.org) Map Design (www.tabd.co.uk); Baldizzone.com 125; Jupiter Images 164, 200/201; Christopher Banks 174/175; Derek Edwards 196; Splashdown Direct 211; Neil Rees 212, 214.